FIFTY
THE CONTEMPORARY THEORISTS

Fifty Key Sociologists: The Contemporary Theorists covers the life, work, ideas and impact of some of the most important thinkers within this discipline. This volume concentrates on those figures whose main writings were based predominantly in the second half of the twentieth century. A–Z entries make this book easy to navigate and figures covered include:

- Zygmunt Bauman
- Pierre Bourdieu
- Judith Butler
- Michel Foucault
- Claude Lévi-Strauss

Interested readers will find the ideas of theorists writing in the nineteenth and early twentieth century discussed in *Fifty Key Sociologists: The Formative Theorists*.

John Scott is a Professor of Sociology at the University of Essex. His most recent books include *Sociology: The Key Concepts* (2006), *Power* (Polity Press, 2001), *Social Theory: Central Issues in Sociology* (Sage, 2006) and, with James Fulcher, *Sociology* (third edition, 2007).

Also available from Routledge

Sociology: The Key Concepts
John Scott
0-415-34406-9

Sociology: The Basics
Martin Albrow
0-415-17264-0

Fifty Key Sociologists: The Formative Theorists
Edited by John Scott
0-415-35260-6

Key Quotations in Sociology
K. Thompson
0-415-05761-2

Cultural Theory: The Key Thinkers
Andrew Edgar and Peter Sedgwick
0-415-23281-3

Cultural Theory: The Key Concepts (Second edition)
Edited by Andrew Edgar and Peter Sedgwick
0-415-28426-0

Social and Cultural Anthropology: The Key Concepts
Nigel Rapport and Joanna Overing
0-415-18156-9

Habermas: The Key Concepts
Andrew Edgar
0-415-30379-6

The Routledge Companion to Feminism and Postfeminism
Edited by Sarah Gamble
0-415-24310-6

The Routledge Companion to Postmodernism
Edited by Stuart Sim
0-415-33359-8

FIFTY KEY SOCIOLOGISTS: THE CONTEMPORARY THEORISTS

Edited by John Scott

LONDON AND NEW YORK

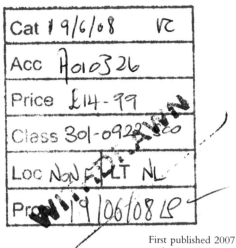
First published 2007
by Routledge
2 Park Square, Milton Park, Abingdon, Oxon OX14 4RN

Simultaneously published in the US and Canada
By Routledge
270 Madison Avenue, New York, NY 10016

Routledge is an imprint of the Taylor & Francis Group, an informa business

© 2007 John Scott for selection and editorial matter; the
contributors for individual entries.

Typeset in Bembo by
Taylor & Francis Books
Printed and bound in Great Britain by
TJ International Ltd, Padstow, Cornwall

British Library Cataloguing in Publication Data
A catalogue record for this book is available from the British Library

Library of Congress Cataloging in Publication Data
A catalog record for this book has been requested

ISBN10: 0-415-35256-8 ISBN13: 978-0-415-35256-7 (hbk)
ISBN10: 0-415-35259-2 ISBN13: 978-0-415-35259-8 (pbk)
ISBN10: 0-203-12890-7 ISBN13: 978-0-203-12890-9 (ebk)

CONTENTS

NOTES ON CONTRIBUTORS

Paul Atkinson is distinguished Research Professor of Sociology at Cardiff University and Associate Director of the ESRC Centre for Economic and Social Aspects of Genomics (CESAGen). His latest book is *Everyday Arias* (AltaMira, 2006), an ethnography of the Welsh National Opera Company.

Les Back is Professor of Sociology at Goldsmith's College, having previously researched at Birkbeck College and the University of London, and taught at the University of Birmingham in the cultural studies department. He has published widely on racism and urban culture and is co-editor of *The Auditory Cultures Reader* (with Michael Bull, Berg Publishers, 2003), *Out of Whiteness: Color, Politics and Culture* (with Vron Ware, University of Chicago Press, 2002), and co-author of *The Changing Face of Football: Racism, Identity and Multiculture in the English Game* (with T. Crabbe and John Solomos, Berg Publishers, 2001).

Peter Baehr is Professor and head of the Department of Politics and Sociology, Lingnan University, Hong Kong. His publications include *The Portable Hannah Arendt* (editor, Penguin, 2000), *Founders, Classics, Canons* (Transaction, 2002) and *Dictatorship in History and Theory* (co-edited with Melvin Richter, Cambridge University Press, 2005).

Patrick Baert is University Senior Lecturer in Sociology and Fellow and Director of Studies in Social and Political Sciences at Selwyn College, Cambridge University. He studied at the Universities of Brussels and Oxford and has been teaching at Cambridge since 1992. His recent publications include *Social Theory in the Twentieth Century* (Polity Press, 1998) and *Philosophy of the Social Sciences: Towards Pragmatism* (Polity Press, 2005).

Janet Borgerson is Lecturer in the University of Exeter School of Business and Economics. She received her PhD in philosophy from the University of Wisconsin, Madison, and completed postdoctoral work in existential phenomenology at Brown University. Her research has appeared in *European Journal of Marketing*, *Advances in Consumer Research*, *Consumption Markets & Culture*, *International Marketing Review*, *Culture and Organisation*, *Journal of Knowledge Management*, *Organisation Studies*, *Gender Work & Organisation*, *Feminist Theory*, *Radical Philosophy Review* and *Journal of Philosophical Research*.

Joan Busfield is Professor of Sociology at the University of Essex. She trained initially as a clinical psychologist at the Tavistock Clinic. Her research has focused on psychiatry and mental disorder, and her main publications include *Managing Madness: Changing Ideas and Practice* (Hutchinson, 1986), *Men, Women and Madness* (Macmillan, 1996) and *Health and Health Care in Modern Britain* (Oxford University Press, 2000). She is the editor of *Rethinking the Sociology of Mental Health* (Blackwell, 2001).

Eamonn Carrabine is Senior Lecturer in the Department of Sociology at the University of Essex. His teaching and research interests lie in the fields of criminology and cultural studies. His books include *Crime in Modern Britain* (with Pamela Cox, Maggy Lee and Nigel South, Oxford University Press, 2002), *Criminology: A Sociological Introduction* (with Paul Iganski, Maggy Lee, Ken Plummer and Nigel South, Routledge, 2004) and *Power, Discourse and Resistance: A Genealogy of the Strangeways Prison Riot* (Ashgate, 2004). He is currently working on a book on *Crime and the Media: Interrogating Representations of Transgression in Popular Culture*.

James J. Chriss is currently Associate Professor of Sociology at Cleveland State University. His main areas of interest are sociological theory, crime and delinquency, the sociology of police and medical sociology. His forthcoming book *Social Control: History and Current Controversies* will be published by Polity Press.

Nick Crossley is Professor of Sociology at the University of Manchester, having previously taught in the Department of Psychiatry at the University of Sheffield. His recent publications include *Intersubjectivity: The Fabric of Social Becoming* (Sage, 1996), *The Social Body: Habit, Identity and Desire* (Sage, 2001), *Making Sense of Social Move-*

ments (Open University Press, 2002) and *Reflexions in the Flesh: Embodiment in Late Modernity* (Open University Press, forthcoming).

Sara Delamont is Reader in Sociology at Cardiff University. She was the first woman President of the British Education Research Association in 1984. Her most recent book is *Feminist Sociology* (Sage, 2003).

Mary Evans has taught sociology and women's studies at the University of Kent since 1971. Her main interests are in narratives about social life and personal experience. At present she is working on the 'stories' told about illness and – quite separately – a study of Jane Austen.

Marcel Fournier is Professor of Sociology at Université de Montréal, Canada, and held the Killam Fellowship and Pathy Chair at Princeton University from 2001 to 2003. He is the author of *Cultivating Differences* (with D. White, University of Chicago Press, 1992), *Quebec Society* (Prentice Hall, 1996), *Émile Durkheim, Lettres à Marcel Mauss* (Presses Universitaire de France, 1998) and *Marcel Mauss: A Biography* (Princeton University Press, 2005).

Sarah Franklin is Professor of Social Studies of Biomedicine and Convenor of the MSc in biomedicine, bioscience and society at the London School of Economics. Her research in the areas of assisted conception, embryo research, cloning, stem cells and the new genetics has been the basis for numerous publications, including *Embodied Progress: A Cultural Account of Assisted Conception* (Taylor and Francis, 1997), *Technologies of Procreation: Kinship in the Age of Assisted Conception* (with Jeanette Edwards, Eric Hirsch, Frances Price and Marilyn Strathern, Manchester University Press, 1998) and *Global Nature, Global Culture* (with Celia Lury and Jackie Stacey, Sage, 2000). Her latest book is *Born and Made: An Ethnography of Pre-implantation Genetic Diagnosis* (in press).

Anthony Heath is Fellow of Nuffield College, Professor of Sociology and head of the Department of Sociology at Oxford University. He is the author of numerous articles and books on rational action theory, education, social mobility and social identities. His most recent publication is *Ireland North and South: Perspectives from Social Science* (co-edited with Richard Breen and Chris. T. Wheelan, Oxford University Press, 1999).

David Howarth is Senior Lecturer in Government, University of Essex. He specializes in discourse theory, South African politics and social movements. His publications include *Discourse* (Open University Press, 2000), *South Africa in Transition* (co-edited with Aletta Norval, Macmillan,1998) and *Discourse Theory in European Politics: Identity, Policy and Governance* (co-edited with Jacob Torling, Palgrave, 2005).

Sevgi Kilic is a social anthropologist with expertise in gender and Islam in the Middle East. She is a lecturer in the Gender Studies Program in the Department of History at the University of Melbourne. Prior to this appointment she was a Senior Research Fellow in the Institute for Women's Studies, Lancaster University, UK.

José López is Assistant Professor in the Department of Sociology at the University of Ottawa. He is author of *Society and Its Metaphors*, co-author with John Scott of *Social Structure* and co-editor with Garry Potter of *After Postmodernism: An Introduction to Critical Realism*. He is currently researching and writing about the language-borne nature of social theorizing and the emergence of ethical discourses concerned with bio- and nanotechnology.

Steven Loyal is Lecturer in Sociology at University College, Dublin. He undertook postgraduate work at the Universities of Sussex and Exeter. His books include *The Sociology of Anthony Giddens* (Pluto, 2003) and *The Sociology of Norbert Elias* (co-edited with Stephen Quilley, Cambridge University Press, 2004).

Nina Lykke is Professor in gender and culture and head of the Department of Gender Studies, Linköping University, Sweden. She was formerly head of the Department of Feminist Studies, University of Southern Denmark. She is the author of *Between Monsters, Goddesses and Cyborgs* (co-edited with Rosi Braidotti, Zed Books, 1996) and *Cosmodolphins, Feminist Cultural Studies of Technology, Animals and the Sacred* (co-authored with Mette Bryld, Zed Books, 2000).

E. Stina Lyon is Professor of Educational Developments in Sociology and Pro Dean in the Faculty of Arts and Human Sciences at London South Bank University. Her research interests include research methodology, the sociology of education, gender, race and ethnicity, and welfare-state ideology. Her present research is focused on the intellectual contributions of Gunnar and Alva Myrdal. She is co-editor of *Methodological Imaginations* (with Joan Busfield, Macmillan, 1996) and *Gender Relations in Public and Private* (with Lydia Morris, Macmillan 1996).

William Merrin is Lecturer in the Department of Media and Communication Studies, Swansea University, having previously taught at Leeds Metropolitan University. He is the author of *New Media: Key Thinkers* (with Nick Gane, Berg Publishers, 2006). He is editor of the *International Journal of Baudrillard Studies* and is working on a book on Jean Baudrillard.

Michael Newman is Professor of Politics and Jean Monnet Professor of European Integration Studies at London Metropolitan University. His publications include *Ralph Miliband and the Politics of the New Left* (Merlin Press, 2002) and *Harold Laski – A Political Biography* (Macmillan, 1993). His latest book is *Socialism – A Very Short Introduction* (Oxford University Press, 2005).

Ann Nilsen is Professor at the Sosiologisk Institutt at the University of Bergen, Norway, where she is also Vice Dean of the Faculty of Social Sciences. She is engaged in comparative research on gender, parenthood and employment. Her publications include *Young Europeans, Work and Family: Futures in Transition* (co-edited with Julia Brannen, Suzan Lewis and Janet Smithson, Routledge, 2001) and 'Individualisation, Choice and Structure: A Discussion of Current Trends in Sociological Analysis' (with Julia Brannen, *Sociological Review* 53(3), 2005).

Lucinda Platt is Lecturer in Sociology at the University of Essex. Author of *Parallel Lives? Poverty among Ethnic Minority Groups n Britain* (CPAG, 2002) and *Discovering Child Poverty* (The Policy Press, 2005), her research focuses on ethnic minority disadvantage and on child poverty.

Carlo Ruzza is Associate Professor of Sociology at the Università di Trento, having previously taught at Essex University, the University of Surrey and Harvard University. He studies environmentalism, social movements and civil society, and is the author of *Europe and Civil Society: Movement Coalitions and European Governance* (Manchester University Press, 2004).

John Scott is Professor of Sociology at the University of Essex, having previously been Professor at the University of Leicester. Specializing in social stratification, economic sociology and social theory, his most recent books include *Power* (Polity Press, 2001), *Sociology* (with James Fulcher, third edn, Oxford University Press, 2007) and *Social Theory: Central Issues in Sociology* (Sage, 2006).

Susie Scott is Lecturer in Sociology at the University of Sussex, with research interests in interaction, performance and everyday life. Her publications include various articles on shyness and a forthcoming book, *Shyness and Society* (Palgrave, 2007).

Wes Sharrock is Professor of Sociology at the University of Manchester. He has published widely on issues of ethnomethodology and social theory, and his books include *Garfinkel and Ethnomethodology* (Sage, 2003), *Understanding Classical Sociology* (with John Hughes and Pete Martin, Sage, 2003) and *Understanding Modern Sociology* (with John Hughes and Pete Martin, third edn, Sage, 2003).

Perri 6 is Professor of Social Policy at Nottingham Trent University, having previously taught at Birmingham University and researched at Demos. He is the author of *Towards Holistic Governance* (with Diana Leat, Kimberly Seltzer and Gerry Stoker, Palgrave, 2002), *E-governance: Styles of Political Judgment in the Information Age Polity* (Palgrave, 2004), *Managing Networks of Twenty First Century Organisations* (with Nick Goodwin, Edward Peck and Tim Freeman, Palgrave, 2006) and *Beyond 'Delivery'* (with Edward Peck, Palgrave, 2006). He is currently studying government policies to shape citizens' behaviour.

Stephen Small is Associate Professor of African American Studies at University of California, Berkeley. He has previously taught at the University of Massachusetts, Amherst, and at the Universities of Warwick and Leicester. His recent publications include *Representations of Slavery. Race and Ideology in Southern Plantation Museums* (with Jennifer Eichstedt, Smithsonian Institution Press, 2002) and *Race and Power. Global Racism in the Twenty-First Century* (with Gargi Bhattacharyya and John Gabriel, Routledge, 2004).

Dennis Smith is Professor of Sociology at Loughborough University and editor of *Current Sociology*, the journal of the International Sociological Association. His books include *The Rise of Historical Sociology* (Polity, 1991), *Zygmunt Bauman. Prophet of Postmodernity*

(Polity, 1999), *Capitalist Democracy on Trial* (Routledge, 1990) and *The Chicago School. A Liberal Critique of Capitalism* (Macmillan, 1988). One of his current research interests is the relationship between globalization and the dynamics of humiliation.

David Swartz is Assistant Professor in the Department of Sociology at Boston University, having previously taught at the Wesleyan University and at the Sorbonne. Author of *Culture and Domination: The Social Theory of Pierre Bourdieu* (University of Chicago Press, 1997) and *After Bourdieu: Influence, Critique, Elaboration* (co-edited with Vera L. Zolberg, Springer, 2004). He is book review editor for *Theory and Society.*

Piotr Sztompka is Professor of Theoretical Sociology at the Jagiellonian University in Krakow, Poland, and the current President of the International Sociological Association (ISA). He is the author of *Trust: A Sociological Theory* (Cambridge University Press, 1999) and co-author of *Cultural Trauma and Collective Identity* (with Jeffrey C. Alexander, Ron Eyerman, Bernhard Giesen and Neil J. Smelser, University of California Press, 2004).

Tiziana Terranova lectures in the Sociology of Media, Culture and Film at the University of Essex. She currently holds a research fellowship at the Università degli Studi l'Orientale in Naples, Italy, as part of the national programme of incentives for the mobility of Italian scholars with residence abroad. She is the author of *Network Culture: Politics for the Information Age* (Pluto Press, 2004).

Paul Terry Since completing his doctorate at Sheffield University in 1999, Paul Terry has taught at a number of schools and colleges in Oxfordshire and Warwickshire. He is currently head of philosophy at the Woodlands School in Coventry.

Kenneth Thompson is Emeritus Professor of Sociology at the Open University, Faculty Fellow at Yale University and Visiting Professor at the University of California, Los Angeles. His numerous publications on social theory and the sociology of culture include *Moral Panics* (Routledge, 1998), *Emile Durkheim* (Routledge, 2002) and *The Uses of Sociology* (co-edited with Peter Hamilton, Blackwell, 2002).

Frank Webster is Professor of Sociology at City University. He previously taught at the University of Birmingham, where he was head of department, cultural studies and Sociology. He is Visiting Professor, Department of Journalism and Mass Communications, at Tampere University in Finland. His publications include *Theories of the Information Society* (second edn, Routledge, 2002), *The Virtual University* (co-edited with Kevin Robins, Oxford University Press, 2002) and *The Information Society Reader* (editor, Routledge, 2004).

Iain Wilkinson is Lecturer in Sociology at the University of Kent, Canterbury. His publications include *Anxiety in a Risk Society* (2001, Routledge), *Suffering: A Sociological Introduction* (Polity Press, 2005) and *Risk Vulnerability and Everyday Life* (Routledge, 2006).

Alford A. Young, Jr is Arthur F. Thurnau Professor and Associate Professor, Department of Sociology and Center for Afroamerican and African Studies, University of Michigan. He is the author of *The Minds of Marginalized Black Men: Making Sense of Mobility, Opportunity, and Future Life Chances* (Princeton University Press, 2004), *From the Edge of the Ghetto: African Americans and the World of Work* (Rowman and Littlefield, forthcoming) and *The Souls of W.E.B. DuBois* (with Elizabeth Higginbotham, Charles Lemert, Manning Marable and Jerry Gafio Watts, Paradigm Publishers, 2006).

INTRODUCTION

The theorists included in this volume comprise those who have made the most important and innovative advances on the formative ideas set out by the theorists included in *Fifty Key Sociologists: The Formative Theorists*. They are 'contemporary' by virtue of the continuing relevance of their theoretical innovations to current sociological work. Their theoretical ideas have picked up from the leading contributions of the formative sociologists and have enlarged their arguments, or they have developed totally new concepts as the basis for their own work.

Contemporary theory should not be seen as something that replaces the earlier, formative theory. It does not make it totally outmoded and moribund. Contemporary theoretical work should, rather, be seen as an extension and elaboration of many themes developed by the formative writers and as broadening the armoury of theoretical tools available to the sociologist. It is for this reason that most courses in social theory have adopted a chronological structure, tracing the development of ideas from the formative to the contemporary.

This theoretical advance has occurred in all the principal areas of social theorizing. Understandings of culture, of social structure, of socialization, of action, and of conflict and change, for example, have all experienced significant debate and theoretical elaboration. Many old ideas have, indeed, been superseded or have been shown to be misleading or partial and have been supplemented by novel theoretical insights. Of all the areas within which social theory has advanced since the formative period, however, two stand out above all others. These are to be found in the works of those writers who have made gender and ethnicity into their central concerns.

Among the formative theorists, Harriet Martineau pioneered the attempt to understand the position of women, and her lead was followed by a small number of other theorists. Such concerns were, however, largely absent from the mainstream of theoretical debate. It was not until the second-wave feminism of the 1970s, however, that novel conceptual ideas concerning gender, sexuality and patriarchy had a major impact within sociology and the wider social sciences. Simone de Beauvoir and Viola Klein were early pioneers of novel approaches to these issues, and their ideas permeated the later research of such diverse writers as Shulamith Firestone, Ann Oakley, Dorothy Smith, Donna Haraway and Judith Butler.

'Race', on the other hand, had not been ignored by the formative theorists, who wrote extensively on the topic. What they wrote on race, however, tended to reflect the then-prevailing biological models of race and ethnicity. Formative theorists such as William DuBois rejected such determinism and stressed the importance of social constructions of race, and it was ideas such as that which inspired a new generation of theorists to explore structures of racialization and racial formation and the processes of inclusion and exclusion with which they are associated. Such writers as Frantz Fanon, C. L. R. James, Paul Gilroy and Orlando Patterson have been leading contributors to these arguments, while those such as William Julius Wilson have explored the empirical consequences of such processes.

Underpinning much work on gender and race have been the theoretical advances that have taken place in the analysis of culture. Culture was always a central matter for social anthropologists and the formative sociologists, but only in the contemporary period has it been the object of sustained and rigorous theoretical attention. Writers such as Basil Bernstein and Mary Douglas are important examples of this new focus of attention, but it is writers influenced by the structuralism of Claude Lévi-Strauss who have had the major impact. Working in the mainstream of structuralism, Roland Barthes made major contributions to theoretical debates, while those such as Michel Foucault and Jean Baudrillard have, in their different ways, pioneered 'poststructuralist' and 'postmodernist' arguments that have helped to reorientate whole areas of debate.

Closely linked to these theoretical advances have been developments in the theorization of race that have gone by the name 'post-colonialism'. This work has looked, in particular, at the imperial contexts of race relations and explored the ideas of ethnic difference and hybridity. Most notable in these discussions have been Edward Said and Gayatri Spivak, both of whom have a background in literary theory.

The inclusion in this volume of key writers from outside the bounds of sociology itself is important. Sociology developed as a discipline focused around the construction of social theory, though this too, was developed in specialized social sciences. For this reason,

I have included in this volume a number of philosophers, social psychologists, anthropologists and others whose ideas have had a major impact on the ideas discussed and debated within sociology itself. Anthropologists Claude Lévi-Strauss and Clifford Geertz, psychoanalyst Melanie Klein, philosopher Gilles Deleuze and primate biologist Donna Haraway all merit inclusion in a volume on key sociologists, even if they and many commentators would refuse the identity of 'sociologist'. It is their ideas and the impact of those ideas within sociological debates that warrant their inclusion in this volume.

My particular selection of key sociologists reflects my own interests and concerns: that is inevitable. I have, however, taken advice in order to ensure that my selection is as representative as possible. My initial selection of writers was referred to a panel of colleagues at Essex University, the leading department of sociology in Britain. Colleagues were asked to vote for those they felt should definitely be included and those they felt should be excluded. They were also asked to identify any further writers whom they felt warranted inclusion in the book. A revised list was produced from these suggestions and this was then, in its turn, sent around the panel for further consideration. Finally, the overall list was divided into two lists – of 'formative' and 'contemporary' writers – and each list was trimmed down to the essential fifty thinkers that it seemed reasonable to include in the definitive list.

The entries in this volume have been produced by a variety of international experts. They vary in style and format, but all take a similar approach. Basic biographical details on the life and career of each theorist place them in their historical and intellectual contexts. Contributors also aim to outline the key ideas and studies undertaken by each writer, showing the ways in which their ideas emerged and developed. I have tried to list each theorist simply by first name and surname, but where they are more conventionally known by an alternative name (e.g. C. Wright Mills and William Julius Wilson) they are listed in that way. Each entry concludes with a listing of the major works of each theorist and some suggestions for further reading. Connections with other theorists are indicated by 'See also' cross-references. These cross-references include references to antecedent writers in the companion volume on *Fifty Key Sociologists: The Formative Theorists*.

Further reading

Baert, Patrick. 1998. *Social Theory in the Twentieth Century.* Cambridge: Polity Press.

Craib, Ian. 1992. *Modern Social Theory: From Parsons to Habermas.* London: Harvester Wheatsheaf.

Scott, John. 2006. *Social Theory: Central Issues in Sociology.* London: Sage.

Scott, John. 1995. *Sociological Theory: Contemporary Debates.* Aldershot: Edward Elgar.

FIFTY KEY SOCIOLOGISTS: THE CONTEMPORARY THEORISTS

LOUIS ALTHUSSER

Louis Althusser was born in Birmandreïs, Algeria, in 1918. In 1939 he successfully wrote the extremely competitive admission exam for the prestigious Ecole Normale Supérieure (ENS) in Paris. Military service, however, prevented Althusser from beginning his studies immediately: the Second World War was to postpone them further. Althusser was captured at Vannes in 1940 and spent the following five years in German prison camps. After the war, Althusser established three attachments that would remain central for most of his remaining life. First, he returned to the ENS, where he would eventually pass his *agrégation* and where he would teach until 1980. Second, he met Hélène Rytman, who would remain his partner in a difficult and turbulent relationship until her tragic death. Third, having broken with Catholicism, he joined the Communist Party of France (CPF), to which he would remain attached for most of his life – though not without some discomfort.

Althusser erupted on to the intellectual scene in 1965 with the publication of *For Marx*, quickly followed by *Reading Capital*. In these texts, Althusser strongly criticized what he considered to be the dogmatic ossification of Marxist theory under the Stalinist orthodoxy, which had reduced social determination to the economic productive forces and so took the form of an economism. Equally, he mounted fierce polemics against Hegelian readings of Marx. Western Marxists had drawn heavily on Hegel, and the de-Stalinization of Marxist communist parties had also encouraged a rapprochement. A critical rereading of Marx's work led Althusser to a new periodization in which he located a 'break' between an 'ideological' young Marx and a 'scientific' mature Marx. Althusser claimed that the move towards a 'scientific' approach had required Marx to abandon Hegel along with the philosophical anthropology and humanism underpinning his pre-1845 writings. Therefore, to defend a Hegelian or humanist reading of Marx was precisely to cut oneself off from Marx's most important scientific achievements, chief among these being a conception of society as a complexly determined totality.

Althusser claimed that he had returned to Marx to differentiate between authentic and ideological Marxisms. The return, however, was not a recovery of something once known but now forgotten. Marx, according to Althusser, had opened up a 'new continent' of scientific knowledge and it was the task of Althusser's books to explore and map the potential theoretically contained in this domain. Curiously, this discovery of the authentic Marx required three non-

Marxist intellectual resources: historical epistemology, Spinozist philosophy and Lacanian psychoanalysis.

From historical epistemology – and more specifically from the work of Gaston Bachelard – Althusser appropriated the notion of the 'break'. This means, first, that science is not an extension of everyday life but breaks from everyday experience by constructing conceptual and theoretical frameworks. These frameworks are then 'materialized' in tools, instruments and experiments. Althusser saw this behind the contrast between science and ideology. The latter is a know-how that reproduces the everyday as common sense in an attempt to stabilize antagonistic relationships, such as that between capital and labour.

The second sense of a break historicizes the first one. For Bachelard, a word is not a scientific concept. What gives a particular word its scientific meaning is its relationships with other concepts. Each concept is embedded in a network of concepts that Althusser termed a 'problematic', and he identified an epistemological break in Marx beginning in 1845 that would develop into a new problematic after 1857. Because different problematics could share words, it was necessary to perform, in Lacan's term, 'symptomatic readings' aimed at extracting the theoretical 'unconsciousness' of the text that structured the types of questions posed and limited the range of possible concepts and answers. The word 'space' does not have the same meaning in Newtonian physics as it does in relativity theory. The meaning in the latter does not build on the former; it breaks with it.

Althusser's symptomatic reading of Marx identified a problematic that broke with humanism and Hegelianism. Humanism, the belief that it is individuals as such who make history, was incompatible with the theoretical anti-humanism of the scientific investigation of social relations found in the later Marx. Associated with Hegelianism was historicism, or the notion that history is the realization of a human essence such as creativity or love of freedom. Historicism presents history as a linear process towards a goal. It is a teleology in which an 'essence' is thought to determine all facets of social life, in what Althusser called an 'expressive totality'. He claimed that 'such and such an element (economic, political, legal, literary, religious, etc., in Hegel) = the inner essence of the whole'.

In *Capital*, Althusser claimed to have discovered that theoretical work had to be seen as a type of production, a practice through which raw materials (for example 'facts', documents, experience, ideologies) are acted upon by a theoretical structure that coherently processes and organizes them. This practical transformation of what he called 'Generality I' by 'Generality II' produces the scientific knowledge that he called 'Generality III'. Thus, theoretic–conceptual work, by breaking with ideology, is the key to the production of scientific knowledge. In later works, however, Althusser would criticize the excessive theoreticism of this approach.

Drawing on Marx, Mao and Lenin, but especially on the materialist philosophy of Spinoza, Althusser claimed that Marx's concept of the mode of production made possible a problematic in which societies could be conceptualized as contradictory and complexly organized totalities in which each element is 'overdetermined' or always already acted upon by a variety of other elements. The different regions (economic, political and ideological) of a society are always both determining and determined by others. There is not one contradiction but a plurality of contradictions that are fused or displaced. This is not a unitary structure but a structure of structures. Althusser saw this not as an expressive, but as a structural causality. He maintained that the economic level or region of relations of production is always determinant in the last instance. He qualified this, however, by saying that, in certain modes of production, other regions could be dominant. Thus, in feudalism it is the political level that is dominant. Nevertheless, '[f]rom the first moment to the last, the lonely hour of the "last instance" never comes'. In other words, the economic region structures a field of mutual determination in which other regions are relatively autonomous. The social formation is a decentred totality. There is no primary or ultimate cause; there is an 'absent cause' or, in Spinozist language, 'the effects are not outside the structure ... the structure is immanent in its effects'.

Althusserianism, notwithstanding its difficult relationship with structuralism, is frequently referred to as 'structural Marxism'. It jolted Marxism and electrified theoretical debate. By the late 1970s, however, it had lost much of its charge. This was due to a concatenation of events: a visceral turn against Marxism in the French academy, changed political horizons and also important internal theoretical problems of Althusser's own position. The latter were recognized by Althusser himself in a number of subsequent self-critiques.

Althusser's legacy has been immense. Outside of his immediate circle – including such as Etienne Balibar, Pierre Machery, Nicos Poulantzas and Michel Pechaux, to name but a few – his writings have been decisive for such scholars as Göran Therborn, Terry Eagleton, Erik Olin Wright, and Stephen Resnick and Richard Wolf. Althusser's emphasis on knowledge as a productive practice has been further developed by Roy Bhaskar as the basis of critical realism. His work on ideology – sketched out in *For Marx* and developed in the essay 'Ideology and Ideological State Apparatuses' – has had a broad influence through sketching out the function of the 'ideological state apparatuses' (such as church, family, education) and their contribution to the reproduction of exploitative social relations. It is another area in which Althusser innovatively draws on Lacanian psychoanalysis to explore ideology as a material practice that constitutes individuals as subjects. Althusser's definition of ideology as 'a representation of the imaginary relationship of individuals to their real conditions of existence' has proven extremely fertile. Althusser's attempt to develop a non-reductionist materialism remains a vital ongoing research programme. Moreover, Althusser was an important contributor to the contemporary Spinozist immanentist materialism associated with, amongst others, **Gilles Deleuze**, Etienne Balibar and Antonio Negri.

Althusser suffered from manic depression. He underwent myriad treatments but none seemed able to prevent periodic collapses, severe depressions and periods of hospitalization. Tragically, in November of 1980, whilst in the midst of a mental crisis, he murdered his wife, Hélène. Deemed unfit to plead, he was committed to a psychiatric institution and did not stand trial for the murder. His academic career came to an end. Released in 1983, he lived in northern Paris in relative isolation until his death from a heart attack on 22 October 1990.

In 1992, Althusser's autobiography was published posthumously. He claimed that, silenced by the absence of a trial for the murder of Hélène, the text allowed him to 'intervene personally and publicly to offer my own testimony'. More than a testimony or a biography, the text is, in Elliot's words, above all 'a re-writing of a life through the prism of its wreckage'. If the 'traumabiography' conceals more than it reveals, other posthumously published texts do shed light on important aspects of Althusser's intellectual and political project. In texts such as 'The Subterranean Current of the Materialism of the Encounter' and 'Machiavelli and Us', Althusser tried to trace and sketch a 'materialism of the encounter', an 'aleatory materialism'. In other words, he posed the question of how we can use theoretical knowledge to contribute to the emergence of something new (such as a fairer society) without seeing this as a preordained event, as the product of voluntarism or an entirely random phenomenon. This was Althusser's challenge to Marxist theory and to social thought more broadly: arguably it is also ours.

See also: Manuel Castells, Ernesto Laclau, Claude Lévi-Strauss.

See also in *Fifty Key Sociologists: The Formative Theorists*: Karl Marx.

Major works

For Marx. 1962–5. London: Allen Lane, 1969.
Reading Capital. 1965–8. With Etienne Balibar. London: New Left Books, 1970.
Lenin & Philosophy and Other Essays. 1971. London: New Left Books.
Essays in Self-Criticism. 1974. London: New Left Books, 1976.
The Future Lasts a Long Time. 1994. London: Vintage.
Machiavelli and Us. London: Verso, 1999.

Further reading

Ted Benton. 1984. *The Rise and Fall of Structural Marxism*. London: Macmillan.
Roy Bhaskar. 1989. *Reclaiming Reality*. London: Verso.
Alex Callinicos. 1976. *Althusser's Marxism*. London: Pluto Press.
Gregory Elliot, ed. 1994. *Althusser: A Critical Reader*. Oxford: Blackwell.
Gregory Elliot. 1987. *Althusser: The Detour of Theory*. London: Verso.
José López. 2003. *Society and Its Metaphors*. London: Continuum.
Warren Montag. 2002. *Louis Althusser*. London: Palgrave.
J. Read. 2003. *The Micro-Politics of Capital*. New York: SUNY.

JOSÉ LÓPEZ

ROLAND BARTHES

Barthes was a groundbreaking French literary critic and cultural theorist with a renowned personal vision who developed structuralist ideas on writing and popular culture into one of the defining intellectual movements of the last century. His contribution to sociology was immense and multifaceted. It stretches from his initial concern with the nature of language and representation by analysing the signifying systems of, amongst other things, fashion, wrestling and the obsessions of historians, through to his later poststructuralist preoccupations with textuality, pleasure and subjectivity. Although there is a tendency to divide Barthes' work into artificial phases or reductive parts (as critic, theorist, writer), this obscures some significant continuities across his thought and the way his own literary style effortlessly shifts from cold, neologistic formalism to warm, playful subversion. Of course, there are changes of direction over his career, but central elements remain constant.

Perhaps the most enduring theme is that of language. Barthes was resolutely critical of the rules of communication, while insisting on the necessity of overcoming the distortions of language. Almost from the beginning he set himself the task of unmasking bourgeois 'common sense' and disturbing the 'what goes without saying' to reveal how the seemingly innocent representations and conventions of everyday life shore up power relations. His target was the 'falsely obvious'. Likewise, he objected to realist literature on the grounds that it pretends to provide faithful representations of the world by concealing the signs of its fabrication. This duplicity is ultimately unhealthy. By seeking to suppress the signifying practices of language, by passing itself off as natural, realism becomes ideological. The significance of the relationship between language and culture, which Barthes examined throughout his work, is one particularly influential example of what the philosopher Richard Rorty has called the 'linguistic turn' in the humanities and social sciences.

Roland Barthes was born in Cherborg, Manche, in 1915 to a middle-class Protestant family. After his father, a naval officer, was killed in battle a year later, Barthes spent his childhood with his mother and grandparents in Bayonne. In 1924 they moved to Paris, where his mother eked out a living as a bookbinder. By all accounts these years were spent in genteel poverty. There are few records left of his school years, but it is clear that he was a bright student as he intended to compete for a place at the prestigious Ecole Normale Supérieure in 1934. In the same year, however, he contracted tuberculosis and the ensuing illness devastated his academic plans. Barthes spent the years 1934–5 and 1942–6 in various sanitoria, but during intermissions from the illness he worked towards university degrees in classical literature, Greek tragedy, grammar and philology, as well as founding a theatrical troupe, beginning to write and forming an antifascist group. With the outbreak of war in 1939, Barthes was exempted from military service and he taught in schools in Biarritz and Paris. However, a relapse during the German Occupation in 1941 meant that he spent most of the next five years in sanitoria in the Alps, where he was able to read avidly and emerge, as he would later say, an existentialist and a Marxist.

After convalescing in Paris he obtained posts teaching French abroad, initially in Romania in 1947. He taught in Egypt two years later, where the lecturer Algirdus Greimas introduced him to modern linguistics. Returning to Paris in 1950 to work in the government's education department, he secured a grant in 1952 to work on a thesis studying the vocabulary of social debate in the early nineteenth century. He made little headway on the thesis, but did publish two books on literary criticism in quick succession: *Writing Degree Zero* and

Michelet. When his contract as a researcher was not renewed he worked for a publisher and wrote regular articles for *Les Lettres nouvelles*, brought together in *Mythologies*. In 1955, however, he obtained a sociological scholarship for a study on fashion, and he eventually published this, twelve years later, as *The Fashion System*. At the end of the scholarship he was appointed to a position at the Ecole Pratique des Hautes Etudes in 1960, becoming the director of studies in 1962 in the 'sociology of signs, symbols and representations'. Barthes remained in this post until he was elected to a chair in literary semiology at the Collège de France in 1976. He died from injuries sustained in a traffic accident outside the Collège in 1980.

Barthes' reputation came to international prominence in a famous quarrel, widely reported in the press, with a traditionalist Sorbonne professor, Raymond Picard, in the mid-1960s. Picard attacked Barthes in a pamphlet, *New Criticism or New Fraud?*, and, in doing so, transformed Barthes, in Culler's words, into the 'representative of everything that was radical, unsound and irreverent in literary studies'. Picard's polemic represents the academic establishment's response to the structuralist 'science of literature' that Barthes had been practising for the last decade or so and which he had elaborated in *Criticism and Truth*.

Barthes had insisted that there were two approaches to the study of French literature, a deadening, positivistic academic criticism and a vigorous, interpretative criticism (soon dubbed the '*nouvelle critique*'). The latter, largely excluded from the university mainstream, made clear its philosophical and ideological leanings, whether these were existentialism, Marxism or psychoanalysis. Academic criticism, on the other hand, claims objectivity and to know the essence of literature by appealing to the ideology of 'common sense'. In addition, academic criticism values knowledge of the author's life and times as it uses this to causally explain features of the text. Interpretative criticism breaks with this mechanics of determination in favour of the logic of signification and does not privilege the accumulation of extra-textual details (on the author's sources, for instance), which can be easily graded by university exams. Instead, interpretation involves an immanent study of the work aimed at revealing the internal relationships of theme, imagery and structure. It is sometimes claimed that the '*nouvelle critique*', for which Barthes was the leading spokesperson, produced a 'Copernican revolution' in literary criticism by removing the author from the centre of scholarship.

As many now recognize, this quarrel was symptomatic of a broader conflict in French intellectual life between two kinds of academic:

the ancient, conservative establishment of Picard and the marginal, modern radicalism of Barthes. There was no confusion over which side to take in the 1960s, and the lines of division were easily drawn. However, the issues posed by the dispute have never been resolved and continue to shape much polemical debate. Nevertheless, the affair established Barthes as a central proponent of structuralist analysis, which was sweeping through French thought at the time. One of the defining features of this movement was the importance given to language in explaining social practice.

The 'linguistic turn' took many directions, but it had its origins in the structural linguistics of Ferdinand de Saussure (first published posthumously in 1915) and in Russian formalist literary critics such as Osip Brik, Roman Jakobson and Viktor Shklovsky. The formalists emerged before the 1917 Bolshevik Revolution, flourished during the 1920s and were effectively silenced by Stalinism. Their innovation was to regard literary language as a set of systematic deviations that distort everyday speech. Consequently, formalists reduced the surface study of literary content to the deep structures of literary form. Saussure's conception of language strongly influenced this understanding of cultural meaning and subsequent developments in structuralism.

Before Saussure, linguists studied how languages developed over time. For Saussure this historical 'diachronic' tracing cannot grasp how things acquire meaning or function in the world. He maintained that language can only be understood relationally, by looking at the relationships between different parts as a 'synchronic' system. Saussure argued that meaning results from a system of structured differences in language. Significance results from the finite rules and conventions that organize language rather than the infinite number of specific utterances that individuals use in speech acts. Saussure anticipated that semiology – the general science of signs – had a wide applicability, but even he would have been surprised by the extent to which his ideas were taken up after his death.

Claude Lévi-Strauss, whose work gave a powerful impetus to structuralism, treated kinship relations, cooking practices and mythic stories as linguistic structures and concluded that the human mind works through binary oppositions to reduce arbitrary data into some kind of order. Likewise, the philosopher and Marxist **Louis Althusser** identified an underlying structure or language of capitalism where individual capitalist societies are regarded as particular speech acts, while Jacques Lacan, an influential psychoanalyst, argued that 'the unconscious is structured like language'. **Michel Foucault** even claimed to have found the structural codes that govern thinking in particular eras in his *The Order of Things*.

Although there were major differences among these thinkers, structuralism did appear to an Anglo-American audience as a single intellectual movement originating from France. It is in this context that Barthes developed semiology into the study of all kinds of sign systems in an effort to describe the underlying structures of a range of human activities. Like other leading figures he would soon distance himself from structuralism, yet much of what was lauded as 'post-structuralism' was already present in these early writings.

For a time, Barthes' clear ambition was to found a structuralist 'science of literature' in an effort to distinguish the approach from the academic criticism that relies on aesthetic discrimination and ideological understandings of 'objectivity' and 'good taste'. He set this out in his most accessible book, *Mythologies*, which contains a collection of short, witty essays on various aspects of popular and high culture as well as an outline of the semiological concepts (like sign, signifier and signified) that inform his analysis. The intention was to demonstrate how images and texts contain complex codes and practices that shore up myths that serve to render particular values (often bourgeois) as natural, universal and eternal. A good example of this approach is contained in his dissection of 'The Writer on Holiday':

> To endow the writer publicly with a good fleshly body, to reveal that he likes dry white wine and underdone steak, is to make even more miraculous for me, and of a more divine essence, the products of his art. Far from the details of his daily life bringing nearer to me the nature of his inspiration and making it clearer, it is the whole mythical singularity of his condition which the writer emphasizes by such confidences. For I cannot but ascribe to some superhumanity the existence of beings vast enough to wear blue pyjamas at the very moment when they manifest themselves as universal conscience, or else make a profession of liking reblochon [a cheese] with that same voice with which they announce their forthcoming Phenomenology of the Ego.

What Barthes is demonstrating, on one level, is how the positivist accumulation of small facts merely serves to heighten reverence for the Great Man of Literature.

It is striking how this piece also announces themes he would develop in his quarrel with academic literary criticism – an enterprise he subsequently condemned through notoriously announcing 'The Death of the Author'. Before this, he had produced a somewhat dense treatise on *The Elements of Semiology*. Here Barthes refined his understanding of the relationship between signifier, signified and myth by drawing a staggered distinction between denotation (literal meaning) and connotation (cultural meaning) in systems of signification. His highly influential essay, 'Introduction to the Structural Analysis of Narrative' – published in 1966 and included in the *Image-Music-Text* collection of essays – provides principles for classifying the numerous narratives circulating in the world. Yet, shortly after, Barthes moved from seeing the literary work as a closed entity with precise meanings and general rules that the critic can decode, to viewing the text as possessing a multiplicity of meanings that cannot be reduced down to a single core or essence. This is introduced in his famous essay on the 'Death of the Author', where he claims that 'a text is not a line of words releasing a single "theological" meaning (the "message" of the Author-God) but a multi-dimensional space in which a variety of writings, none of them original, blend and clash'.

The shift in direction is partly explained by other theoretical developments. In particular, Jacques Derrida's deconstruction of the stable binaries of structuralism and his insistence that meaning is continually deferred are a clear influence. Julia Kristeva's concept of intertextuality, which rendered the author anonymous and held that a text is a derivation and transformation of other, earlier texts, informed Barthes' poststructuralism. Barthes' most ambitious analysis in this mode is the exhaustive commentary on Balzac's short story 'Sarrasine', where he breaks the text down into small units to explain how they carry many different meanings simultaneously.

Indeed, the issues explored in *S/Z* shaped his subsequent work, which addressed the twin concerns of the hedonistic pleasures of the text and the personal subjectivity of the reader. These themes are pursued in three books written before his death: the autobiography *Roland Barthes by Roland Barthes*, the fragmentary *A Lover's Discourse* and the mournful *Camera Lucida*. These last books moved even further away from traditional criticism to challenge conventional distinctions between critic and creator, fact and fiction, literature and language. For instance, his autobiography eschews normal conventions by being arranged alphabetically rather than chronologically. It will come as no surprise to learn that he even reviewed it – and concluded that the author 'has only been able to say one thing: that he is the only person who is unable to speak truthfully about himself'.

Assessing such an oeuvre is no easy task and it is clear that Barthes exasperated his followers as much as his detractors by his almost ceaseless search for new and fashionable positions. Nevertheless, his early work is amongst the founding statements of cultural studies and his attention to the distorting role of myth in modern society remains seminal. Although Barthes presented his semiology as a thorough scientific method, this was not carried over into practice. He did not explain why his semiotic interpretation is to be preferred over others – this proved to be particularly problematic, since his later work stresses the multiplicity of meaning.

Another troubling tendency in the method is the reduction of cultural phenomena down to underlying structures, thereby glossing over surface complexity. At times it is hard not to share Picard's view that much of what is being presented is a spurious scientificity that implies a rigour that is largely absent. Indeed, when I read Barthes I am more persuaded by the surface style of his arguments than the attempts at reducing meaning to abstract formulae (as in his *Elements of Semiology*). The playful nature of his later writings, which became more concerned with desire, pleasure and subjectivity, anticipates some of the themes explored by postmodernist and feminist interrogations of identity. Dismissed by some as self-indulgence, this work nevertheless offers a subtle and nuanced understanding of the fragmented self whose sociological evaluation is long overdue.

See also: Louis Althusser, Michel Foucault, Claude Lévi-Strauss.

See also in *Fifty Key Sociologists: The Formative Theorists*: Emile Durkheim, Ferdinand de Saussure.

Major works

Writing Degree Zero. 1953. New York: Hill and Wang, 1977.
Michelet. 1954. New York: Hill and Wang, 1987.
Mythologies. 1957. London: Village, 1993.
Elements of Semiology. 1964. New York: Hill and Wang, 1967.
Image-Music-Text. 1966. London: Fontana, 1977.
Criticism and Truth. 1966. London: Athlone Press, 1987.
The Fashion System. 1967. London: Jonathan Cape, 1985.
S/Z. 1970. London: Jonathan Cape, 1975.
Roland Barthes by Roland Barthes. 1975. London: Macmillan, 1977.
A Lover's Discourse: Fragments. 1977. London: Jonathan Cape, 1979.
Camera Lucida: Reflections on Photography. 1980. London: Fontana, 1984.
Susan Sontag, ed. A Barthes Reader. New York: Hill and Wang, 1982. Contains extracts from many of his works.

Further reading

Graham Allen. 2003. *Roland Barthes*. London: Routledge.
Louis-Jean Calvet. 1994. *Roland Barthes: A Biography*. Cambridge: Polity Press.
Jonathan Culler. 1983. *Roland Barthes*. London: Fontana.
Rick Rylance. 1994. *Roland Barthes*. London: Harvester Wheatsheaf.

EAMONN CARRABINE

JEAN BAUDRILLARD

Jean Baudrillard is a philosopher whose work emerges out of, radically develops and ultimately questions the established sociological tradition. Born in Reims, France, in 1929, he taught language in provincial *lycées* before moving into sociology. In 1966 he completed a thesis with Henri Lefebvre at Nanterre University of Paris X, where he lectured in sociology before retiring in 1987 to concentrate on his writing and public lecturing. His earliest publications on literary theory and in the pro-situationist journal *Utopie* were followed by a series of books and essays developing an original critique of post-war, western consumer and media society. He has extended and continuously redeveloped this project throughout his career in over thirty books and many interviews and articles, becoming one of the most important – and controversial – contemporary thinkers and cultural commentators.

Baudrillard's first books, *The System of Objects* and *The Consumer Society*, draw on a number of traditions: Roland Barthes' semiotic analysis of popular culture; the analysis of the penetration of social control and 'alienation' throughout everyday life and leisure in Henri Lefebvre, Herbert Marcuse and Guy Debord; Thorstein Veblen's discussion of competitive 'conspicuous consumption'; the analysis of technology in Jacques Ellul and Gilbert Simondon; the discussion of contemporary electronic media culture in Daniel Boorstin and Marshall McLuhan; and the Freudian analysis of the meanings of cultural objects. His books present a picture of contemporary consumer society as defined by the reduction and transformation of 'symbolic' meaning and relationships into 'semiotic' elements. The latter are combined to produce sign-objects that are organized into a structural system controlled by a code of signification, each sign being unilaterally appropriated and consumed by its user for its specific, culturally produced meanings.

Against this mode of communication, its semiotic production of the individual and the 'totalitarian' control of experience, Baudrillard defends the symbolic. The latter is a lived, bilateral and immediately actualized mode of relation, intellectually derived from Durkheimian social anthropology in its radical line of descent through Durkheim, Marcel Mauss and Henri Hubert, to the College of Sociology and the work of Georges Bataille and Roger Caillois. Their analysis of tribal festivals and gift relations provides the model for that mode of 'symbolic exchange' that Baudrillard sees as historically replaced and simulated in the West but also as surviving within it as a latent and explosive demand. Baudrillard's work can best be understood as following from this opposition and the spiralling together of its terms. His entire career has been committed to the dual, critical project of tracing the accelerating processes of the semiotic world and searching for surviving symbolic forces that resist, subvert and reverse it.

Baudrillard's early critique of consumption is tied to a broader critique of 'general economy' – the interlinked processes of the sign and the commodity. In *For a Critique of the Political Economy of the Sign*, he advances a poststructuralist critique of these categories, demonstrating how each relies upon an external referential category – 'the real' and 'use value' – to ground and naturalize its processes and how this category is actually an internal product of their own operation. This leads to a renewed defence of the symbolic as an ineffable realm beyond significatory value and to a further analysis of the semiotic world. This is pursued in the theorization of a contemporary 'structural revolution in value' in which the sign absorbs its own referent to produce a 'reality' from the play of its own signifiers. Baudrillard's early claims regarding the semiotic simulation of the symbolic develop, therefore, into a broader concern with the combination of semiotic elements to produce our entire experience of the 'real'.

These ideas are famously extended in *Symbolic Exchange and Death* in a Foucaultian sketch of the historical transformations of the sign – and the production of the real – from the Renaissance, through industrial society, to the contemporary 'code-governed' world. Despite its later adoption, simplification and banalization in debates around postmodernism, this theory of 'the orders of simulacra' and of simulation constitutes an important contribution to social theory. It historically and philosophically grounds a critique of the contemporary processes of consumer and media society through the recovery and foregrounding of the ancient concept of the 'simulacrum' – the efficacious, demonic image that takes on the force of the real. His subsequent analysis of the contemporary reproduction of the real, its forced 'hyperreality' and abolition of social relations, meaning and investment remains powerful and inspired. As his later discussion of the impact of modelled simulacra upon our experience demonstrates, however, his adoption of this concept is essentially critical: aiming to expose the simulacrum's penetration throughout everyday life and its functioning as a mode of social control, pacification and integration.

Baudrillard's most famous contribution to sociology is *In the Shadow of the Silent Majorities* (1978), where he reworks his historical theorization of the passage from symbolic to semiotic societies, focusing upon the consequences of modernity's production of social relations. Ultimately the overproduction, generalization and saturation of 'the social', as well as of 'information' and 'meaning' in our communicational world, leads, he argues, to the 'implosion' and destruction of these categories. Baudrillard explains the loss of the social through its absorption into the idea of 'the masses', a simulacrum produced by the speed and impact of informational systems and whose reality is unknowable outside the systems of social communication and representation that construct it. The result is not only a critique of sociology's ongoing project of studying the social but also a radical attack on its methodological pretensions to objective and scientific knowledge, as Baudrillard highlights the processes of simulation that it relies upon. Though his concept of the masses has attracted criticism, for Baudrillard it remains a positive simulacral force, operating both through passive absorption and silence and through active 'hyperconformity' to destabilize social structures.

Through *Forget Foucault*, *Seduction* and *Fatal Strategies*, Baudrillard escalates again his image of a western 'productive' order, bound to the materialization of the real. This theme leads to an increasing emphasis upon new media and an emerging critique of 'virtuality' in later texts such as *The Perfect Crime*. This is closely linked with a critique of western 'non-events' and of the West's global, trans-political project of controlling and domesticating all external, symbolic sources of opposition – ideas fruitfully explored in his writings on the 1991 Gulf War, on 9/11 and on the Afghan and Iraq Wars. Books such as *The Gulf War Did Not Take Place*, *Power Inferno* and *The Intelligence of Evil* have ensured that his controversial voice and original interpretation and critique of western society have remained at the centre of contemporary debates concerning the processes and operations of western societies.

Whilst early discussions of Baudrillard were dominated by the issue of 'postmodernism', provoking many hostile and simplistic readings of his work, a more sophisticated critical literature has since emerged to reflect its complexity and explore its contribution to a variety of debates and disciplines. If, however, Baudrillard has become an unavoidable figure today, he remains a controversial one. His anti-empiricism, extreme and subjective analyses, his debt to radical sociological traditions and avant-garde and marginal theory, and the epistemological and methodological contradictions of his analysis of simulacra are problematic for sociology. So too is his methodology. However, his radical methodological principle of 'theoretical violence' – employing an escalating 'speculation to the death' to expose and oppose the escalating simulacral processes producing our world and experience – arguably leads to a more insightful, original and critical theory than many more traditional disciplinary approaches.

See also: Judith Butler.

See also in *Fifty Key Sociologists: The Formative Theorists*: Theodor Adorno.

Major works

The System of Objects. 1968. London: Verso, 1996.
The Consumer Society. 1970. London: Sage, 1998.
For a Critique of the Political Economy of the Sign. 1972. St Louis, MO: Telos Press, 1981.
The Mirror of Production. 1973. St Louis, MO: Telos Press, 1975.
Symbolic Exchange and Death. 1976. London: Sage, 1993.
In the Shadow of the Silent Majorities. 1978. New York: Semiotext(e), 1983.
Simulations. 1981. New York: Semiotext(e), 1983.
Fatal Strategies. 1983. London: Pluto Press, 1990.
The Gulf War Did Not Take Place. 1991. Sydney: Power Publications, 1995.
The Perfect Crime. 1995. London: Verso, 1996.
The Spirit of Terrorism. 2001. London: Verso, 2002.
The Intelligence of Evil. 2004. Oxford: Berg, 2005.

Further reading

Michael Gane. 1991. *Baudrillard's Bestiary: Baudrillard and Culture*. London: Routledge.
Michael Gane. 1991. *Baudrillard: Critical and Fatal Theory*. London: Routledge.
Michael Gane. 2000. *Jean Baudrillard. In Radical Uncertainty*. London: Pluto Press.
William Merrin. 2005. *Baudrillard and the Media. A Critical Introduction*. Cambridge: Polity Press.

WILLIAM MERRIN

ZYGMUNT BAUMAN

Zygmunt Bauman is an accomplished practitioner of the sociological imagination. His self-imposed task has been to provide his readers with an intellectual map and a moral compass with which to negotiate the latest phase of modernity, one in which belief in the big promises of 'progress' and universal betterment made by politicians has greatly diminished. This phase, sometimes called 'postmodernity', is one of great uncertainty about the self and society. In analysing this condition, Bauman has drawn upon several traditions, including French structuralist anthropology, the Frankfurt school of critical theory from Adorno to **Habermas**, the revisionist Marxism of Gramsci and Lukács, and the frontier radicalism of American sociologists such as **C. Wright Mills**.

Bauman, born in Poland in 1925, moved to the USSR at the beginning of the Second World War at the age of fourteen. By the age of eighteen he was fighting in the Polish division of the Red Army against Hitler's German army. Returning to Poland after the war, Bauman served as a political officer in the Polish army during the late 1940s and early 1950s and in 1948 he married Janina Lewinson. He was dismissed from his position during an anti-Jewish purge in 1953, and subsequently became a revisionist intellectual, teaching at Warsaw University. Bauman decided to emigrate to the West in 1968 following another anti-Jewish campaign orchestrated by the regime, during which he was castigated as a public enemy.

Since 1968, Bauman has built yet a third career, this time in the West. By 1971 he was professor of sociology at Leeds University. He published five books during the 1970s, four during the 1980s and has published many more since his official retirement in 1990. Bauman won the Amalfi Prize for *Modernity and the Holocaust* (1989), in which he focused on the tendency of modern bureaucracies to neutralize the moral sensitivity of those who work in them, permitting brutal measures to be enacted against groups that do not 'fit in' to the social and political blueprints of those who rule.

Zygmunt Bauman made his 'turn to postmodernity' in the mid-1980s. Since then, one of his preoccupations has been to explore the nature of the postmodern habitat in which, he argues, we are destined to live. In Bauman's view, this habitat is occupied by rootless strangers disoriented by an overload of ambivalence and by warring neo-tribes asserting competing 'truths'. Bauman's message to postmodern men and women is: accept responsibility for making your own choices in life with no other guidance but your own judgement and your own sense of what is 'right'. This is coupled with a chal-

18

lenge: look inside yourself and be aware of your inborn inclination to be-for-the-Other, to respond to the Other's mute demand for care. Bauman argues that our innate tendency to express moral concern and identify with the Other's wants is stifled in modernity by positivistic science and dogmatic bureaucracy. If the Other does not 'fit in' to modernity's approved classifications, it is liable to be extinguished.

Bauman did not always have an extremely pessimistic view of modernity's potential for producing good outcomes. Before Bauman made his 'turn to postmodernity', for over a quarter of a century his efforts had been focused on the prospects for 'improving' modernity. He developed a strategy for making modernity democratic and socialist: freer, more equal, more just. This strategy, which drew on Marx, Gramsci and Habermas, gave a leading role to intellectuals, especially sociologists. Their task was to encourage open and informed dialogue among social groups, leading towards the identification of shared interests. Dialogue would be one aspect of creative praxis leading in the direction of a socialist utopia.

In fact, as early as the mid-1960s, while he was still teaching and researching as a leading sociologist in communist Poland, Bauman was developing the arguments for which he has become famous. In his published work he was, for example, making three major claims: that ideology, reinforced by bureaucracy, encourages conformity and neutralizes the sense of personal moral responsibility; that it is a very challenging task to plan society effectively when cultural homogeneity has been undermined by subcultural heterogeneity; and that everyone must take responsibility for their own moral choices. Over two decades later, these arguments were central to *Modernity and the Holocaust, Legislators and Interpreters* and *Postmodern Ethics,* respectively. In other words, some of the elements of Bauman's sociology of postmodernity were already present in the work he carried out in his earlier manifestation as a sociologist who did not look beyond modernity but, instead, sought his utopia within its bounds.

During the 1960s and early 1970s Bauman explored the dynamics of the triangular relationships among the state bureaucracy, the people and the intellectuals. He hoped that, under the influence of persuasive intellectuals, bureaucratic planners would become enlightened teachers.

In fact, the social contract between the peasantry and the bureaucracy was so strong and so central to Polish society that Bauman and those who shared his aspirations were unable to act as an effective third force. Neither the peasantry nor the bureaucrats felt any enthusiasm for progressive intellectuals who spoke about freedom and seemed to relish uncertainty.

When he emigrated to the West, Bauman retained his commitment to the goal of socialism. Along with this commitment went a strategy and a critique, both initially developed in Poland. The strategy was to continue exploring the opportunities involved 'objectively' in unfolding historical situations, East and West, in the hope that a progressive analysis might be heard at the right time. This analysis would include a positive vision of the better society offered by socialism, a vision to inspire praxis.

The critique was initially directed against the socio-political order created in Poland during the 1960s by an unenlightened bureaucracy and a highly conformist population. Bauman pointed out that state socialism had failed to confront three challenges: preventing moral anaesthesia, coping with subcultural heterogeneity and encouraging a sense of personal moral responsibility. When Bauman mounted the same critique against western capitalist societies during the 1980s and 1990s, it played a different role in his overall argument.

In the 1960s Bauman argued that the deficiencies just listed were practical matters that could be dealt with as long as the correct strategies were adopted by leaders who were competent and clear sighted. However, during the late 1980s and early 1990s Bauman took a much more absolutist line: the prevalence of moral anaesthesia made modernity unacceptable: subcultural heterogeneity contributed to a climate of ambivalence that fatally undermined belief in modernity; the challenge of assuming personal moral responsibility was too daunting for modern men and women to confront as a matter of course. In other words, these issues were no longer practical matters that could be handled within the context of socialist modernity but *fundamental flaws that made modernity unacceptable.*

What had changed between 1966 and the late 1980s was that Bauman had lost his confidence that the kind of socialism he wanted could be brought into existence. He tried hard to make it work, intellectually at least. In *Socialism. An Active Utopia* Bauman focused upon the nature of communism and capitalism. At the same time, in *Towards a Critical Sociology*, he concentrated upon the complex relationships between culture and sociology. Bauman deconstructed Marxist socialism as intellectual theory, political regime and social order, looking in particular at the role of culture and intellectuals, and the part played by power, especially bureaucratic power.

His critical analysis had four parts: the communist regimes had pursued industrialization instead of socialism; they had made the ruling party a self-perpetuating establishment and tried to atomize civil society, the source of corrective criticism; meanwhile, western consumerism seduced the population of capitalist societies into supporting that system; and, finally, the stability of capitalism had acquired a cultural foundation.

Bauman's objective has been to bring about a social existence in which rational and emancipated human beings exercise their freedom in a creative fashion. He wanted to encourage a process of dialogue within civil society. His hope was that intellectuals such as himself would encourage ordinary people to take an informed, rational and active part in making society freer, more equal and more just.

During the early 1980s, major social changes were underway in both East and West with the arrival of Solidarity in Poland and Margaret Thatcher in Britain. When Bauman published *Memories of Class*, he believed that the whole system of social production and satisfaction of needs was in an acute crisis and that the time was ripe for bringing into being a thoroughly democratic society in which citizens played a much more active part in running their own affairs. In other words, the early 1980s were a time of hope for Zygmunt Bauman and his writings from this period were optimistic. However, Bauman's programme of creative dialogue and action depended on a reconstruction of the political sphere. The idea was that as society became more democratic, the central state would take less responsibility for regulating the details of social life. Instead, local assemblies of various kinds would become more powerful. The everyday lives of most people would become more 'political.' Men and women would make more decisions collectively as citizens in their localities.

The discovery that active citizenship and participatory democracy were easily swamped by consumerism and the power of global capitalism presented serious difficulties for Bauman's intellectual strategy. Bauman had learned his socialism, both old style and new style, in the context of a highly developed public sphere headed by a powerful central state. This had been the case in pre-war Soviet Russia, post-war socialist Poland and also, to a lesser degree, in Western European societies before the 1980s, during the period of corporatist management of the Keynesian welfare state.

By the time he published *Freedom*, Bauman had diagnosed the condition of the people, both East and West, as being a form of captivity or disablement, although he does not use these terms. In the East the people were repressed by the state. In the West they were seduced by consumerism. Either way, the obstacles to creative socialist praxis were enormous. The world was full of half-finished or disintegrating 'modern' projects. Many occupants of this disconnected world lived in a thoroughly confused state, not understanding what was going on. At some point in the mid-1980s Bauman placed these facts at the centre of his vision. In other words, he discovered post-modernity.

Bauman has stopped trying to find ways of making modernity 'work'. He thinks that great schemes of modernity are most harmful when they are most effective. In practice, Bauman believes, the amount of harm legislators can do has been diminished since the state has gone into semi-retirement. In any case, national governments have been forced to bow to the power of multinational and transna-tional corporations as these institutions have grown larger, more powerful and more demanding.

As Bauman argues in *Globalisation: The Human Consequences*, in this new globalized world no one is in control and the whole planet is in a state of high risk. However, consumers can buy short-term comfort in the marketplace. Consumerism seduces us into accepting the deeply unsettling condition of postmodernity. It does not stop us being anxious. However, it offers us a range of pre-packaged short-term solutions for our sense of dissatisfaction.

The experience of migration and exile fundamentally changed Bauman's relationship with the societies he studies and writes about. Having been an 'insider' he became an 'outsider'. He is a little more 'distanced' from his subject. Bauman's later work is not filled with concrete social groups who live in specific ways in particular places. Instead, it is populated with archetypes: tourists and vagabonds, strollers and players, consumers and flawed consumers, rich and poor. These are abstract entities, personifications of different perspectives, plights and strategies. In his hands, the Jews become the prototypes of the archetypes. He presents their situation as being a microcosm or condensation of the situation of *all* men and women in post-modernity: rootless strangers in an ambivalent world.

Bauman has made an intellectual voyage from the pursuit of the progressive within modernity to the search for humane survival within postmodernity. As Bauman sees it, a change in objective conditions has produced the postmodern habitat in which he and the rest of us are forced to dwell. His fundamental approach remains the same: to encourage open communication and creative action. Indi-vidual action can be creative in the sense that when 'I' enact care for the 'Other' I strengthen the tissue of interpersonal solidarity in which ethical behaviour resides.

Compared to the more optimistic programme of the 1970s, Bau-man's ethical challenge to the inhabitants of the postmodern habitat is more diffident, presented in a less exhortatory manner ('the choice is yours'). He expects less. The impulse is conservatory, protecting the seed for a future sowing. It is a programme for the winter rather than the spring.

In the early twenty-first century, Bauman has continued to hold his view, already well developed in the 1960s, that culture is the key arena in which the structure of society is determined. Equally long-standing has been his conviction that intellectuals, especially sociologists, should stay close to ordinary men and women, injecting a critical perspective on the deeply conservative and potentially oppressive conventions of 'common sense'. He has continued to do this in a stream of books.

See also: Ülrich Beck, Anthony Giddens, Jürgen Habermas.

See also in *Fifty Key Sociologists: The Formative Theorists*: Theodor Adorno, Karl Marx.

Major works

Between Class and Elite. 1960. Manchester: Manchester University Press, 1972.
Spoleczeństwo, w ktorym żyjemy. 1962. Warsaw: Książka i Wiedza.
Zarys marksistowskiej teorii spoleczeństwa. 1964. Warsaw: Państwowe Wydawnictwo Naukowe.
Culture as Praxis. 1973. London: Routledge & Kegan Paul.
Socialism: The Active Utopia. 1976. London: George Allen and Unwin.
Towards a Critical Sociology: An Essay on Common-Sense and Emancipation. 1976. London: Routledge & Kegan Paul.
Hermeneutics and Social Science: Approaches to Understanding. 1978. London: Hutchinson.
Memories of Class: The Pre-history and After-life of Class. 1982. London: Routledge & Kegan Paul.
Legislators and Interpreters. 1987. Cambridge: Polity Press.
Modernity and the Holocaust. 1989.Cambridge: Polity Press.
Modernity and Ambivalence. 1991. Ithaca, NY: Cornell University Press.
Intimations of Postmodernity. 1992. London and New York: Routledge.
Postmodern Ethics. 1993. Cambridge: Polity Press.
Postmodernity and Its Discontents. 1997. Cambridge: Polity Press.
Consumerism and the New Poor. 1998. Buckingham: Open University Press.
Globalisation. The Human Consequences. 1998. Cambridge: Polity Press.
In Search of Politics. 1999. Cambridge: Polity Press.
The Individualized Society. 2000. Cambridge: Polity Press.
Liquid Modernity. 2000. Cambridge: Polity Press.
Community. 2000. Cambridge: Polity Press.
Society under Siege. 2002. Cambridge: Polity Press.
Wasted Lives. 2003. Cambridge: Polity Press.

Liquid Love. 2003. Cambridge: Polity Press.
Identity. 2004. Cambridge: Polity Press.
Europe. An Unfinished Adventure. 2004. Cambridge: Polity Press.
Liquid Life. 2005. Cambridge: Polity Press.

Further reading

Peter Beilharz. 2000. *Zygmunt Bauman: Dialectic of Modernity.* London: Sage.
Tony Blackshaw. 2005. *Zygmunt Bauman.* London: Routledge.
Dennis Smith. 1999. *Zygmunt Bauman: Prophet of Postmodernity.* Cambridge: Polity Press.

DENNIS SMITH

SIMONE DE BEAUVOIR

Simone de Beauvoir was born in Paris in 1908, the elder of two daughters of bourgeois parents. Beauvoir's intellectual abilities were apparent from an early age and the change in her family's economic circumstances was such that the young Beauvoir – contrary to the expectations about young bourgeois women of the time – was allowed to train for a career. The profession she chose was that of teacher of philosophy, and it was during this training that she encountered the secular, critical world of European philosophy – a world inhabited not just by ideas that challenged those of her former milieu but by the person of Jean-Paul Sartre, the man with whom she was to form a complex, life-long relationship.

The names of Beauvoir and Sartre are linked in the majority of writing about Beauvoir; the reverse is less often the case. This statement touches on many of the key features of both Beauvoir's work and work about her. Beauvoir and Sartre did share a common commitment to the development and articulation of the philosophical school of existentialism, both had life-long commitments to left-wing politics and both wrote fiction as well as non-fiction. But for many years Beauvoir was a woman whose ideas were essentially less original than those of her male partner, a woman who wrote the twentieth century's greatest book on women (*The Second Sex*) but who drew theoretical inspiration from a male writer.

Part of the complexity of situating Beauvoir in intellectual history is thus to recognize the ways in which changes in the way we write intellectual biography are shaped by other changes in social under-

24

standing. Beauvoir began to write (both fiction and non-fiction) in the 1940s: her first published work was the novel *She Came to Stay* (1943), which was followed by the philosophical essays *Pyrrhus and Cineas* (1944) and *The Ethics of Ambiguity* (1948). Previous accounts of Beauvoir's work have always emphasized the biographical nature of Beauvoir's fiction. *She Came to Stay*, for example, is often 'read' as a work of fictional revenge on the woman who challenged Beauvoir's relationship with Sartre. But such a reading was based on the assumption that women, rather than men, drew their inspiration from their own lives and that Beauvoir's work – both fiction and otherwise – was never anything other than an attempt to help to illustrate the ideas of Sartre.

The assumptions that underpinned this gendered account of intellectual creativity were to be challenged – although not perhaps fully discussed until years later – by the publication in 1949 of *The Second Sex*. In this work Beauvoir voiced the now famous comment that 'women are made and not born'. Beauvoir did not trespass into those places where **Judith Butler** and others were to take this idea some thirty years later, but what she did do was to suggest that men (and Man) are the definitive norm of human existence. Women are, she argued, born into a world which allows full human agency only to men and in which women are condemned to lives of subservience and inactivity. For readers in the twenty-first century *The Second Sex* poses a number of problems, not least the very much more ambiguous accounts of masculinity and femininity which now prevail. Amongst the other problematic aspects of *The Second Sex* is its reliance on somewhat outdated accounts of human biology, its assumption that the normative world of femininity is that of bourgeois France in the middle of the twentieth century and – perhaps most significantly – the assumption that masculinity is as unproblematic as femininity is apparently problematic. Beauvoir flatly rejects the work of Freud and hence she is unsympathetic to the idea that human sexuality is nothing if not unstable.

For all this, *The Second Sex* was (and is) a genuinely revolutionary work, in that it had the courage to challenge the taken-for-granted ideas not just of one culture but of an entire intellectual and social tradition – that of post-Enlightenment Europe – and ask for a change in the way that human beings related to one another. If more changes seem to be demanded of women than men, we are nevertheless asked to consider the possibilities of a social world in which women and men do not have to act out demeaning roles of superiority and inferiority. The emphasis on the inherent 'play acting' and 'performance' which

Judith Butler and others were later to explore owes a great deal to Beauvoir's recognition of the personal prisons created by the internalization of gendered scripts.

In the history of twentieth-century ideas Beauvoir's *The Second Sex* has an iconic status as one of the great books of feminism: it is what Mary Wollstonecraft's *The Vindication of the Rights of Woman* was to the eighteenth. But the 150 years between the publication of the two books – one at the end of the Enlightenment and the other towards the end of modernism – suggests some of their similarities rather than disparities, and in particular the way in which both authors work within a framework of binary difference between male and female. Equally, both Beauvoir and Wollstonecraft emphasize the centrality of education and work to the shift in gender relations: at times Beauvoir, not unlike Wollstonecraft, comes close to making women's entry into public employment the be all and end all of female emancipation. For generations born to the expectation (not to mention the necessity) of women's participation in employment, this call has less of the emancipatory promise than Beauvoir assumed. The experience, and the accompanying discourse, which is absent from Beauvoir is that of motherhood; it is a part of human existence that has little place in her world.

Paradoxically, it was the death of her own mother that led Beauvoir to write what many critics regard as her most powerful book. *A Very Easy Death*, the account of the death of her mother, is part of Beauvoir's considerable autobiographical work (the other four volumes are *Memoirs of a Dutiful Daughter*, *The Prime of Life*, *Force of Circumstance* and *All Said and Done*).

Various publications after Beauvoir's death in 1986 have challenged some of the exclusions, evasions and inconsistencies of Beauvoir's autobiography, but few have questioned the veracity of *A Very Easy Death*. There is little in Beauvoir's subsequent work to suggest that she wished to explore the reasons for the impact of her mother's death, but we can note the coincidence of the event and Beauvoir's increasing involvement with explicitly feminist politics.

French feminism (in the work of writers such as Hélène Cixous and Monique Wittig) argued that women had to recognize their essential difference from men, and from male intellectual systems. Beauvoir was never prepared to concede this point: for her, language and to a very significant extent intellectual systems were gender neutral. What she did do, however, was to take a very prominent part in campaigns about reproductive rights and violence against women.

The last years of Beauvoir's life were marked by a degree of estrangement from Sartre, who was to marry a much younger woman towards the end of his life. However, Sartre and Beauvoir have become, both individually and as a couple, part of the intellectual and political history of the twentieth century.

The novel for which Beauvoir won the Prix Goncourt in 1955 (*The Mandarins*) gave something of an account of the dynamic between them, an account which did not minimize the sorrows and the difficulties of women and men attempting to maintain loyalties to both personal and political ideals. Beauvoir has, of course, become globally famous for her study of women (although she also investigated in her work *Old Age* another binary division, that between old age and youth), yet, in sum, we might see that her work is more crucially concerned with an issue that late-twentieth-century feminists have identified as crucial to the situation of women: the question of ties to others and the impact of our actions on others. Throughout her long career, Beauvoir worked on the issue that has become part of the work of sociologists and social psychologists such as **Anthony Giddens**, **Ülrich Beck** and Carol Gilligan: the question of how interpersonal relations can be lived in ways which allow the freedom of one individual without depleting the freedom of the other. Beauvoir helped us to see the gendered nature of this problem.

See also: Judith Butler.

Major works

Beauvoir was a prolific writer and her key texts are:

Fiction

She Came to Stay. 1943. New York: W. W. Norton, 1999.
The Mandarins. 1954. New York: W. W. Norton, 1999.

Autobiography and biography

Memoirs of a Dutiful Daughter. 1959. New York: Harper Perennial, 1974.
The Prime of Life. 1962. New York: Marlowe and Company, 1992.
Force of Circumstance. 1965. New York: Marlowe and Company, 1992.
A Very Easy Death. 1965. New York: Pantheon, 1985.
All Said and Done. 1979. New York: Marlowe and Company, 1993.
Adieux: Farewell to Sartre. 1984. New York: Pantheon, 1985.

Philosophy and social theory

The Ethics of Ambiguity. 1948. New York: Citadel Press, 1966.

The Second Sex. 1949. Harmondsworth: Penguin, 1972.

Some extracts can be found in Margaret Simons' edited collection *Simone de Beauvoir: Philosophical Writings.* Champaign, IL: University of Illinois Press, 2004.

Further reading

Mary Evans. 1985. *Simone De Beauvoir: A Feminist Mandarin.* London: Tavistock.

Deidre Bair. 1990. *Simone de Beauvoir: A Biography.* New York: Summit Books.

Toril Moi. 1993. *Simone de Beauvoir: The Making of an Intellectual Woman.* Oxford: Blackwell.

MARY EVANS

ÜLRICH BECK

Ülrich Beck, born in 1944, is primarily known for his groundbreaking thesis on 'risk society'. He argues that a fundamental break is taking place within the social history of modernity; a break marked by the dissolution of older forms of 'industrial society' and the rise of a new risk society. Beck claims that earlier generations of industrial societies were blind to the ecological hazards of modernization and that a social consciousness of large-scale industrial hazards is beginning to exert a heavy influence upon people's cultural attitudes and social behaviours in the emergent risk society. This is particularly apparent in relation to chemical pollutants, nuclear technologies and genetic engineering. The new 'risk consciousness' results from a perception, encouraged by the mass media, that we are living through a time where the environmental costs of industrialization are beginning to outweigh the social benefits. The frames of reference that shape Beck's approach to social theory, as well as his terms of political analysis, are rooted in the belief that, where the denizens of industrial society are blind to the uninsurable risks of modernization, those of the risk society must come to terms with possible futures in which the threat of 'self-annihilation' looms large upon the cultural horizon.

Beck holds that the novelty of the situation demands a revision of the language of social science so as to create concepts that are more suited to grasp the reality of the world in which we now find ourselves. He maintains that many longstanding sociological concepts, such as 'social class', 'the family household', gender roles' and 'the nation-state' are now outdated and exist only as 'zombie categories'. Indeed, he holds strongly to the view that we have arrived at a point in our social development where the so-called 'classical' frameworks of sociological analysis developed by writers such as Max Weber and Emile Durkheim no longer provide us with any significant insights into the major transformations that are shaping the overall structure and quality of life in contemporary societies. Accordingly, his writings may be seen as a forthright attempt to furnish sociology with theories of society that are more in tune with contemporary cultural sensibilities.

Beck's publications have done a great deal to establish the idea of risk as a core concept in sociological analysis. He has used this concept as a means to initiate a variety of critical debates on the essential character of contemporary society, culture and politics. Beck's focus on 'risk' is used not only to bring sociological attention to bear upon myriad problems relating to ecological hazards, but also to present a broad vision of social life where individuals increasingly experience a pronounced sense of insecurity with regard to everyday matters of love and work. While he argues that people's awareness of risks is intimately related to their knowledge about threats to the environment, he also acknowledges the extent to which 'risk consciousness' results from experiences of 'flexible' forms of employment and shifting patterns of family life. Accordingly, along with writers such as **Anthony Giddens** and **Zygmunt Bauman**, he presents the 'risk society' as a 'runaway world' of rapid social change: a world where individuals are continually forced to negotiate their basic terms of self-identity, cultural meaning and social belonging. He argues that, more than ever before, people are inclined to think about and approach every aspect of their lives through a calculation of risk.

'Risk consciousness' comprises a cultural sensibility rooted in processes of 'individualization' and 'reflexive modernization'. The majority of people now find that contemporary social and economic arrangements afford no time or space for traditional patterns of work and family life. As a result, individuals are increasingly forced to make anxious choices about how to live their lives. It is claimed that such an intensifying process of 'individualization' is at once a source of and a response to a further process of 'reflexive modernization'. Beck maintains that individuals are not only increasingly inclined to reflect critically upon the value and purpose of their lives, but also more likely to be primed to engage in wider critical debates over political organization and established ideals of social progress. Accordingly, while critical thinking may well result from a growing knowledge about the threat of ecological catastrophe, the culture for such thinking is at the same time nurtured by everyday social circumstances of pronounced insecurity.

In the final analysis, a great deal of Beck's sociological commentary is designed to provoke further debate over the possibilities that exist within a 'risk society' for radical social change. There is a strong polemical orientation to his work. He makes explicit his concern for the development of a new 'radicalized' modernity guided by the ideals of 'ecological enlightenment'. Following on from his conviction that western industrialization has brought us to the brink of global environmental catastrophe, a great sense of urgency characterizes his search for any erstwhile developments that indicate a propensity for society to reform itself (particularly in its use of technology and science) so as to secure our planetary survival. While it is possible to recognize a 'utopian' element within his social theory, this is far removed from the Marxist ideals that inspired earlier generations of critical theorists. Whilst seeking to promote a new 'cosmopolitan' perspective on international politics and law, he argues that our best hopes for the future rest on the possibility of involving an increasingly powerful transnational community of non-governmental organizations within the key political decisions confronting global society. On this account, the seeds for radical social change are already being sown by organizations such as Greenpeace, Genewatch, Oxfam and Amnesty International. It is according to the intensity of our shared fears for the future that opportunities may increase for these seeds to germinate and flourish.

Considerable controversy surrounds Beck's work. First, some object to the strong 'realism' that characterizes his depiction of environmental hazards and, in particular, his failure to engage with the analytical complexity of existing sociological debates concerning the social construction of our cultural understandings of risk. Second, empirical studies of risk perception have found little evidence to support Beck's favoured representation of the ways in which individuals are liable to experience and make sense of potential risks to themselves and others. Finally, some are inclined to take issue with the historical narrative which frames his account of the novelty of a 'risk society'; and all the more so where this leads him to argue that 'classical' sociological theory holds no value for understanding contemporary social developments. Nevertheless, there is no doubting the fact that his works are now widely recognized as indispensable for engaging with the task of theorizing today's world. Ülrich Beck is a prime example of a *Zeitgeist* sociologist. Whilst the majority of commentators may adopt a largely critical stance towards the central claims of his thesis, it is all too clear, nevertheless, that he is widely regarded as having significantly advanced the capacity for sociological theorists to engage with the task of 'thinking society anew'.

See also: Zygmunt Bauman, Anthony Giddens.

See also in *Fifty Key Sociologists: The Formative Theorists*: Karl Marx.

Major works

Risk Society: Towards a New Modernity. 1986. London: Sage, 1992.
Ecological Politics in an Age of Risk. 1988. Cambridge: Polity Press, 1995.
The Normal Chaos of Love. 1990. With Elizabeth Beck-Gernsheim. London: Polity Press, 1995.
Ecological Enlightenment: Essays on the Politics of the Risk Society. 1991. Atlantic Highlands, NJ: Humanities Press, 1995.
The Reinvention of Politics: Rethinking Modernity in the Global Social Order. 1996. Cambridge: Polity Press.
Democracy Without Enemies. 1997. Cambridge: Polity Press.
World Risk Society. 1997. Cambridge: Polity Press, 1999.
Power in the Global Age. 2005. Cambridge: Polity Press.
Cosmopolitan Vision. 2006. Cambridge: Polity Press.

Further reading

Barbara Adam, Ülrich Beck and J. van Loon, eds. 2000. *The Risk Society and Beyond: Critical Issues for Social Theory*. London: Sage.
Ülrich Beck and Johannes Willms. 2004. *Conversations with Ülrich Beck*. Cambridge: Polity Press.
Gabe Mythen. 2004. *Ülrich Beck: A Critical Introduction to the Risk Society*. London: Pluto Press.
Iain Wilkinson. 2001. *Anxiety in a Risk Society*. London: Routledge.

IAIN WILKINSON

HOWARD S. BECKER

Howard Saul Becker is one of the most influential figures in the symbolic interactionist tradition. Born in 1928 and raised in Chicago, he studied there for all three of his degrees and spent most of his career working at Northwestern University, before moving to the University of Washington in 1991. He is now retired and lives in San Francisco with his wife, photographer Dianne Hagaman. Becker is most famous for his studies in the sociology of deviance, but he has also researched and written extensively in areas such as education, the arts and qualitative methodology. Unlike **Goffman**, Mead and others in this theoretical tradition, Becker is happy to define himself as an interactionist: he was a graduate student in the thriving sociology department of the University of Chicago, and often refers to his mentors Everett C. Hughes and Herbert Blumer.

Another great influence in Becker's life has been music. In the 1950s, he played as a jazz pianist in various Chicago bars and nightclubs, and he was a member of a jazz band, the Bobby Laine Trio. Becker asserts that he started playing the piano long before he became a sociologist, and his work often demonstrates the influence of one upon the other. His first paper, 'The Professional Dance Musician and His Audience', was published in 1951, the year that he completed his PhD, but he continued to write about the subject as late as 2000, in an article on 'The Etiquette of Improvisation'. In Becker's view, playing live music is a social activity that involves interacting with other players and the audience and that follows certain unspoken rules which only become evident when they are broken. This may happen, for example, when a band member plays too many choruses or fails to pick up on another player's cues.

Perhaps the most famous piece of research that Becker carried out was his 1953 study of marijuana users, published first as an article and eventually in the book *Outsiders*. This research was not intended to provide any policy recommendations about drug addiction and crime control, but served rather as an exercise in interactionist theory and methods. The dominant view at the time was that drug users were a distinct group of people with a distinct psychological profile. By contrast, Becker argued that anyone could potentially drift into the habit if they experienced a certain sequence of interaction. It follows that sociologists should, therefore, study the social process of *becoming* a marijuana user, as with any other deviant identity, and should see this in terms of the meanings that it holds for the individual. Becker identified three main stages through which people became progressively committed to a 'deviant career' of marijuana use: they must first learn the technique of smoking, then learn to perceive the effects of the drug and finally interpret the feelings as pleasurable.

This study of drug use formed the basis of Becker's perspective on the sociology of deviance, often referred to as 'labelling theory'. This theoretical approach developed in the 1960s as a response to the conventional models of crime then dominant. Becker argued that deviance was not a quality inherent in a particular type of person or behaviour, but was rather a label attributed to those who break the rules in a particular social setting: thus, the same act can be deviant in one context but not in another. This relativist definition of deviance therefore asked not 'Who are the deviants?' or 'What is deviant behaviour?' but, rather, why certain kinds of action are seen as deviant in the first place. It asks: 'deviant to whom?' and 'in relation to which social norms?' Labelling theory focuses on the way in which interactions between rule makers and rule breakers lead some people into a deviant career and change their sense of self-identity. Labels such as 'thief' or 'drug addict' can create a 'master status' that dominates the way that people see each other. Other sociologists, such as Stan Cohen and Jock Young, built on this approach to show how the mass media contributed to these public perceptions of deviance by creating 'folk devils' and stirring up 'moral panics'. Labelling theory has been criticized for being too sympathetic towards deviants, assuming them to be the passive victims of a punitive society, and not explaining why some people are motivated to break social rules in the first place. It continues, nevertheless, to be an influential perspective in the sociology of deviance.

Another key area of research for Becker was that of 'student culture', or the way in which people are socialized into the norms and values of college life. With Blanche Geer, he conducted a study of students at medical school, university and vocational trade schools that informed their books *Boys in White* and *Making the Grade*. They showed that, whereas college students felt some degree of autonomy over the way they organized their political and social activities on campus, they felt relatively powerless about controlling their academic success. Becker and his co-workers argued that such feelings of subjection led to the development of a supportive student culture that helped these young people cope with uncertainty. In particular, their anxieties were channelled into concerns about flunking courses or failing to maintain their grade-point averages. Becker revised the book in 1995, examining the effects of increasing bureaucracy and administration upon university life.

In 1982, Becker published *Art Worlds*, a study of the social context in which artwork is produced. This was based on his own experiences as a jazz pianist and photographer and on his empirical research on painters, art dealers, classical composers, poets and literary editors. Becker's argument here was that art is a collective activity, involving a whole network of people as well as the individual 'artist'. Works of art are embedded in these 'art worlds' of production, distribution and consumption, and artists are constrained by factors such as the availability of materials, changing technologies and artistic conventions and the 'rules of the game' that govern their art. The final work of art that reaches its audience is, then, the product of a long social process of negotiation among the various members of an art world.

Alongside these substantive topics, Becker has also maintained an interest in research methods and epistemology. He has written about techniques of participant observation, interviewing, case studies and digital imaging, and was one of the first to discuss the impact of computers on academic work. In 1967, Becker engaged in a contentious debate with **Alvin W. Gouldner** about value freedom in the social sciences, arguing that sociologists could not and should not claim to be objective. In his paper 'Whose Side Are We On?', Becker argued that personal interests inevitably shape the way researchers select topics to study and questions to ask, and so this should be acknowledged in sociological work. The idea of value-free, non-political research is a myth, as sociologists must necessarily take sides in social conflicts. Furthermore, given that most social research serves the interests of dominant groups, the sociologist had a duty to take the side of the relatively powerless, such as deviant outsiders. This approach came to be referred to as a 'sociology of the underdog'.

Throughout all of his work, Becker has written exceptionally clearly, communicating theoretical ideas in a direct and accessible manner. He is also a very humorous writer, and his various books and papers are a delight to read. This style of writing is one that he has consciously developed and that he discusses in his books on study skills, *Writing for Social Scientists* and *Tricks of the Trade*. In these books, Becker debunks some of the common myths about academic writing that intimidate students and professors alike. In particular, he explains that no one writes perfectly first time, but rather 'good writing' results from continuous redrafting.

On his personal website, Becker has described how he has often been confused with a sociologist called Howard Paul Becker, who had a colourful family history. The figure known to friends and admirers as 'Howie' is a different character altogether, and has led a remarkable life. From jazz pianist and photographer to researcher, theorist and professorial guru, Becker has earned his place amongst the most influential sociologists.

See also: Erving Goffman.

See also in *Fifty Key Sociologists: The Formative Theorists*: Charles Cooley, George Herbert Mead, Albion Small.

Major works

Boys in White: Student Culture in Medical School. 1961. With Blanche Geer, Everett Hughes and Anselm Strauss. Chicago: University of Chicago Press.
Outsiders: Studies in the Sociology of Deviance. 1963. New York: Free Press.
'Whose Side Are We On?' 1967. *Social Problems* 14.
Making the Grade: The Academic Side of College Life. 1968. With Blanche Geer and Everett Hughes. New York: Wiley. Revised edn with new introduction published in 1995.
Art Worlds. 1982. Berkeley, CA: University of California Press.
Writing for Social Scientists: How to Start and Finish Your Thesis, Book, or Article. 1986. Chicago: University of Chicago Press.
Tricks of the Trade: How to Think About Your Research While You're Doing It. 1998. Chicago: University of Chicago Press.
'The Etiquette of Improvisation'. 2000. *Mind, Culture and Activity* 7.

Further reading

Stan Cohen. 1972. *Folk Devils and Moral Panics: The Creation of the Mods and Rockers*. London: MacGibbon & Kee.
Jock Young. 1971. *The Drugtakers*. London: McGibbon & Kee.

SUSIE SCOTT

BASIL BERNSTEIN

Basil Bernstein was one of the most original British sociologists of the second half of the twentieth century. He was remarkably creative, and continued to produce challenging work to the very end of his life. Although his work is most simply categorized as falling within the sociology of education, it really defies such easy categorization. Grounded in a synthesis of empirical inquiry and conceptual elaboration, Bernstein's sociology owed as much to European traditions of social theory as to the British sociology of education with which he was most often associated. While his contributions received recognition in the United Kingdom – especially towards the end of his career – he was more widely recognized internationally, enjoying a major reputation in North America, Spain, Portugal, Latin America,

Australia and Scandinavia. Over the course of his intellectual career, one can trace the transition in Bernstein's thought from a form of structuralism inspired by Durkheim and Mauss to an individual version of poststructuralism.

Born in 1924, he began his career as a family caseworker and went on to study sociology at the London School of Economics in 1947. After qualifying, he worked as a teacher but became a research assistant in the University of London in 1960. He moved to the Institute of Education in 1962, where he spent the rest of his career and became Karl Mannheim Professor of Sociology in Education. Bernstein remained intellectually productive until his death in 2000. He was firmly rooted in some of the recurrent preoccupations of British sociology of education – notably the relations of schooling and social stratification – although his approach differed markedly from that of most of his British colleagues. His work owed more to a European, especially French, style of thought, although he always attempted to marry his general theoretical schemas to empirical evidence.

Even those who are relatively well versed in Basil Bernstein's sociology are not always aware that his earliest work included some speculations on psychotherapy. Before he worked out his sociolinguistic theories of socialization in home and school, or his models of pedagogic discourse, he wrote about the psychotherapeutic encounter as a device for the differential generation of narratives, experiences and identities. One can detect in that early work the possibilities for a semiotic analysis of talk and technologies of subjectivity. In his last work he began to sketch a vision of the 'totally pedagogized society', a social formation generated by discursive principles of life-long learning, global information networks, pervasive state-sponsored credentialism, self-improvement and an obsession with training. Between those two chronological poles of his intellectual career Bernstein developed a remarkably consistent set of sociological preoccupations. He wanted to understand, and to research, how social actors are differentially positioned, how socially distributed semiotic resources differentially enable the construction of knowledge and experience, and how institutions are structured so as to act as selective agencies of reproduction.

Bernstein's was a daring undertaking. Although it was grounded in the sociology of education, his intellectual programme was always extended beyond the sociology of schooling. Indeed, he was often impatient with colleagues whose vision of a possible sociology of education he found rigidly narrow. His was a singularly bold attempt to create a thoroughly sociological analysis of education, in all its forms, in the tradition of Durkheim, and drawing inspiration from Marx and Mead along the way. It was never easy for Bernstein's readers and students to discern the lineaments of his thought and to distinguish the key elements of his intellectual programme. While his teaching and conversation could be inspirational, his written work could be forbidding, complex and convoluted. In consequence, he was often misrepresented. Too many textbooks contain gross caricatures of his ideas. Critics all too often attacked those misrepresentations rather than engaging with Bernstein's ideas at first hand.

He became famous – notorious in some quarters – by virtue of his early work on language, class and socialization. In a series of works he and his co-workers in his Sociological Research Unit explored relationships between types of language use, social class and gender. In essence, the research suggested that there were subtle but important differences between social classes, or class fractions, and the symbolic means of expression available to them. It was argued that different kinds of language use create different kinds of identity, different kinds of experience and different orders of meaning. The development of different kinds of language use was related to modes of socialization in Bernstein's general theory. The key distinction was between 'positional' and 'personalizing' modes of domestic organization and primary socialization. These, Bernstein postulated, reflected – and in turn reproduced – distinctive kinds of orientation to language, meaning and identity. The positional type and its associated language types (not to be confused with dialects) Bernstein held to be characteristic of the working class and the 'old' middle class. The personalizing type generated the characteristic social realities of the 'new' middle class. The latter is defined as those occupational groups concerned primarily with symbolic work and cultural production (in education, the media, personnel, advertising and so on), whereas the old middle class is concerned primarily with material production, trade and commerce. Bernstein thus implicates language and socialization in the creation of different domestic and social types. Positional systems depend upon overt means of social control: clearly defined social roles and identities that are largely determined by social position (such as those of sex and generation). Personalizing, new-middle-class systems, on the other hand, are regulated by identities and meanings that are individually negotiated, and in which the boundaries of gender and generation are permeable and themselves available for negotiation. These ideas were summarized in his distinction between 'restricted' and 'elaborated' codes. These were thought of as underlying structural principles, rather than specific language types. In this empirical research programme on socialization, Bernstein was one of the few sociologists of his generation to pay sustained attention to gender, and to the domestic sphere.

Bernstein extended his model, based on ideal-typical modes of socialization, into the field of educational institutions. In doing so, he developed a systematic account of the relations between school organization, curriculum and pedagogy. This provided a suggestive analysis of how the social frameworks of school knowledge, in turn, generate student and teacher identities, subject loyalties and orientations to school knowledge. Bernstein suggested that what might loosely be called 'progressive' modes of educational organization and pedagogy – with looser boundaries and more flexible teaching – were congruent with the general worldview of the 'new' middle class, while more tightly bounded arrangements were congruent with that of the old middle class. Contestations over schooling could, therefore, be seen in terms of symbolic contestations between representatives of different class fractions. Bernstein's ideas were developed through the concepts of 'classification', relating to the organization of curriculum, and 'framing', relating to the organization of pedagogy. Again, Bernstein used his idea of generative 'codes' to express these systemic relations. These ideas were especially influential in the 1970s, when the so-called new sociology of education turned analytic attention towards the contents of education rather than educational systems themselves. The inspirations of Bernstein and the new sociology of education were, however, poles apart. Although the ideas were developed entirely independently, there was a convergence between Bernstein's ideas on school knowledge and those of **Pierre Bourdieu** on how educational knowledge implicitly operates as a principle of social and cultural stratification.

In the 1980s and 1990s Bernstein developed further his ideas on 'pedagogic discourse'. In a series of remarkable essays, he intensified his analysis of the organizing principles of educational knowledge and the principles of pedagogic practice. He produced a number of sophisticated analyses of the principles ('pedagogic devices') underlying different pedagogies. These analyses remain linked to class-based beliefs and practices as they are played out in the domain of education. Although his main interests were in schooling rather than higher education, Bernstein's ideas were especially valuable in illuminating the anthropology of the academy. His interests in symbolic boundaries between domains of sacred and profane knowledge are perfectly adapted to decoding the social, moral and sentimental order of professional and academic education. Recent changes in knowledge-practices in universities are perfectly amenable to Bernsteinian analysis, not least the almost obsessive move towards ever-greater insistence on explicit criteria, accountability and practical 'skills'.

See also: Mary Douglas.

See also in *Fifty Key Sociologists: The Formative Theorists*: Emile Durkheim.

Major works

Most of Bernstein's books consist of previously published essays brought together with additional new material.

Class, Codes and Control, Vol. I. 1971. London: Routledge & Kegan Paul.
Class, Codes and Control, Vol. II, Applied Studies Towards a Sociology of Language. 1973. London: Routledge & Kegan Paul.
Class, Codes and Control Vol. III, Towards a Theory of Educational Transmission. 1976. London: Routledge & Kegan Paul. Second edn, 1977.
Class, Codes and Control, Vol. IV, The Structuring of Pedagogic Discourse. 1990. London: Routledge.
Pedagogy, Symbolic Control and Identity: Theory, Research, Critique. 1996. London: Taylor and Francis. Revised edn, London: Rowman and Littlefield, 2000.

Further reading

Madeleine Arnot. 2001. 'Bernstein's Sociology of Pedagogy: Female Dialogues and Feminist Elaborations'. In K. Weiler, ed. *Feminist Engagements*. New York: Routledge.
Paul Atkinson. 1985. *Language, Structure and Reproduction*. London: Methuen.
Special issue: 2002. *Basil Bernstein's Theory of Social Class, Educational Codes and Social Control. British Journal of Sociology of Education* 23.
S. Morais, I. Neves, B. Davies and H. Daniels, eds. *Towards a Sociology of Pedagogy: The Contribution of Basil Bernstein*. New York: Peter Lang, 2001.
J. Muller, B. Davies and A. Morais, eds. 2004. *Reading Bernstein, Researching Bernstein*. London: Routledge Falmer.
A. Sadovnik, ed. 1995. *Knowledge and Pedagogy: The Sociology of Basil Bernstein*. Norwood, NJ: Ablex.

SARA DELAMONT AND PAUL ATKINSON

PIERRE BOURDIEU

Pierre Bourdieu was a prolific thinker and social scientific researcher. Author of over thirty-five books and 400 articles, appearing in several languages, Bourdieu founded and directed a journal, *Actes de la recherche en sciences sociales*, and a series of books (*Le Sens common*) for over twenty-five years, and in 1996 he launched a new publishing venture, *Raisons d'agir*, that continued after his death. He developed a distinctive conceptual language, such as 'habitus', 'cultural capital', 'field' and 'symbolic violence', that is now widely referenced in sociology and anthropology. His empirical work spans a broad range of subjects, from the ethnography of peasants in Algeria to sociological analysis of nineteenth-century artists and writers, marriage patterns in his native Béarn region, modern universities, language, consumer and cultural tastes, analysis of class and politics, and sources of misery and poverty amid affluence in modern French society. Bourdieu was both a major social theorist and an empirical researcher with an uncanny ability to combine abstract social theory and critical empirical inquiry. His most widely known work, *Distinction*, was ranked in a 1997 survey by the International Sociological Association as the sixth most important social scientific work of the twentieth century; *The Logic of Practice* was ranked fortieth and *Reproduction in Education, Society and Culture* forty-eighth. The only other French thinkers to make it into the top fifty were Emile Durkheim and **Michel Foucault** (see http://www.ucm.es/info/isa/books/). Many of his works were collaborative, as Bourdieu also directed his own research centres at the Ecole des Hautes Etudes en Sciences Sociales and the Collège de France. Given the number of close associates who worked with him over the years and the much larger network of social scientists drawing direct influence from him in their work, it is no exaggeration to say that Bourdieu founded a veritable school of sociology, the most important in France since Emile Durkheim.

His appeal, however, was not limited to the profession of sociology. He was also a politically committed intellectual. His public engagements, particularly during his last several years, led him to become by the late 1990s the leading public intellectual of social scientific stature at the head of the anti-globalization movement in France and in other Western European countries.

Pierre Bourdieu was born in 1930 into a lower-middle-class family in the remote rural region of Béarn in Southwestern France. A particularly gifted and industrious student, he gained entrance to the prestigious and academically elite Ecole Normale Supérieure. There, he prepared for the *agrégation* in philosophy. Bourdieu experienced his schooling not only as a miraculous survivor of strenuous academic selection, but also as a cultural and social outsider of the elite Parisian intellectual world. Indeed, his self-perception of being an outsider in the French intellectual world informed, throughout his life, his sharply critical attitude towards this very world in which his phenomenal rise to intellectual renown occurred.

His teaching career in philosophy was interrupted in 1955 by military service in Algeria, where he was eventually able to obtain a teaching position at the Faculty of Letters in Algiers and where he began his social scientific work as a 'self-taught' ethnographer of the Kabyle peasant communities. This fieldwork experience directly informed his early work: on *The Algerians*, numerous articles and his trademark theory of practices in his most famous 'theoretical' work, *Outline of a Theory of Practice*, and its revised formulation as *The Logic of Practice*.

Opposition to the French colonial war effort led to his return to Paris. He did not follow the approved path towards a university professorship by writing the state doctoral dissertation, but, after a brief teaching assignment in the university he became one of the directors of studies at the Ecoles des Hautes Etudes en Sciences Sociales and made his subsequent career in research centres and seminar rooms rather than university lecture halls.

The 1964 publication of *The Inheritors* (co-authored with Jean-Claude Passeron) was influential in shaping a critical student consciousness during the May 1968 student revolt, but it was translated much later into English without any comparable attention or influence. In 1970 Bourdieu, again with Passeron, published the landmark book – initially his best-known work in English – *Reproduction: In Education, Society and Culture*. This became one of the contemporary classics in the sociology of education. Extensive surveys of French consumer practices, cultural tastes and lifestyles culminated in the book *Distinction: A Social Critique of the Judgement of Taste*, which helped Bourdieu gain access in 1981 to the chair of sociology, held earlier by Marcel Mauss and Raymond Aron, at the Collège de France, the pinnacle of French intellectual life. The 1980s brought to fruition his cumulative empirical and critical investigations of the French university and elite system of the *grandes écoles* in two major works: *Homo Academicus* and *The State Nobility*. A major study of the historical rise of artistic fields in France led to *The Rules of Art*. His call for a critical and reflexive practice of sociological investigation would find expression in 1992 in the widely read *An Invitation to Reflexive Sociology* (co-authored with Loïc Wacquant). He directed a collaborative and massive interviewing project of lower-middle-class individuals on the theme of social suffering and exclusion for the

1993 publication of *The Weight of the World*, and in the same year he received the esteemed French Centre National de Recherche Scientific Gold Metal for outstanding contributions to scientific research. Several subsequent and important books in the 1990s included *On Television, Pascalian Meditations, Masculine Domination, Acts of Resistance* and *Firing Back*. His last major research project on public housing policy in France led to the 2000 publication of *The Social Structures of the Economy*. Several of his books appeared on best-seller lists, giving him an influential voice well beyond the social scientific research community. He died in 2002.

Bourdieu proposed a sociology of power, with a specific focus on how the symbolic dimension of domination contributes to the maintenance and enhancement of social inequality by masking its underlying social, economic and political realities. His sociology of 'symbolic power' addresses the important topic of relations between culture, social structure and action. Whether he was studying Algerian peasants, university professors and students, writers and artists or church leaders, a central underlying preoccupation emerged: how do stratified social systems of hierarchy and domination persist and reproduce intergenerationally without powerful resistance and without the conscious recognition of their members? The answer to this question, Bourdieu argued, can be found by exploring how cultural resources, processes and institutions hold individuals and groups in competitive and self-perpetuating hierarchies of domination. He advanced the bold claim that *all* cultural symbols and practices, from artistic tastes, style in dress and eating habits to religion, science and philosophy – even language itself – embody interests and function to enhance social distinctions. His theory of symbolic power reconceptualized the relations between the symbolic and material aspects of social life by extending the idea of economic interest to the realm of culture. There are symbolic interests just as there are material interests. He conceptualized culture as a form of capital ('cultural capital') with specific laws of accumulation, exchange and exercise.

The struggle for social distinction, whatever its symbolic forms, is for Bourdieu a fundamental dimension of all social life. Social class struggles are classification struggles. The larger issue, then, is one of power relations among individuals, groups and institutions (particularly the educational system). Indeed, for Bourdieu power is not a separate domain of study but stands at the heart of all social life. The successful exercise of power requires legitimation, so he also proposed a theory of 'symbolic violence' and 'symbolic capital' that stressed the active role that symbolic forms play as resources that both constitute and maintain power structures. For Bourdieu, interest and culture stand not in fundamental opposition but are relationally linked; the pursuit of material interest is inseparable from a cultural understanding of just what that interest might be and culture, even in its most abstract and idealized expression, is never devoid of vested interest.

The focus of his work, therefore, is on how cultural socialization places individuals and groups within competitive status hierarchies; how relatively autonomous fields of conflict lock individuals and groups in struggle over valued resources; how these social struggles are refracted through symbolic classifications; how actors struggle and pursue strategies to achieve their interests within such fields; and how in doing so actors unwittingly reproduce the social stratification order. Culture, then, is not devoid of political content but, rather, is an expression of it.

Bourdieu also offered a 'theory of practice'. By thinking of human action as practices, Bourdieu placed the emphasis on what humans actually do rather than what they say they do or what formal theoretical models impute to their patterned activities. He argued that most human action flows out of a practical sense of things. It is guided by his key concept of habitus, those deeply seated, enduring and transposable dispositions that are derived from previous socialization, that are embodied as well as cognitive and that operate to generate and organize practices. This gives action a strategic character, since it occurs under conditions of uncertainty through time and is situated in space. By strategy Bourdieu means – often to the confusion of his critics – that action for the most part is not consciously calculated; nor is it closely governed by rules: it is structured improvisation in a practical sense, rather than rational calculation.

Practices occur in structured arenas of conflict called 'fields'. This central concept in Bourdieu's sociology connects the action of habitus to the stratifying structures of power in modern society. Bourdieu conceptualized modern society as an array of relatively autonomous but structurally homologous fields of production, circulation and consumption of various forms of cultural and material resources. Practices stem from the intersection between habitus and field. Fields, therefore, mediate the relationship between social structure and cultural practice.

Bourdieu also offered a systematic reflection on the epistemological underpinnings of social science practices. An orienting theme throughout Bourdieu's work warns against the partial and fractured views of social reality generated by the fundamental subject/object dichotomy that has plagued social science from its very beginning. The binary oppositions, such as theory versus empirical observation, quantitative versus qualitative methods, micro- versus macro-sociology, causal explanation versus interpretative understanding and materialism versus idealism, operate as social – indeed political – as well as conceptual classifications that undergird narrow and rigid divisions between the disciplines, subfields and theoretical schools. They 'haunt, like theoretic ghosts, the academic mind', dividing the social sciences into warring camps where research was frequently reduced to posturing for one side or the other. For Bourdieu, the solution requires practising a genuinely critical and reflexive social science that systematically relates agents and structures and situates all social scientific inquiry within the broader context of power relations that embrace researchers as well as the object of their investigations. To this end, Bourdieu proposed an epistemological vigilance that calls for critical reflection on the theoretical and methodological practices of the researcher and scientific community as well as the practices of those who are the object of research in every substantive empirical investigation. Thus, Bourdieu called for 'reflexivity', a systematic and rigorously self-critical monitoring of the cognitive and social conditions that make social scientific work possible.

Finally, Bourdieu thought of the practice of sociology as 'socio-analysis', where the sociologist is to the 'social unconscious' of society as the psychoanalyst is to the patient's unconscious. The social unconscious consists of those unacknowledged interests that actors follow as they participate in an inegalitarian social order. Since, according to Bourdieu, it is the 'misrecognition' of those embedded interests that is the necessary condition for the exercise of power, he believed that their public exposure would destroy their legitimacy and open up the possibility for altering existing social arrangements. By exposing those underlying interests that bind individuals and groups into unequal power relations, sociology becomes an instrument of struggle that is capable of offering a measure of freedom from the constraints of domination. Here Bourdieu's sociology intersects with critical theory and politics. He thought of his work as a mode of political intervention.

Bourdieu's work has been frequently criticized. Just six recurring criticisms are mentioned here. First, though not a rigid social and cultural reproduction theorist, as a few critics superficially charge, Bourdieu's strength clearly lay in identifying patterns of continuity and reproduction, rather than moments of creativity or abrupt change. Second, if one of the strengths of Bourdieu's work lay in identifying ways in which action is interested, even when it appears not to be, he leaves little place for disinterested judgement by treating all actions as strategies stemming from the intersection of habitus with fields. Third, the concept of habitus both carries more theoretical weight than many critics would like to see and has been difficult for many to empirically document with any precision. Fourth, Bourdieu's introduction of agency into structuralist analysis does not grant the degree of actor autonomy that many critics would like to see. Many would grant culture more autonomy from the structural moorings that Bourdieu stressed. If the concept of 'field' usefully mediates and transcends crude expressions of the class determinism of cultural life, a kind of field determinism emerges as practices of actors appear to reduce to field position. Fifth, the concept of field does not offer enough insight into how institutions, particularly the state, actually work. And sixth, Bourdieu's stress on transcending the subjective/objective dualism tended to reinstitute the very opposition that he contested, as opposing viewpoints are frequently categorized and reduced to one side of that dichotomy.

Bourdieu's influence in the social sciences has been substantial, interdisciplinary and international. He has had a major influence on Anglophone anthropology, sociology of education, sociology of culture and cultural studies. Key elements of his conceptual language, such as social and cultural reproduction, cultural capital, habitus, field and symbolic power and violence, have already become part of the working vocabulary of many social scientists. Yet frequently his concepts have been theorized outside a research context and abstracted from the relational framework in which Bourdieu developed them. They offer their best insights when used relationally and applied in actual empirical research. Perhaps his greatest influence in the English-speaking world has been in social theory, where his theory of practice has become a significant reference point in contemporary theorizing. This is ironical in that Bourdieu saw himself as an empirical researcher who combined abstract theory with mundane empirical data. His influence on empirical research has been greatest in the sociology of culture and in the broader interdisciplinary field of cultural studies. His influence in the sociology of education also has been very strong, his concept of cultural capital and reproduction perspective having been widely discussed and researched. Though *Distinction* is widely studied and cited, its impact on the sociology of stratification has been more limited.

Bourdieu's analysis of how symbolic classifications obscure class power and provide the tools for social distinctions represents a key contribution to contemporary sociologies of culture and stratification. Indeed, Bourdieu's reformulation of the problem of ideology and false consciousness stands as one of his central contributions to the study of class and power in modern societies. He, more than any other contemporary sociologist, has provided a powerful theoretical approach to the study of culture, bringing it into a central place in contemporary sociology. He has contributed to the development of a vibrant and growing subfield of sociology of culture and, more broadly, to the interdisciplinary field of cultural studies.

See also: Louis Althusser, Claude Lévi-Strauss.

See also in *Fifty Key Sociologists: The Formative Theorists*: Emile Durkheim.

Major works

The most complete listing of his works can be found at http://www.iwp.uni-linz.ac.at/lxe/sektktf/bb/HyperBourdieu.html.

The Algerians. 1958. Boston, MA: Beacon Press, 1962.
Reproduction in Education, Society and Culture. 1970. With Jean-Claude Passeron. London: Sage, 1977.
Outline of a Theory of Practice. 1972. Cambridge: Cambridge University Press, 1977.
Distinction: A Social Critique of the Judgement of Taste. 1979. Cambridge, MA: Harvard University Press, 1984.
The Logic of Practice. 1980. Stanford, CA: Stanford University Press, 1990.
Language and Symbolic Power. 1982. Cambridge, MA: Harvard University Press, 1991.
Sociology in Question. 1984. Thousand Oaks, CA, and London: Sage Publications, 1993.
Homo Academicus. 1984. Stanford, CA: Stanford University Press, 1988.
In Other Words: Essays Toward a Reflexive Sociology. 1987. Stanford, CA: Stanford University Press, 1990.
The State Nobility: Elite Schools in the Field of Power. 1989. Stanford, CA: Stanford University Press, 1996.
The Craft of Sociology: Epistemological Preliminaries. 1991. With Jean-Claude Chamboredon, Jean-Claude Passeron, Beate Krais and Richard Nice. Berlin and New York: Walter de Gruyter.
An Invitation to Reflexive Sociology. 1992. With Loïc J. D. Wacquant. Chicago: University of Chicago Press.
The Rules of Art. Genesis and Structure of the Literary Field. 1992. Stanford, CA: Stanford University Press, 1996.
The Field of Cultural Production: Essays on Art and Literature. 1968–93. New York: Columbia University Press, 1993.

On Television. 1996. New York: New Press, 1998.
Acts of Resistance. Against the Tyranny of the Market. 1998. New York: The New Press.
The Weight of the World. 1997. Cambridge: Polity Press, 1999.
Pascalian Meditations. 1997. Stanford, CA: Stanford University Press, 1999.
Masculine Domination. 1998. Stanford, CA: Stanford University Press, 2001.
The Social Structures of the Economy. 2000. Cambridge: Polity Press, 2005.
Firing Back: Against the Tyranny of the Market. 2001 New York: The New Press, 2003.

Further reading

Craig Calhoun, Edward LiPuma, and Moishe Postone, eds. 1993. *Bourdieu: Critical Perspectives.* Chicago: University of Chicago Press.
Bridget Fowler. *Pierre Bourdieu and Cultural Theory: Critical Investigations.* 1997. Thousand Oaks, CA: Sage Publications.
Richard Jenkins. 2000. *Pierre Bourdieu.* London: Routledge.
Derek Robbins. 1991. *The Work of Pierre Bourdieu: Recognizing Society.* Boulder, CO, and San Francisco: Westview Press.
Derek Robbins. 2000. *Bourdieu and Culture.* Thousand Oaks, CA: Sage Publications.
David Swartz. 1997. *Culture and Power: The Sociology of Pierre Bourdieu.* Chicago: University of Chicago Press.
David Swartz and Vera L. Zolberg, eds. 2004. *After Bourdieu. Influence, Critique, Elaboration.* Dordrecht: Kluwer Academic Publishers.

DAVID SWARTZ

JUDITH BUTLER

Philosopher, phenomenologist and gender theorist, Judith Butler (born in 1956) offers complex, rhetorically brilliant and diligently comprehensive thinking and writing on issues such as the formation of the human subject or self, the productive and destructive power of language and Hegelian philosophy's continuing relevance. Butler's work stands against essentialist understandings of identity and existence, culture and biology, and the relationships between gender and sex. In other words, all aspects of femininity link to the female and masculinity links to the male. Her interrogation and insightful analysis of concepts from Sigmund Freud and French philosopher **Michel Foucault** have led to formative insights and fundamental innovations in many fields, providing, as well, elaborations and extensions in the realm of phenomenology – the study of the movement of consciousness through time, including how things appear to us.

Butler's work – radical as it may seem – responds to and engages with classic questions of ontology (the study of being), epistemology (the study of knowing) and philosophy of language. After studying philosophy as an undergraduate in the 1970s at Bennington College in Vermont and Yale University, Butler travelled on a Fulbright Scholarship to Heidelberg University in Germany, attending the lectures and seminars of philosopher Hans-Georg Gadamer and reading continental philosophy. Back at Yale for graduate training, she occasionally attended lectures by theorists Jacques Derrida and Paul de Man – not without ambivalence, apparently. Butler earned her PhD in philosophy under Maurice Natanson, an influential and well-respected phenomenologist and Husserl scholar who had studied with Alfred Schutz.

Three years after publishing her PhD thesis as a book on the French reception of Hegel, Butler became infamous for *Gender Trouble: Feminism and the Subversion of Identity*. Notoriously difficult reading, *Gender Trouble* became an academic best-seller. Moreover, the book emerged as a founding text in queer theory and was adopted by many as an argument for understanding gender as a performance – and hence worn, or not, rather like a particularly theatrical concatenation of clothing. Although clearly offering other contributions to the emergent field, Butler has made clear that such an understanding seriously miscomprehends and misrepresents the arguments of the book, arguments that were often read without any recognition of their connections to Hegelian or basic phenomenological questions.

Butler joined others in the phenomenological tradition who have explored the meanings, interrelations and ontological status of binary oppositions – and the limits of their intelligibility – such as finite and infinite, being and nothingness, self and other, and white and black in an 'antiblack' world. Driven by similar theoretical concerns, Butler has sought to understand these paradoxes and complexities, often in relation to masculinity and femininity in the formation of the gendered subject. According to Butler, the subject's intelligibility or legibility is limited by the available, and simultaneously forbidden, closed off or 'foreclosed' sets of repetitive normative behaviours and gestures that she calls 'performative iterations'. In interrogating the way 'constraints' produce domains of intelligibility, such as the other acting as boundary or limit for the self, Butler writes:

> This latter domain is not the opposite of the former, for oppositions are, after all, part of intelligibility; the latter is the

excluded and illegible domain that haunts the former domain as the spectre of its own impossibility, the very limit of intelligibility, its constitutive outside.

Performative iterations are not simply the acting out of ways of being in the world. Iterations appear as 'a regularised and constrained repetition of norms' that produce identities and foreclose others, maintaining the illusion of natural categories of being and behaviour, including gender.

Butler's use of the term 'performative' remains technical, derived from semiotic insights into the linking of words and things, or between words and other language-based signs. Thus, semiotics, the science of signs, and other theories of language play a fundamental role in building a cohesive and coherent model of subject formation. The individual subject comes into being as a 'linguistic occasion', taking form from language and gestures: produced with body positions, speech acts, reflective processes and other performative behaviour. Thus, the function that the performative plays cannot be captured by the word 'performance'. However, it is interesting to recall **Erving Goffman**'s work on *The Presentation of Self in Everyday Life*, in which the performing of aspects of identity, and how the self copes with this performance, form a crucial function in producing a 'self' to be presented.

Butler always reminds us of the lack of presence or essence of a subject or self, the lack of 'a being behind the doing'. This is a familiar point in existential philosophy: 'existence precedes essence' or 'doing comes before being'. For Butler, 'being' will never attain solidity, completeness or essence; and 'existence' is active and ever in iteration. Thus, there is never a subject, or self, who *does* the performing: performative iterations bring the subject into being. For Butler, 'this repetition is not performed *by* a subject; this repetition is what enables a subject and constitutes the temporal condition for the subject'. Iteration calls attention to the lack of an original, 'natural' or ideal category that exists prior to an appearance, instantiation or iteration.

Butler's work on subject identity constitution through performative iterations demonstrates fundamental aspects of her theoretical perspective. If a structure, ideal or subject identity must be iterated, Butler argues, then it is not absolute or ideal, as the existence is in the iteration, this endless repetition. Re-signification or iteration is necessary. Butler takes her lead from Derrida, arguing that iterability counters a structuralist essentialist ideal, for example in waiting for a moment to arrive. The iteration of anticipation in the waiting is all of the 'moment' that really exists. In fact, anticipation of the moment that we await creates the moment: waiting for Godot, as it were. Lack of ideals, generally, functions similarly, including the ideal of gender. Identities via iteration form over time and through repeated performances of socially constructed characteristics and appropriate gestures and signs; yet this notion provides openings for contingent or chance occurrences. Butler requires that we note the *potential production of difference* emerging from required modes of behaviour. Such differences and deviations may be subversive but are not necessarily to be understood as intentional forms of resistance. For Butler, the hope that emerges in this scenario is something like this: if typical iterations elide, alter and shift, then the previously recognized definitive category – the apparent ideal – may be altered as well, opening up possibility for diverse gestures and characteristics, demonstrating contingency and allowing change over time.

Currently the Maxine Elliot Professor of Rhetoric and Comparative Literature at the University of California at Berkeley, Butler stands outside her academic home field of philosophy and writes, arguably, for a broader audience, creating spaces for rethinking the history of ideas and expanding notions of everyday lived experience, as well. She has websites, fanzines, university courses and PhD theses dedicated to her ideas and the possibilities people have derived from her work.

See also: Michel Foucault, Erving Goffman.

See also in *Fifty Key Sociologists: The Formative Theorists*: Alfred Schutz.

Major works

Subjects of Desire. 1987. New York: Columbia University Press.
'Foucault and the Paradox of Bodily Inscriptions'. 1989. *Journal of Philosophy* 86.
Gender Trouble: Feminism and the Subversion of Identity. 1990. New York: Routledge.
Bodies that Matter: On the Discursive Limits of "Sex". 1993. New York: Routledge.
The Psychic Life of Power: Theories of Subjection. 1997. Stanford, CA: Stanford University Press.
Undoing Gender. 2004. New York: Routledge.
Giving an Account of Oneself. 2005. New York: Fordham University Press.

Various extracts can be found in Sara Salih, ed. 2004. *The Judith Butler Reader*. Oxford: Blackwell.

Further reading

Jacques Derrida. 1978. 'Structure, Sign, and Play'. In *Writing and Difference*. Chicago: University of Chicago Press.
Lewis Gordon. 1995. *Bad Faith and Antiblack Racism*. Atlantic Highlands, NJ: Humanities Press.
Maurice Natanson. 1986. *Anonymity: A Study in the Philosophy of Alfred Schutz*. Bloomington, IN: Indiana University Press.

JANET BORGERSON

MANUEL CASTELLS

Manuel Castells was born in Spain in 1942. He was educated in Catalonia, but his study of economics and law at the University of Barcelona was interrupted when he felt compelled to flee Spain for political reasons at the age of twenty. This was the time of the Franco dictatorship (1936–75) and Castells was active on the left. He went into exile in France and took a doctorate at the University of Paris in 1967. He was teaching at the university when the student rebellion of 1968 took place. Participation in *les événements* of 1968 led to efforts to have him expelled from France, but an active campaign, helped by his doctoral supervisor **Alain Touraine**, enabled him to remain.

Castells spent the academic year 1969–70 in Canada, at the University of Montreal, but returned to Paris to continue his work in urban sociology and published his first major book, *The Urban Question*, in 1972. This Marxist analysis had an enormous effect, turning upside down the then staid field of urbanism. He was employed at the prestigious Ecole des Hautes Etudes en Sciences Sociales, Paris, between 1970 and 1979, then moving to the University of California, Berkeley, where he was professor of city and regional planning and professor of sociology. As democracy returned to Spain, Castells increased his contacts with his home and, since the late 1980s, has held positions at the Universidad Autónoma de Madrid and the Open University of Catalonia. Late in 2003 he left Berkeley and took up the Wallis Annenberg Chair of Communication Technology and Society, University of Southern California, and he now divides his time between Los Angeles and Barcelona. He is married to the Russian sociologist Emma Kiselyova.

Castells is best known as one of the world's leading urbanists. His books, notably *The Urban Question*, *The City and the Grassroots*, *The Informational City* and (with Peter Hall) *Technopoles of the World*, secured his pre-eminence in this field. Between 1996 and 1998, however, he published a trilogy, *The Information Age*, that went beyond concern for cities to offer a comprehensive, coherent and encyclopaedic account of the state of the world today. These volumes were received with great acclaim, Castells being compared to Max Weber and Karl Marx. They have been translated into over twenty languages and have helped make Castells one of the best known of contemporary social analysts.

Though he came from a Francoist family, Castells occupies the left in politics. His work has also been marked by the engaged quality found in such influential social scientists as Ralf Dahrendorf, Daniel Bell and **C. Wright Mills**. This does not colour his intellectual work, but it drives it. Lately he has contented himself with being an expert advisor who maintains detachment from political affairs, but concern for social justice motivates his intellectual inquiry.

Early in his career he was much influenced by Marxism, especially by the structuralist version advocated by **Louis Althusser**. A structural approach has remained with Castells: he continues to emphasize the importance of economics and production, though he also pays much attention to culture and politics. He has moved away from his youthful concern for class as central to social analysis, stressing since the mid-1980s the importance of social movements and groups such as gay activists, environmentalists and feminists as agents for change. He might be regarded as a 'post-Marxist' thinker because of this.

Castells describes himself as an empirical sociologist. A striking feature of his writing is its saturation in substantive detail and evidence. This means that he prioritizes evidence over theory. Castells is theoretically informed, but he advocates 'disposable theory', to emphasize his antipathy towards the abstract theorizing that periodically enters social sciences. His work is also notably interdisciplinary: though a sociologist he is at home with a vast range of literature from other fields, which he does not hesitate to use.

Castells is undoubtedly best known now for *The Information Age* (1996–8). This 1,500-page trilogy is empirically packed, yet presents a holistic account of the state of the world. It may be seen as an exercise in 'grand narrative', a big-picture analysis of how we live today. Its theme is the relations between integration of the world in networks alongside accompanying fragmentations and divisions. It focuses on issues of structure (work, organization and economy), Volume II on culture (identities, social movements, media) and Volume III on macro social issues such as global crime chains, the European Union and the Far East.

The core argument of the book is that restructuring, driven by the economic crises of the 1970s, coincided with the development of an 'informational mode of development' – essentially the growth of information and communications technology (ICT) to produce a novel society. While Castells refers to 'informational capitalism' and the 'information age', he is uncomfortable with the argument that information alone distinguishes the current epoch. Most important is the ability of networks now to permeate all human activities. The 'information flows' this allows lead Castells now to favour the term 'network society', facilitated – but not determined – by ICT.

Networks have grown alongside the tendential process of globalization, such that they now allow planetary action in real time (for example in corporate decision-making, in media coverage of sports, in political campaigns, in e-mail conversations). This accelerates the pace of change, competitive edge and the flexibility of organization. It stimulates the 'network enterprise' that devolves power to innovators and experts who work on projects, driven less by bureaucratic pressures and more by peer esteem operating in horizontal relations. Networks also make the nation-state less capable of controlling affairs, yet simultaneously compelled to act in timely and appropriate ways (for example, lawless states suffer when networks of capital bypass them).

Castells identifies major consequential changes in stratification. Male manual workers are massively reduced, displaced by non-manual, often female, labour, and their central role in radical politics declines. 'Informational labour' (the work of those who are networked, with attendant education and capabilities, constantly retrained, lying at the heart of innovation) expands and occupies a central position in all spheres from entertainment to agitation. 'Generic labour' (undertaken by the working class) is constantly threatened by technological design and reorganization, and is readily automated or relocated. Finally, there are the unskilled and/or irrelevant, at the fringes of the network society, surviving as cheap labour in peripheral areas, as an underclass in ghettoes or ignored as in parts of Africa such as Sudan and Chad.

Information flows are increasingly global, but they are not placeless. They move through, and are created in, particular places that are the nodes of the network society. Such informational cities have distinctive features – of culture, image, stratification, education and technology – that have been brilliantly examined by Castells, notably in his concepts of 'milieux of innovation' and 'bipolarization'. He suggests that public policies and political action will be critical for the quality of urban life, urging people to 'act globally, think locally'.

There are echoes of Marshall McLuhan's concern for the cultural import of new media technologies. It is Castells' view that access to the network is a prerequisite of participation in today's world, since to be off the net is to risk exclusion. This is especially evident in his accounts of social and political movements. These are presented as increasingly global, media sophisticated and led by informational labour, as with feminist or human rights groups.

The Information Age trilogy has a strong claim to being the single most impressive sociological study in over a generation. Its energy and range, its attention to detail combined with theoretical coherence, its substance and practical pertinence account for its enormous influence and critical acclamation.

See also: Louis Althusser.

See also in Fifty Key Sociologists: The Formative Theorists: Karl Marx.

Major works

The Urban Question. 1972. London: Edward Arnold, 1977.
The City and the Grassroots. A Cross-Cultural Theory of Urban Social Movements. 1983. Berkeley, CA: University of California Press
The Informational City. Information Technology, Economic Restructuring and the Urban-Regional Process. 1989. Oxford: Blackwell Publishers.
Technopoles of the World. The Making of 21st Century Industrial Complexes. 1994. With Peter Hall. London: Routledge.
The Information Age: Economy, Society, and Culture. Volume I: The Rise of the Network Society. 1996. Oxford: Blackwell. Revised edn, 2000.
The Information Age: Economy, Society, and Culture. Volume II: The Power of Identity. 1997. Oxford: Blackwell. Revised edn, 2004.
The Information Age: Economy, Society, and Culture. Volume III: End of Millennium. 1998. Oxford: Blackwell. Revised edn, 2000.
The Internet Galaxy. Reflections on the Internet, Business, and Society. 2001. Oxford: Oxford University Press.

Further reading

Frank Webster and Basil Dimitriou, eds. 2004. Manuel Castells: Masters of Modern Social Thought. 3 vols. London: Sage.

FRANK WEBSTER

RANDALL COLLINS

Many sociologists are creatures of the moment, agitated by the latest storm – postmodernism, deconstruction, academic feminism – only to see it become the languid breeze of orthodoxy. Equally, most self-styled sociological theorists never produce sociological theory; instead they remain commentators on the work of other people. In both these respects, as in others, the work of Randall Collins (born in 1941) is strikingly different. For over four decades, Collins has pursued an agenda that, while absorbing novel ideas, is notable for its stamina and coherence. A dedicated student of sociology's classical heritage, he is no curator, for Collins persists in the unfashionable belief that sociological theory is cumulative. We are learning more about society – learning it more comprehensively and with greater sophistication – than ever before. We are making scientific progress. This contention is at odds with a widespread view that sociology is little more than a kaleidoscope of perspectives, none demonstrably better than the others. As for the classics, read them, Collins says, not only as models of creative thinking. Read them principally for clues and propositions that enable us to work out, systematically, a variety of connections: notably between the micro and macro, and between solidarity (a type of conflict) and conflict (a type of solidarity).

Collins' work is typically associated with 'conflict theory', a school of thought whose predecessors include Karl Marx, Max Weber, Georg Simmel and Lewis Coser. Essentially, this theory states that social life is characterized by the attempts of social actors to maximize their advantages over others. Agents struggle to monopolize resources or to share them. What we call 'society' is a network of dominant and subordinate interest groups in perpetually shifting alignment. 'Conflict' must be understood in its broadest sense. It includes not only visible, dramatic events, such as strikes, demonstrations, terrorist attacks, revolutions and wars. It also embraces the normal social order of everyday life: for instance social rituals that distinguish in-group from out-group, rules governing legitimate sexual activity, belief systems that stipulate what is normal and what is heretical.

The above characterization only hints at the range and complexity of 'conflict theory'. But in Collins' case the sketch is inadequate for another reason. Collins is, above all, an integrative theorist. His work combines several other traditions: Durkheimian, dramaturgical, interactionist, utilitarian ('rational choice'). Similarly, he has for many years sought to work out the manifold relationships between local, personal, everyday events, on the one hand, and large, world-shaping forces, on the other. **Erving Goffman** and Max Weber, polar types in many ways, are among his great heroes. Collins' cardinal rule of sociological method is this: study individuals by studying the situations they are in, for it is the situation, not the individual, which shapes conduct, emotion and thinking. In addition, Collins sees the 'macro' order not as a layer of reality hovering above the 'micro' or superimposed upon it, but as the outcome, extension and seepage of multiple 'micro' interactions unfurling through space and time. Osmosis rather than hierarchy is the key principle of the micro–macro relationship.

While Collins' work is still very much in progress, he has already made four important contributions to sociology. These concern credentialism, intellectual networks, geopolitics and interaction rituals.

Collins was an early analyst of credential inflation, a concern that was already evident in his doctoral thesis on education and employment (completed in 1969 at the University of California, Berkeley). To understand the meaning of credential inflation, consider the paradox that while increased access to education is supposed to improve people's position in the labour market, it has not produced a more equal society. Why is this? Collins shows it is because credentials (diplomas, degrees at the undergraduate and postgraduate level, and many sub-degree modes of certification) function largely like money. Increase the money supply and you encourage inflation. The same is true of credentials. It transpires that education is one market among others. Where the supply of certified people for a particular job is plentiful, its market price will be commensurately depressed. Hence, it is expected today that most non-manual workers should have an undergraduate degree. This signals a major change from the mid-twentieth century, when universities were an elite privilege and when degrees were rare. As such, they were a potent source of market leverage. No longer. One way to revive this leverage is to create a market in new credentials at the graduate level – MBAs for instance. Soon, however, that market too becomes saturated and a new niche is required to distinguish the good from the average. And so the process goes on. Meanwhile, education becomes more costly for the individual. It requires greater investment (more time and money spent) at the tertiary level, for a stable or diminishing return.

Another longstanding and related interest of Collins lies in the nature of intellectual creativity. Again, he first took up this topic as a student at Berkeley. Just over 30 years later, the project came to fruition in Collins' *Sociology of Philosophies: A Global Theory of Intellectual Change*. In this massive cross-cultural study, Collins argues that intellectual networks are the key to explaining such otherwise mysterious attributes as creativity, reputation, influence, greatness and even thought itself. The animating force of intellectual life is conflict: conflicts of positions, conflicts over intellectual resources and conflict for control of the 'attention space' (audience interest) within which ideas are articulated and become socially persuasive. And depending on the intellectual area or discipline involved, this attention space is severely restricted – usually to no more than five or six relevant schools of thought or current debates. Great intellectuals are those with large quantities of drive, initiative and ambition, an 'emotional energy' (EE) that is not free-floating but requires social conditions to sustain it. These include a person's location in the white heat of a controversy, previous or contemporary links with prestigious teachers and ready access to media – universities, think tanks, publishing houses, televisions stations, internet blogging sites – that allow ample scope for communication. Accordingly, EE ebbs and flows in intensity to the degree its protagonists are at the centre of the cultural fray. Those who possess EE are likely to cultivate more of it in a value-added spiral as their careers progress. However, EE may also dissipate when a thinker overreaches himself or herself or when the stakes of the debate in which she or he has been focally implicated change.

Collins' geopolitics begins from a recognition that in the modern world people's lives are strongly influenced by the state – by the political institutions of government, parliament, civil service and the security apparatuses. In turn, states inhabit a world system composed of other states, endlessly jockeying for power and influence. The study of inter-state relations is known as geopolitics. This requires us to suspend the common reflex to look at the state, and the society over which it governs, from the 'inside', examining its domestic complexion (its constitution, political parties, taxation policy, legitimacy, for instance). Geopolitical writers insist that a deeper understanding of states requires that they are looked at from the outside in, exploring how a state is placed in the state system as a whole, the challenges and competition for power it faces from other states, and the alliances that are necessary for its survival.

Collins has studied these issues intensely, measuring the dynamics of ethnicity, democratic modernization and revolution over long periods of time. His most famous contribution, though, lies in the prediction he offered, in 1980, of the breakdown of the Soviet Union that finally occurred in 1992. The prediction was based on a series of geopolitical principles that Collins first enunciated in the mid-1970s. These specified the conditions under which the territorial power of states expands or contracts. For instance, states which border many other states tend to find themselves weaker over time than states that border few or no neighbours as a result of such geographical barriers as seas, mountains and so on. Equally, states that become overextended are likely to see themselves strained for resources and prone to disintegration. On this basis, linked to other geopolitical principles, Collins ventured the forecast that a particular constellation of events was likely to trigger major losses in Soviet territory. It did. The more general point is that the fate of any country is to be understood by the dynamics of the state system in which it operates.

The above considerations make it appear that Collins is above all a macro-theorist. That impression is misleading. As much, if not more, of his work has been devoted to explaining the emotional foundations of social life. As Collins pictures them, such emotions are situated in social rituals or what he calls interaction ritual chains. Four basic ingredients define interaction rituals. First, two or more people must be co-present: bodily assembled and able to charge up a situation with excitement and significance. Second, interaction rituals require a boundary that demarcates insiders from outsiders, lending participants a privileged sense of inclusiveness. A third feature of interaction rituals is that all parties to the encounter train their attention on a common object or activity and become mutually aware they are doing so. Finally, interaction rituals require that participants share a common mood or emotional experience. Where these elements combine successfully, four outcomes are discernible: (1) individuals feel solidarity with one another; they imagine themselves to be members of a common undertaking; (2) they are infused with a feeling of exhilaration, achievement and enthusiasm (emotional energy again) which induces initiative; (3) interaction ritual membership generates collective symbols that are assigned sacred qualities; it follows (4) that violations of these symbols provoke righteous indignation towards, and sanctions against, those guilty of transgression. Interaction rituals, in short, are what hold society together in 'pockets of solidarity'. They are what give individuals an identity and a purpose. Collins has applied interaction ritual theory to a variety of phenomena: anti-smoking movements, acts of sexual intercourse, responses to terrorist attacks and other rituals of violence.

In sum, few authors have Collins' range of interests or analytical acuity. Fewer still have such a large command over historical and empirical data. And no one since Durkheim has more effectively demonstrated sociology's explanatory reach. Develop more than one specialism and grasp their interrelationships, Collins advises his students; avoid polemics and the temptations of the latest craze; contribute to sociology's x-ray vision; get on with the task of building a discipline that, of all the social sciences, has the most to offer the ambitious thinker.

See also: Erving Goffman.

See also in *Fifty Key Sociologists: The Formative Theorists*: Georg Simmel, Max Weber.

Major works

Conflict Sociology: Toward an Explanatory Science. 1975. New York: Academic Press.
The Credential Society: An Historical Sociology of Education and Stratification. 1979. New York: Academic Press.
Weberian Sociological Theory. 1986. Cambridge: Cambridge University Press.
Theoretical Sociology. 1988. San Diego, CA: Harcourt Brace.
The Discovery of Society. 1992. With Michael Makowsky. New York: McGraw Hill.
Four Sociological Traditions. 1994. New York: Oxford University Press.
The Sociology of Philosophies: A Global Theory of Intellectual Change. 1998. Cambridge, MA: Harvard University Press.
Macro-History: Essays in Sociology of the Long Run. 1999. Stanford, CA: Stanford University Press.
Interaction Ritual Chains. 2004. Princeton, NJ: Princeton University Press.

PETER BAEHR

GILLES DELEUZE

Gilles Deleuze is a French philosopher, born in 1925 in Paris, where he lived for almost all of his life. He studied philosophy at the Sorbonne, where he also taught history of philosophy between 1957 and 1964. He held other teaching positions at the University of Lyon, the University of Vincennes (at the behest of his good friend **Michel Foucault**) and finally at the University of Paris VII, where he stayed until his retirement in 1987. He took his own life in 1995, in the final stages of a serious pulmonary illness from which he suffered for almost thirty years.

Author of monographic studies of classical philosophers from Kant, Spinoza and Leibniz to Hume, Bergson and Nietzsche, his mode of reading was that of a commentary that, in the words of Patton, doubled 'the original text in a manner which subjects it to maximal modification: repetition and differentiation'. Deleuze never subscribed to claims about the death of philosophy and held to the idea that philosophical systems 'have in fact lost absolutely none of their power. All the groundwork for a theory of so-called open systems is in place in current science and logic.' Thus his philosophical work can be seen as an open system characterized by a permanent modification of an array of concepts that are inflected differently according to different subject matter.

Although he is usually described as a poststructuralist philosopher, Deleuze had significant differences with poststructuralist thinkers such as Jacques Derrida (in as much as Deleuze broke with hermeneutics) and substantial disagreements with Jacques Lacan (whom he explicitly attacked in his work with Felix Guattari). In addition to his philosophical monographs, he wrote two important books on cinema (*Cinema I* and *Cinema II*), an original reading of Michel Foucault's work (*Foucault*) and several books on literature and painting. He also produced two slim booklets on Kafka (*Kafka: Toward a Minor Literature*) and philosophy (*What Is Philosophy?*), where he set out to discuss the differences between philosophy, science and art.

Gilles Deleuze is, however, probably most famous for his collaborative work with psychiatrist and political activist Felix Guattari, with whom he co-authored the two influential and widely read volumes of *Capitalism and Schizophrenia: Anti-Oedipus* and *A Thousand Plateaus*. These can be considered as the first texts of philosophy to conceptually engage with the political events of 1968.

One of the most relevant aspects of Deleuze's philosophy in relation to sociological thinking is his critique of the idea that philosophy is basically concerned with epistemological questions – that is, with the relation between thinking, truth and knowing. In his first major philosophical work, *Difference and Repetition*, Deleuze creatively deconstructed some fundamental assumptions of western philosophy. In particular, he tackled what he called the dogmatic or orthodox image of thought from Plato and Descartes to Kant and Russell. This image subordinates thinking to knowledge and knowledge to truth. Such knowledge is guaranteed by the harmonious cooperation of the faculties, fixes the identity of the subject and thus ensures the recognition of the object. He also called this logic the form of representation: '*Everybody knows, no one can deny* is the form of representation and the discourse of the representative'. Following Nietzsche, he claimed that this mode of philosophy is unable to break with doxa or opinion and is thus unable to grasp the genetic power of thinking, its capacity to follow not so much a logic of representation as one of *invention*. For Deleuze, thinking is not characterized by an intrinsic good will, but is something that is forced on us from the outside, from the power of the encounter with the outside. Philosophy is thus continuously challenged by the appearance of the event, that is, by that which cannot be reduced to a given state of affairs.

Deleuze maintained that the dogmatic image of thought has made philosophers unable to think what lies outside the domain of knowledge, representation and truth. As an alternative to the orthodox image of thought, he advocated a flat ontology of lines, surfaces, planes, folds, sets, intensive variations and divergent/convergent series. Such an ontology is not subordinated to or derived from an identity, not reduced to a form of re-presentation, but introduces a principle of discontinuity and metamorphosis. It focuses on multiplicity as a substantive, as opposed to the multiple as an attribute of the 'One'; on the event as virtuality, as distinct from the actuality of a state of affairs; on a body as defined by its relations of speed and capacity to affect, rather than by the perception of a subject; and on becoming or intensive duration, as opposed to simple movement. Deleuze found inspiration for this mode of thinking in a minor tradition of philosophers from Lucretius and the Stoics to Nietzsche, Spinoza, Bergson, Leibniz and Whitehead.

Of particular interest is Deleuze's philosophy of difference, becoming and multiplicity that he constructed from his reading of Spinoza, Nietzsche and Bergson. Here, difference is not conceived in terms of a spatial, external relation between separate beings, but in terms of internal, temporal processes of differentiation marked by intensive leaps between states. In this, he also followed Gilbert Simondon's critique of the opposition between individual and structure as compared to the ontological priority of processes of individuation. Deleuze's philosophy of becoming can be considered as an implicit critique of the Hegelian dialectics, which he praised for having introduced movement into being, but which he rejected for having conceived of difference as external negation and mediation. Unlike his contemporary Jacques Derrida, however, he did not see this intensive difference as an effect of writing, but as belonging to being itself, understood as a positive process of affirmation and expression. Based on this ontology, Deleuze constructed his critique of the subordination of multiplicity to the One in western metaphysics – where the multiple as intensive manifold is usually subordinated or derived from the superior unity of multiplicity. Deleuze thus distinguished between two types of multiplicities: discrete and continuous. Discrete multiplicities are not affected by the fact of division, whereas continuous multiplicities change when they are divided. Western metaphysics is held to have been preoccupied mostly with discrete multiplicities that do not pose any problem of internal differentiation or becoming. Continuous multiplicities can be explained only by assuming tendencies that give rise to processes that do not exhaust their potential to become. In his later work with Guattari, this becoming was more fully developed.

Finally, in his collaboration with Guattari Deleuze held that language does not designate or represent the world but entails an active intervention into heterogeneous assemblages of words and things. As such, and in spite of his association with postmodernism, Deleuze's work constitutes an alternative to postmodern theories that grant representations the exclusive power to mediate social experience. Instead, he argued that what postmodernists would call representations (such as words and images) enter heterogeneous assemblages that connect social, biological, technical, cultural and physical elements – none of which is granted exclusive ontological priority, but all of which must be grasped together in their combined capacity to produce material effects (including effects of meaning). Language is thus inseparable from the existence of collective assemblages of enunciation that productively bring it into being. Words do not represent objects because they are themselves material entities. He can thus be characterized, as Alliez has argued, as a 'constructivist' rather than a 'constructionist'. Like his co-writer Felix Guattari, and in spite of his reputation as a poststructuralist, he thus preferred hyper-structuralists like the Danish linguist Louis Hjemslev to the linguistic semiotics of Ferdinand de Saussure.

See also: Michel Foucault.

See also in *Fifty Key Sociologists: The Formative Theorists*: Ferdinand de Saussure.

Major works

Difference and Repetition. 1968. New York: Columbia University Press, 1994.
Capitalism and Schizophrenia: Anti-Oedipus. 1972. With Felix Guattari. New York: Viking, 1977.
Capitalism and Schizophrenia: A Thousand Plateaus. 1980. With Felix Guattari. Minneapolis, MN: University of Minnesota Press, 1987.
Cinema I, 2 vols. 1983–5. London: Athlone Press, 1989.
Foucault. 1986. Minneapolis, MN: University of Minnesota Press, 1989.

Further reading

Eric Alliez. 2004. *The Signature of the World: What Is Deleuze and Guattari's Philosophy?* London: Continuum.

Constantin V. Boundas. 1996. 'Deleuze–Bergson: An Ontology of the Virtual'. In Paul Patton, ed. *Deleuze: A Critical Reader*. Oxford: Blackwell.

Michael Hardt. 1993. *Gilles Deleuze: An Apprenticeship in Philosophy*. Minneapolis, MN: University of Minnesota Press.

Paul Patton, ed. 1996. *Deleuze: A Critical Reader*. Oxford: Blackwell.

Gilbert Simondon. 1989. *L'Individuation psychique et collective. A la lumière des notions de forme, information, potentiel et metastabilité*. Paris: Editions Aubier.

TIZIANA TERRANOVA

MARY DOUGLAS

Mary Douglas, born in 1921, is the most influential social theorist working in the Durkheimian tradition. Anyone working on the sociology of knowledge, 'culture', institutions, forms of social organization, risk and social fear, or religion has no choice but to engage with her work.

Born Mary Tew to a family of Irish descent but whose father worked in British colonial administration, she was brought up as a Catholic and attended a convent school for girls, which nurtured the faith in which she has remained but also provided her with a profound and astute sensibility for the nature and merits of hierarchical organization and its peculiar capabilities for managing the symbolic order. She married in 1951 James Douglas, then a civil servant, who would later become both an important political advisor and a theorist of voluntary organizations. Studying anthropology at Oxford brought her under the influence of the greats of British social anthropological thought. After Durkheim, Marcel Mauss, Henri Hubert and Maurice Halbwachs, to whose work she was introduced at Oxford, her major influences were her teacher, Edward Evans-Pritchard, the Oxford school of social anthropology, the social linguist **Basil Bernstein** and, latterly, the philosopher Nelson Goodman. For much of her life, she was associated with the school of anthropology at University College London, initially working closely with the leading Africanist Daryll Forde. During the late 1970s, she went to work on social fears with Aaron Wildavsky during his brief and fruitful but controversial presidency of the Russell Sage Foundation in New York. She then accepted the Avalon Chair of the Humanities at Northwestern University on the outskirts of Chicago.

Initially an Africanist anthropologist interested in religion, Douglas has ranged widely over core sociological questions in the developed world. Her principal ethnographic fieldwork was conducted among the Lele people in what is today the Congo. In the 1960s, in *Purity and Danger*, now a classic of social science, she argued that ideas of pollution and taboo and other boundary-violating practices are sustained by underlying dynamics of social organization. It was also the first major statement of her sociology of knowledge and classification. The 1970s saw her examine, among other things, consumption practices around goods, food and drink as ritual activities to sustain social distinctions, especially in *The World of Goods*.

In *Cultural Bias* and *Essays in the Sociology of Perception*, Douglas produced major restatements of her taxonomy of types of social organization – the so-called 'grid and group' model. In *How Institutions Think*, she drew on Durkheim, Ludwig Fleck and Halbwachs to show that classification, social memory and forgetting are the work of institutions, not individual psychology. During the 1980s, she published a series of works on social fears, or what had by then come to be known as 'risk perceptions', including the controversial *Risk and Culture*, arguing that different types of social organization in any type or scale of society will yield similar thought styles and styles of social fear. Her argument that ancient religious and modern environmental ideas of pollution had much in common was regarded as provocative.

In the 1990s (so much for 'retirement'!), as well as returning to each of these themes and most especially to issues of classification, she also published a series of studies of anthropological interpretations of the Books of Numbers and Leviticus, in which she argued that the literary forms of these works are best explained by the respectively sectarian and hierarchical social contexts in ancient Israel in which their authors worked. In addition to continuing to publish on all of these issues and overseeing new editions of all her major books, she has published a full presentation of her theory of personhood and agency in *Missing Persons*, several articles engaging with aspects of recent economic theories of institutions, and a radical recasting of her theory of 'enclaving'.

Douglas' central arguments begin in a sociology of knowledge that focuses on the systems of classification, styles of reasoning, patterns of perception, memory and aspiration, planning horizons, beliefs, values, understandings of nature and the world, tastes in consumption, worldviews and styles of emotion. People develop the categories that they do in order to solve, or at least cope with, the organizational problems they face. This view enables Douglas to peel away from the Durkheimian tradition the Parsonian notions of societies being held together by norms, showing norms to be emergent upon organization.

Those organizational problems are, Douglas argues, the product of institutional processes, of which tacit, implicit, informal institutions are generally far more important than explicit, palpable, openly recognized, formal rules. People, in any society, think institutionally, and the differences in thought style are to be explained by differences in the elementary forms of their institutions. In *Primitive Classification*, a work of great importance for Douglas, Durkheim and Mauss developed the basic thesis that 'the classification of things reproduces [the] classification of [people]', and that those classifications are the work of institutions. In particular, rival ideas of nature are developed as trump cards in arguments by which people seek to hold others to account under the institutions to which they are committed. This provides the basis of the cultural theory that underpins the general taxonomy of institutional forms that Douglas developed.

Douglas believes functional explanation to be necessary, but, contrary to functional*ism*, she insists that the institutions for which bodies of knowledge can be shown to be functional are in endless conflict, thus explaining historical change. Institutional processes can best be thought of as driven by varying forms and degrees of what Durkheim called social integration and social regulation. Social integration is seen as establishing 'group' organization, drawing more or less closely defended boundaries and accountabilities of membership and 'attachment'. Social regulation is seen as establishing a 'grid' organization that draws tighter or looser, structuring constraints and accountabilities of rule and role or discipline. This is the famous 'group/grid' matrix. Cross-tabulating these dimensions – as Durkheim lamentably failed to do in *Suicide* and the lectures on *Moral Education* – yields the four basic 'solidarities' of hierarchy, enclave, individualism and isolate life. These forms can be found at every level and scale of human organization, in societies and organizations using both simple and advanced technologies, and throughout history, and each yields distinct biases in classification, perception and memory. For this idea, Bernstein's matrix cross-tabulating elaborated and restricted codes in one dimension and personal and positional styles of control in families in the other was an important precursor. However, the resulting types are not closely matched, and Douglas never takes such classifications as those of class as given in the ways that Bernstein still did in the 1970s. For Douglas, Bernstein's work was a springboard rather than a model to follow.

Following Durkheim, Douglas argues that institutional processes are fundamentally ritual in character. Indeed, ritual is part of the way in which institutions explain classification, and is not itself explained by ideas. In ritual, people enact the classification systems of their institutions, so serving to reinforce them.

At the core of Douglas' methodology is the analysis of things that are anomalous within people's systems of classification. The ritual and cognitive ways in which institutions handle anomalies in the classification systems they cultivate and support provide the social scientist with the most important evidence about their true character. The key to understanding any system of social organization is to examine what it rejects, what it cannot recognize and how it handles those things that are anomalous between acceptance and rejection. Such things are likely to acquire the ambivalence of being sacred, at once precious and dangerous. In her early work, Douglas examined the ambiguous status in Lele society of the scaly anteater, or pangolin, showing that the Lele used it symbolically to organize one of the most anomalous groups in their society. In the 1980s and 1990s, she used the same method of examining ways of handling problems that fit uneasily within the classifications of different groups in the West to explain both the varieties of social fears about the environment and the practices of conspicuous and modest consumption.

Stated so baldly, it may not be obvious just how scandalously controversial are these claims. Her hostility to the idealism of much American sociology, her insistence that culture must itself be explained represent a sharp challenge. Many critics of Douglas have failed to distinguish her sociology of knowledge from relativism, despite her clarification in the 1990s that there are the tightest possible institutional constraints on what people can viably think. Contrary to the idealism of social constructionism and postmodernism, Douglas argues that people cannot and do not construe their environment in any way whatsoever. Although institutions will protect people from the possible practical inconveniences of some kinds of ideas, a very wide range of possible construals will quickly prove unviable: real dangers cannot be imagined away without shins being bruised. In recent years, she has clarified her argument using Nelson Goodman's 'irrealist' theory of similarity in classification as the product of institutions, where tight constraints are placed on the range of possible thought styles. Her Durkheimian arguments also challenge methodological individualists such as Elster, who, however much they may deviate from classical rational choice theory, can never allow institutions to be anything other than aggregations of individual preferences. Rejecting 'cultural dope' versions of structuralism, Douglas is, however, entirely consistent in insisting on seeing individuals 'in the active voice' and criticizing modern utilitarians for leaving persons out of their accounts. Agency, the active role of persons and the range of variation in agency cannot be understood save by reference to the institutional processes that give meaning, efficacy and even the possibility for that agency.

No one has taken more seriously than Douglas the central claim of mid-twentieth-century British social anthropology that humankind is essentially one. Douglas specifically rejects Weberian arguments that modernity is a period marked by a distinctive rationality: Douglas denies that there is anything distinctive at the most fundamental level about the forms of organization and rationality to be found in the West since the Renaissance or the Enlightenment. Neither the assertion of uniqueness in historicism nor that of the 'thick description' of cases presumed to be distinctive can be accepted. For Douglas, contrary to the view of thinkers such as **Randall Collins**, there can be no need for separate micro- and macro-sociology. Again, Douglas denies that religion exhibits fundamentally different forms of rationality, organization and ritual from those found in other spheres of life. Indeed, when institutions develop commitments that are sufficiently serious in any sphere of life, they will develop characteristics that can helpfully be understood by exploring their investment with sacred characteristics. Douglas' methodology of focusing on anomalies and organization clearly distinguishes her views from those of idealists like Serge Moscovici and Roy D'Andrade or the cultural evolutionists who write about 'memes', both of which schools tend to see 'social representations' as indefinitely various, freely floating and as communicated by contagion.

Douglas has been criticized for a lack of philosophical precision in her sociology of knowledge, and for a failure exactly to define how far she is a determinist and a structuralist about institutions. Although this may be at least partly just, she has made strenuous efforts to be clearer, and her position is probably now robust against the earlier criticisms. Risk scholars have complained of her reductionism. Her sympathy with hierarchy has been criticized by many as being biased in ways that her own theory ought to preclude. Although her insistence on the centrality of ritual has attracted sympathy from Goffmanians such as Randall Collins, it is rejected by both the rational choice and the constructionist traditions.

Her two-by-two matrix yielding the four elementary forms of institution and social solidarity has been by turns misunderstood, ignored or dismissed as quirky, too simple or unnecessarily complex. Yet many of its critics rely upon even cruder categories. Too often the taxonomy is mistaken for the Durkheimian theory underlying it. Perhaps the key uncertainty in her work about the 'grid–group' model remains the question of whether the dimensions are continuously differentiable or a matter of binary distinction: her followers have tended to the latter view, but the debate continues.

Douglas' matrix has influenced a small school of researchers and scholars who have demonstrated in an astonishingly wide variety of fields the predictive power of the hypotheses about cognition, affect, ritual and material culture expected to be associated with each of the solidarities and with each of the possible hybrids. Michael Thompson, who completed his PhD under Douglas, went on to build a sophisticated cybernetic theory of social dynamics and of the viability of institutions around the taxonomy, which has been widely influential in its own right and partially accepted by Douglas. Steve Rayner, another of her doctoral students, jointly developed the most important methodological statement of her whole approach, while Mars' *Cheats at Work* has become a modern classic. Perhaps the most famous scholar to work with Douglas, as well as with Thompson, and to apply the taxonomy was the political scientist Aaron Wildavsky. Although Wildavsky probably never really accepted Douglas' institutionalism, too often treating the taxonomy as if it identified worldviews that could be used as independent variables rather than the dependent ones that Douglas has always insisted they are, his applications were innovative and controversial.

After the exhaustion of postmodernist attempts to allow infinite variation in ideas and to claim that ideas explain all, and since much rational choice work seems arid and inadequate at the level of meaning and mechanism, and when Durkheimian ideas are once again being reasserted, Douglas' work provides one of the most promising, powerful and coherent directions now available for sociological theory.

See also: Basil Bernstein.

See also in *Fifty Key Sociologists: The Formative Theorists*: Emile Durkheim, Maurice Halbwachs, Marcel Mauss.

Major works

(As Mary Tew) 'Peoples of the Lake Nyasa Region'. 1950. In Daryll Forde, ed. *Ethnographic Survey of Africa: Eastern Central Africa, Part 1*. London: International African Institute; Oxford: Oxford University Press.
The Lele of the Kasai. 1963. London: International African Institute, 1977.
Purity and Danger: An Analysis of the Concepts of Pollution and Taboo. 1966. London: Routledge & Kegan Paul.
Natural Symbols: Explorations in Cosmology. 1970. London: Routledge & Kegan Paul.
Rules and Meanings, ed. 1973. Harmondsworth: Penguin.

Implicit Meanings: Selected Essays in Anthropology. 1978. Second edn. London: Routledge, 1999.

Cultural Bias. 1978. London: Royal Anthropological Institute. Reprinted in Mary Douglas, *Essays in the Sociology of Perception.* London: Routledge & Kegan Paul, 1982.

The World of Goods: Towards an Anthropology of Consumption. 1979. With Baron Isherwood. London: Routledge & Kegan Paul.

Evans-Pritchard: His Life, Work, Writings and Ideas. 1980. Brighton: Harvester Press.

In the Active Voice. 1982. London: Routledge & Kegan Paul.

Risk and Culture: An Essay on the Selection of Technological and Environmental Dangers. 1982. With Aaron Wildavsky. Berkeley, CA: University of California Press.

Essays in the Sociology of Perception. 1982. London: Routledge & Kegan Paul.

Risk Acceptability According to the Social Sciences. 1985. London: Routledge & Kegan Paul.

How Institutions Think. 1986. London: Routledge & Kegan Paul.

Risk and Blame: Essays in Cultural Theory. 1992. London: Routledge.

In the Wilderness: The Doctrine of Defilement in the Book of Numbers. 1993. Oxford: Oxford University Press.

Thought Styles: Critical Essays on Good Taste. 1996. London: Sage.

Missing Persons: A Critique of Personhood in the Social Sciences. 1988. With S. Ney. Berkeley, CA: University of California Press.

Leviticus as Literature. 1999. Oxford: Oxford University Press.

Further reading

Richard Fardon. 1999. *Mary Douglas: An Intellectual Biography.* London: Routledge.

S. Hargreaves Heap and A. Ross, eds. 1992. *Understanding the Enterprise Culture: Themes in the Work of Mary Douglas.* Edinburgh: Edinburgh University Press.

M. Thompson, R. J. Ellis and Aaron Wildavsky. 1990. *Cultural Theory,* Boulder, CO: Westview Press.

J. G. Gross and Steve Rayner. 1986. *Measuring Culture: A Paradigm for the Analysis of Social Organisation.* New York: Columbia University Press.

Aaron Wildavsky, Sun-Ki Chai and Brendon Swedlow. 1998. *Culture and Social Theory.* New Brunswick, NJ: Transaction Publishers.

PERRI 6

NORBERT ELIAS

Elias' approach has been characterized as 'figurational' sociology – he preferred the term 'process sociology' – and he was renowned for his theory of 'civilizing processes'. A figurational approach holds that human beings are born into relations of interdependence and that the social structures they form with each other have emergent dynamics that cannot be reduced to individual actions or motivations. These emergent dynamics shape the growth, development and trajectory of individuals' lives. Figurations are in a constant state of flux and transformation, and long-term transformations in human social figurations are largely unplanned and unforeseen. Elias sees the development of knowledge taking place within such figurations.

Elias was born of Jewish parents on 22 June 1897 in Breslau, then in Germany, but now the Polish city of Wroclaw. He served as a young soldier during the First World War and then studied medicine and philosophy, graduating with a doctorate in philosophy in 1922. He moved to Heidelberg, where he worked with Alfred Weber (Max's younger brother) before becoming academic assistant to Karl Mannheim in Frankfurt in 1929. The rise of the Nazis caused him to flee to Paris in 1933, but he settled in England in 1935 and took a research fellowship at the London School of Economics. Three years research at the British Museum allowed him to complete what is considered his masterpiece, *The Civilising Process*, published obscurely in Switzerland in 1939 and not published in English until 1978. In 1954, he took an academic post at Leicester University, and he later held university positions in Ghana, Frankfurt, Bielefeld and Amsterdam. He died on 1 August 1990, aged ninety-three.

His first work, completed in the 1930s but not published until 1969, was *The Court Society*, which examined the social pressures facing the 'court nobility' during the reign of Louis XIV. He saw the court rationality of the nobility, in which rank and prestige determined expenditure, as contrasting with the economic rationality of the bourgeoisie, where consumption was subordinated to income. The analysis of court society provided a crucial corrective to Max Weber's discussions of instrumental and value rationality, as well as qualifying Marx's simple binary contrast between feudalism and capitalism. These same theorists were the focus of *The Civilising Process*, which drew on Marx, Mannheim, Weber, Simmel and Freud to offer an investigation of psychological and behavioural transformations among the secular upper classes in the West. These, he showed, were integrally tied to processes of internal pacification and state formation. He asked how it was that certain classes in the developing nation-states of Western Europe came to think of themselves as 'civilized' and how this became generalized as a badge of western superiority over non-western cultures.

Elias charted long-term transformations in manners, behavioural codes and thresholds of repugnance concerning bodily functions, all of which involved an internalization of social restraints. His work traced the establishment of a characteristic habitus, involving increasing superego restraints over affective impulses and drives (including violent behaviour), as a compelling aspect of court society. Upper-class manners and affective sensibility, through processes of distinction and imitation, became generalized as examples of polite behaviour and were gradually diffused through other strata. This blind and unplanned – but nevertheless structured and directional – transformation of manners is the primary subject of volume I of *The Civilising Process*, though Elias was not concerned simply with a history of manners. In volume II he turned to state formation and the 'sociogenesis' of the absolutist states and showed how the internalization of restraints and the resulting transformation in behavioural codes were intimately connected with transformations in the division of labour, demographic shifts, societal pacification, urbanization and the growth of trade and a money economy. Growth in the urban money economy facilitated, but also critically depended upon, the power and the monopoly of violence achieved by the central state authority. Greater access to these economic circuits gave access to increased military resources relative to the landed warlord nobility, whose principal source of economic and military power was control over finite and depreciating land assets. This shifting power ratio transformed a formerly independent warrior class into an increasingly dependent upper class of courtiers. Greater pacification facilitated trade and economic growth, which in turn underwrote the economic and military power of the central authority and led to growing power for the middle classes. When declining aristocratic power and increasing middle-class power were approximately equal, monarchs were able to lay claim to 'absolute power'. In their newly pacified domains, and particularly within the court, these developments systematically rewarded more restrained patterns of behaviour. External restraints, associated with the authority relations of state formation, were gradually and increasingly internalized as self-restraints, resulting in a characteristic shift in habitus and personality structure.

Far from being a universal theory of development or of moral and cultural progress, as some commentators have implied, *The Civilising Process* offers a delimited account of the different trajectories of development in Britain, France and Germany, and the genesis and subject matter of the book cannot be understood without reference to Elias' experience of the social and political crisis of German society and the global impact of the rise of Nazism. Elias' later writings develop and expand upon this same theme. His contribution to the sociology of sport in *Quest for Excitement* applies the idea of western civilizing processes to the links between the 'parliamentarization' of English politics and the codification of sports such as boxing, foxhunting and cricket. Elias argues that civilizing processes involve, as one of their aspects, processes of routinization which lead to feelings of emotional staleness in people. As a result, institutions have developed which perform a de-routinizing function through movement, sociability, excitement and identification. This brings about the common features of 'highbrow' activities, such as the arts, and 'lowbrow' activities, such as sports. In *The Germans* he brought his analysis up to date, presenting a prequel and elaboration of his comparative investigation of state formation and psychogenesis during the early modern period. His central concern was the development of a German national habitus imbued with militaristic qualities and how this formed an important basis for the rise of Nazism.

The best introduction to his theoretical approach is *What is Sociology?*, where he reiterates his claim that sociologists must avoid treating single individuals or whole societies as static givens. This, he held, is a reflection of inappropriate language and conceptualization that reduces processes to states. A *scientific* sociology also requires that the *homo clausus* ('closed person') view underlying methodological individualism be replaced with an orientation towards pluralities of 'open people'. This is the basis of a relational view of power as linked to the functions individuals have for one another. Recognizing that an individual's psychology and 'way of seeing' emerges from the figurational matrices in which she or he is a participant allows Elias to problematize and historicize traditional philosophical epistemologies that assume an adult western male as the basis for a supposedly universal theory of knowledge.

One of the most important aspects of Elias' work related to problems that philosophically minded sociologists refer to as epistemology but which Elias himself preferred to conceptualize as a sociological theory of knowledge. In *Involvement and Detachment*, *The Symbol Theory*, and *Time: An Essay*, Elias sought to combine a Comtean theory of knowledge with a sociology of knowledge processes. A historical sociology of the knowledge process shows that earlier stages of human development were characterized by animistic, magico-mythical ideas and feelings with high degrees of fantasy and 'involvement'. Over many millennia, a steady shift in the balance from emotional involvement towards 'detachment' has made possible a steadily increasing reality-congruent understanding (Elias avoids using the word 'truth') of 'natural forces', and a correspondingly greater degree of control over and reduced danger from these forces. Knowledge of social processes, however, has remained relatively less autonomous and people are still very much at the mercy of 'social forces'. Sociologists, Elias concluded, need to create professional procedures and conventions, like those at work in the natural sciences, that will, to a degree, insulate the knowledge process from wider social processes and allow researchers to build up stocks of knowledge that can be of practical use.

Elias' ability to combine micro and macro accounts of social processes, to transcend the individual–society dichotomy, to combine profound theoretical insight with a staggering breadth of empirical evidence and to provide a consistently rigorous social and historical account of the world is amply demonstrated both in *The Civilising Process* and in his study of a single Austrian composer (*Mozart: Portrait of a Genius*). This ensures his place in the pantheon of great sociological thinkers.

See also: Zygmunt Bauman.

See also in *Fifty Key Sociologists: The Formative Theorists*: Karl Mannheim, Georg Simmel, Max Weber.

Major works

Early Writings. Collected Works, Volume 1. Various dates. Dublin: University College Dublin Press, 2005.
The Court Society. Collected Works, Volume 2. 1933. Dublin: University College Dublin Press, 2005.
The Civilizing Process. Volume 1: The History of Manners. 1939. Oxford: Blackwell, 1978.
The Civilizing Process. Volume 2: State Formation and Civilization. 1939. Oxford: Blackwell, 1982.
The Society of Individuals. 1939. London: Continuum, 1991.
The Established and Outsiders: A Sociological Inquiry into Community Problems. 1965. With John Scotson. London: Sage, 1994.
What Is Sociology? 1969. London: Hutchinson, 1978.
Time: An Essay. 1984. Oxford: Blackwell, 1992.
Quest for Excitement. 1986. With Eric Dunning. Oxford: Blackwell.
The Germans. 1989. Oxford: Blackwell, 1996.
The Symbol Theory. 1991. London: Sage.
Mozart: Portrait of a Genius. 1991. Berkeley, CA: University of California Press, 1993.

Further reading

Stephen J. Mennell. 1989. *Norbert Elias: An Introduction.* Dublin: University College Dublin Press.
Peter Reinhart Gleichmann, Johan Goudsblom and Hermann Korte, eds. 1977. *Human Figurations.* Amsterdam: Amsterdams Sociologisch Tijdschrift.
Johan Goudsblom. 1977. *Sociology in the Balance.* Oxford: Blackwell.
Steven Loyal and Stephen Quilley. 2004. *The Sociology of Norbert Elias.* Cambridge: Cambridge University Press.

STEVEN LOYAL

FRANTZ FANON

Born in 1925 in Martinique, Fanon went to fight for France in the Second World War. He remained in France after the war, studying medicine from 1947 to 1953 and specializing in psychiatry. Aimé Césaire, one of the best-known black thinkers in France, was his teacher and he introduced Fanon to the philosophy of negritude (a movement of black thinkers in France and Africa that highlighted black creativity and African values) and to the need to embrace aspects of his personality that the white colonizer had persuaded him to renounce. Césaire also encouraged Fanon to read Hegel, Marx, Lenin and Jean-Paul Sartre. Though Fanon disagreed in fundamental ways with the existentialism of Sartre and the negritude of Césaire, they remained life-long friends. Between 1953 and 1956 he practised medicine in a psychiatric hospital at Blida-Joinville in Algeria, at that time still a colony of France. Here he treated patients who had been tortured by the French Special Forces. His increasing outrage at the hostility of French doctors towards Algerian patients led him to resign his position. He was expelled from Algeria in 1957 and worked for the Algerian nationalist National Liberation Front in Tunisia, where he participated in the All African People's Conference of 1958. He was briefly the Algerian ambassador to Ghana, before he developed and succumbed to leukaemia in 1961.

A psychiatrist by training, Fanon's ideas were shaped by his work in psychiatric hospitals in the French colonies of Algeria and Tunisia, by the experience of having fought in the Second World War and by his studies of psychology, philosophy, politics and colonial struggles. He experienced first hand the refusal by France to honour and respect its African subjects. Fanon strongly believed that the pathological conditions that he identified in individuals were directly caused by the social conditions of colonial domination. He explored how the social and cultural circumstances of oppressed peoples – those living under the political, economic and cultural domination of the French Empire – created feelings of psychological inadequacy and self-doubt. For him, the solution to such problems was not psychological but social: in order to address the mental state of the individual, one had to change the social conditions under which that individual lived. Fanon was staunchly against cultural assimilation, which he saw as destroying the soul and psychology of the assimilated. He had much to say about the French language, which he saw as one of the primary cultural mechanisms used to dominate the colonized.

His first major work, *Black Skin, White Masks*, is an existential, psychological and socio-economic analysis of the effects of colonization on the colonized black people of Martinique. He described how socio-economic inequality and racism gave rise to an inferiority complex and a desire to whiten themselves (socially and literally) among black people, rich and poor. He described how black people in Martinique, taught to be ashamed of their skin and all it suggested of barbarism, savagery and cultural backwardness, sought to wear white masks. Fanon stated 'the Negro, having been made inferior, proceeds from humiliating insecurity through strongly voiced self-accusation to despair'. Psychological well-being for the black man, said Fanon, is not possible in a racist culture. In this analysis Fanon focused on the role of language in dominating black thought: the valorization of the French language was accompanied by the stigmatization of Creole forms of French. The French language was a primary mechanism through which to inscribe European civilization into the consciousness of the colonized. This led to dehumanization. He saw powerful black people in Martinique as complicit in the colonial process, while also suffering from its effects. He felt that only the peasantry could be the source of liberation. The book closely addressed the issues of sexual relations between black men and white women, and white men and black women, offering the conclusion that the primary motivation of black men pursuing white women was their inferiority complex: 'By loving me, she proves that I am worthy of white love. I am loved like a white man. . . . I marry white culture, white beauty, white whiteness'.

The Wretched of the Earth represents the culmination of Fanon's social and political philosophy and in it he articulated a theory of liberation rooted in violent action based on an analysis of political developments across the Third World, especially Africa. Because oppression under colonization was effected through force and violence, then it is only through the use of violence by the oppressed that liberation will occur. For Fanon, violence in support of political and cultural liberation is a positive force that is both psychologically empowering and strategically sound, from the point of view of the oppressed:

> At the level of the individuals, violence is a cleansing force. It frees the native from his inferiority complex and from his despair and inaction; it makes him fearless and restores his self-respect.

Violence of this kind reaffirms the humanity of the oppressed through a process of catharsis and political change. The liberation of the mind, and the escape from mental inferiority, led to the political liberation of the nation. The poorest people, the peasantry, in other words the wretched of the earth, had nothing to lose in this struggle. Critics said that his ideas were utopian and impractical – that the power of the colonizers was too great. But Fanon argued that even if they failed the efforts would be mentally liberating and purifying.

Two collections of Fanon's essays were published posthumously. *Studies in a Dying Colonialism* is an account of his role and involvement in the Algerian War of Independence and the essays address the specifics of white French domination in Algeria and the role of medicine under colonialism. *Toward the African Revolution* consists of pieces written while in Tunisia working with the Algerian independence movement.

Fanon's writings had a major impact on revolutionaries and were influential in many anti-colonial struggles. AfricanAmericans who organized the Black Panthers in the United States in the 1960s – and who saw themselves as victims of internal colonialism – were inspired by his writings. His writing style is direct, the images he evokes are compelling, and his writing has a power and an impact often absent from academic writing: 'I do not carry innocence to the point of believing that appeals to reason or to respect for human dignity can alter reality'. That is why he called for violence.

His writings are still widely read in departments of cultural studies and ethnic studies across the USA. For postcolonial analysts, Fanon's insights have relevance to understanding the continued nature of racial and cultural subordination in Africa and Asia after political independence. Many of his ideas have been developed further by analysts such as Ngugi Wa Thiong'o, **Edward Said** and Homi Bhabha in discussions of postcolonial theory.

Fanon's influence is diverse and diffuse. For sociologists in western countries, preoccupied with economic and political inequalities,

Fanon's work reminds us of the role that culture – racist culture – plays in these processes and of the consequences for the psychological make-up of black or Asian people in Britain, the United States and elsewhere. Reading Fanon provides insights into the psychological goals of a movement such as Rastafarianism and on the emphasis on black language in black musical forms like hip hop and reggae.

See also: Edward Said.

See also in *Fifty Key Sociologists: The Formative Theorists*: Karl Marx.

Major works

Black Skin, White Masks. 1952. New York: Grove Press.
The Wretched of the Earth. 1961. New York: Grove Press.
Toward the African Revolution. 1964. New York: Grove Press.
Studies in a Dying Colonialism. 1965. New York: Grove Press.

Further reading

Lewis R. Gordon, T. Denean Sharpley-Whiting and Renee T. White, eds. 1996. *Fanon: A Critical Reader*. Oxford: Blackwell.
David Macey. 2000. *Frantz Fanon: A Biography*. New York: Picador Press.
Irene L. Gendzier. 1973. *Frantz Fanon: A Critical Study*. New York: Pantheon.

STEPHEN SMALL

SHULAMITH FIRESTONE

Born in 1945 in Ottawa, Canada, and educated at the Art Institute of Chicago, where she received a master's in fine art, Shulamith Firestone was one of the founders of the women's liberation movement in the 1960s. She was a member of New York Radical Women and of the Redstockings, and she wrote for the radical feminist journal *Notes*. In 1970 she published *The Dialectic of Sex: The Case for Feminist Revolution* – one of the most influential of the feminist manifestos, standing alongside Betty Friedan's *The Feminine Mystique*, Kate Millet's *Sexual Politics* and Germaine Greer's *The Female Eunuch*.

Firestone was one of the first feminist theorists to fuse the insights of Marxism, feminism and psychoanalysis into a sophisticated critique linking the structures of gender inequality to those of economic stratification, environmental degradation and the politics of scientific knowledge. In a manner that was later to become a hallmark of feminist writing in the 1970s, Firestone drew powerful and intimate connections between the emotional politics of normative hetero-sexuality, compulsory femininity and the institutionalization of gender inequality in the workplace and beyond. In turn, she linked the toll of a 'society saturated with sexual polarity' to racism, class inequality, excessive consumption and industrial decline.

Like subsequent (and previous) feminist theorists, Firestone targeted 'the culture of romantic love', 'the Beauty Ideal', and the cultivation of femininity as imitative and inauthentic and as root sources of women's lack of self-esteem and devalued status in society. Equally influenced by Friedrich Engels and **Simone de Beauvoir**, she saw the excesses of industrial capitalism as inextricable from the structures of gender, marriage, childhood and the traditional family through which children were seen to 'belong' to their parents. She argued that 'capitalism intensified the worst aspects of patriarchalism', while the biological family preserved them both.

In contrast to her frequent association with the view that mastery of reproductive technology would prove an ultimate liberating force in society, Firestone's argument was in many respects the opposite. Indeed it is on the topic of the 'revolutionary' consequences of technology that she is the most accurately prescient about the forms of social change, and intransigence, that she sought to explicate. Her argument about technology is, at turns, most sharply focused on its potentially transformative capacities and on its propensity to fail, much as later risk society theorists have argued its 'dialectic' is defined.

Thus, in contrast to her frequent depiction as a proponent of technological determinism, her arguments emphasize the social embeddedness of technology, and consequently the social limits to its growth. Indeed, in an era when a new technological device is more likely to be described as revolutionary than a peace agreement or a social movement, Firestone's theoretical contributions to the study of technology are particularly apt.

For Firestone, it was the revolutionary capacity of technological progress that established a fundamental link between feminism and radical ecology because, in her view, the imperative for greater techno-logical control over both production and reproduction would eventually become a matter of human survival, against which biology could no longer be protected as a 'moral' question. 'Thus', she argued,

> In terms of modern technology, a revolutionary ecological movement would have the same aim as the feminist movement: control of the new technology for humane purposes, the establishment of a beneficial 'human' equilibrium between man and the new artificial environment he is creating, to replace the destroyed 'natural' balance.

In this way, Firestone envisaged technology both as an agent of and a salvation from social and environmental degradation. She argued, however, that science and technology could not achieve these ends in the absence of radical social change. It was for this reason, in her view, that a feminist revolution was the necessary condition for 'establishing a new ecological balance' by presenting 'an alternative to the oppressions of the biological family' and thus enabling 'a total redefinition of the economy'.

To further these aims, Firestone advocated progressive social evolution away from the rigid and moralistic biologism nostalgically imagined to underpin the 'naturalness' of gender, parenthood and reproduction. Thus, while she famously argued, like de Beauvoir, that women's experience of childbirth is 'barbaric', so she abhorred the inhumane and diminishing conditions of factory workers that she saw as legitimated within the naturalizing logic of capitalism. For both these and other ills she sought technological, sociological and philosophical solutions, primarily focusing on control of production ('cybernation') and of reproduction (through artificial means).

Firestone's 'cybernetic socialism' anticipates not only the work of Judith Butler in her challenge to the naturalization of gender binarism, but also that of **Donna Haraway** in her rejection of the anti-technology orientation of 1970s ecofeminism, which is the founding gesture for the birth of her famously illegitimate cyborg figure. Haraway's influential writings – like Firestone's dedicated to a mix of technological optimism and pessimism and prone to revolutionary manifestos – share many of Firestone's most powerful insights about the influence of gendered narratives on technological development, the capacity for technological innovation to reinforce social inequality and the ironic co-presence of its opposite capacity to alter or subvert established social patterns.

As Firestone predicted, reproductive technology and information technology are good places to look for both of these, and other, examples of technological 'revolutions' that were constrained in their revolutionary potential more by social forces than by their own limitations. In contrast to the oft-repeated characterization of Firestone's argument as having put too much faith in the capacity of new reproductive technologies to liberate women, her assessment of their potential precisely anticipated that they would reinforce gender polarity if their use was not accompanied by a radical redefinition of gender, parenthood and the family. As she presciently warned, 'in the hands of our current society and under the direction of current scientists (few of whom are female or even feminist), any attempt to use technology to "free" anybody is suspect'.

Firestone is less well known for her second book, *Airless Spaces*, published thirty years after the first edition of *The Dialectic of Sex*. Like a documentary bookend to her earlier accounts of the degrading effects of social stratification and inequality, to which she imagined a possible revolution and its almost inevitable failure, *Airless Spaces* is a terse series of almost cinematic vignettes of Firestone's experiences of a marginal and peripatetic existence, in which she moves in and out of work and is frequently institutionalized. With a keen eye, she depicts the often surreal quotidian worlds of her friends and acquaintances, many of whom share her marginal way of life and its attendant risks of addiction, destitution, suicide and depression. In the same powerful voice, and with the same relentless insight into the costs of structural inequality, but in language that offers analysis in the form of description, she takes a revolutionary look at her own and others' lives on the margins.

From her powerful theoretical account of gender, technology and social change authored in the midst of a period of revolutionary social movements, to her stark portrait of late-twentieth-century social exclusion thirty years later, Firestone's contributions remain pivotal feminist accounts of gender, inequality and the structural patterns of social exclusion.

See also: Simone de Beauvoir, Judith Butler, Donna Haraway.

See also in *Fifty Key Sociologists: The Formative Theorists*: Karl Marx.

Major works

The Dialectic of Sex – the Case for Feminist Revolution. 1968. New York: Bantam.
Notes from the First Year. 1968. New York: New York Radical Women.
Airless Spaces. 1998. New York: Semiotext(e).

SARAH FRANKLIN

MICHEL FOUCAULT

One of the most influential thinkers of the twentieth century, Foucault's work has had a seismic impact in such fields as criminology, cultural studies, history, philosophy, political theory and psychiatry, as well as sociology. Foucault's inter-disciplinary studies of, amongst other things, madness, medicine, knowledge, punishment, institutions and sexuality have significantly altered how sociologists now approach these topics. Even though Foucault was not a sociologist, his work confronts and confounds some of the central issues in sociology. He is best described as a historian of systems of thought, a title that he chose himself and that exemplifies how his own approach to the social distinctively blends history and philosophy. At the same time, the phrase carefully differentiates his work from conventional disciplinary boundaries and traditions.

At the heart of his thinking lie certain key themes, which he later claimed had been driven by the goal of creating 'a history of the different modes by which, in our culture, human beings are made subjects'. Closely tied to this questioning of the human subject lie the joint concerns of power and knowledge. In his early work Foucault sought to grasp how the human and social sciences historically became possible, while his later writings came to regard power as a discursive system of knowledge that shapes institutional practices in specific sites, such as asylums, barracks, factories, prisons and schools. Foucault's thinking marks a decisive break with Marxism for many commentators, while his understanding of subjectivity challenges theories that place human beings at the centre of analysis. These ideas have generated considerable controversy, as they both involve a rejection of a political project that aspires to emancipation and undermine a phenomenological philosophy that privileges the autonomous subject.

Paul-Michel Foucault was born to a rich family in 1926 in the provincial French city of Poitiers, where he was educated initially in local state schools and subsequently at a Catholic school. He left Poitiers in 1945 for an elite school in Paris to prepare for the entrance exams into the Ecole Normale Supérieure, where he studied philosophy and received his *licence de philosophie* in 1948. A year later he obtained a *licence de psychologie* and began a career as a trainee psychologist in a Parisian psychiatric hospital while also working at Fresnes prison performing admission tests on prisoners. He became a lecturer at the University of Lille in 1952, and this research and teaching experience led to the publication of a book on *Mental Illness and Personality*. His career over the next two decades took him to universities in various countries, including Sweden, Poland, Tunisia and Germany. It was at the University of Hamburg that he completed, in 1961, his doctorate on madness, which established his reputation as a scholar and earned him a professorship in philosophy at the University of Clermont-Ferand in 1964. In 1970 he was elected to France's leading academic institution, the Collège de France, where he remained until his death from AIDS in 1984.

The intellectual landscape in which Foucault developed his ideas was dominated by the pillars of Marxism and phenomenology. He has explained how 'people of my generation were brought up on these two forms of analysis, one in terms of the constituent subject, the other in terms of the economic in the last instance, ideology and the play of superstructures and infrastructures'. In making his break with these orthodoxies, Foucault drew on the emerging structuralist forms of analysis that extended ideas in linguistics to cultural and social phenomena. Important examples of this new approach include the anthropologist **Claude Lévi-Strauss's** examination of the underlying structures of kinship relations, the literary critic **Roland Barthes'** application of structuralist methods to popular culture and the philosopher **Louis Althusser's** radical reinterpretation of Marxism to develop a theoretical 'anti-humanism' that profoundly influenced Foucault.

Although he was subsequently to deny any connection, it is clear that Foucault's early work bears the imprint of structuralism. Consequently, it is helpful to divide his work into two distinct phases. The first is what he called that of the 'archaeologies', work that remains influenced by the general structuralist preoccupation with language but includes a broadened understanding of discourse. The second, later writings are his 'genealogies', which mark a break with these earlier studies and are strongly informed by the nineteenth-century philosopher Frederick Nietzsche's sceptical understanding of history.

Foucault's early work traced changing modes of thought in relation to different kinds of knowledge. His first major study, *Madness and Civilisation*, was an abridged version of his doctoral thesis. Foucault charted the relationship between madness and reason, surveying the changing reactions to madness in terms of the ways in which thinking about rationality changed dramatically from the medieval period, through the Enlightenment's 'Age of Reason' and into the nineteenth century. This is Foucault's most straightforwardly historical work, but the issues it raised continued to inform all his subsequent research. *The Birth of the Clinic* takes a much narrower historical focus and examines the changing nature of medical knowledge at around the time of the French Revolution. Up until this point, conventional medical history had argued that medicine finally broke free of fantasy and superstition to arrive at the objective truth about the body and disease. However, the argument that Foucault makes is that what are usually considered as the strange and bizarre practices of the past are in fact governed by structural codes of knowledge. The radical implication of this claim is that what we regard as the meaningful truth claims of modern medicine are also governed by similar arbitrary structures.

These themes are further developed in Foucault's *The Order of Things*. The book humorously opens with a passage from 'a certain Chinese encyclopaedia', where it is written that:

> animals are divided into: (a) belonging to the empire, (b) embalmed, (c) tame, (d) sucking pigs, (e) sirens, (f) fabulous, (g) stray dogs, (h) included in the present classification, (i) frenzied, (j) innumerable, (k) drawn with a very fine camelhair brush, (l) *et cetera*, (m) having just broken the water pitcher, (n) that from a long way off look like flies.

What is demonstrated here, Foucault explains, is both the 'exotic charm of another system of thought' and also 'the limitation of our own, the stark impossibility of thinking *that*'. So, his intention is not to make the past bizarre, but to make the present strange. Foucault's grand goal is to find the structural codes of knowledge that govern particular eras. Consequently, he divides western thought into three distinct periods: the Renaissance, the Classical Age and modernity. Each of these eras is governed by what he terms a single 'episteme' – the implicit conceptual structure that provides the horizons of thinking in these different epochs.

By the time that Foucault came to write *The Archaeology of Knowledge*, it is evident that he was dissatisfied with structuralism, and he spends a good part of the book trying to distance himself from it. The book began as a treatise on the 'archaeological' method that he had been developing in the previous work. The distinctive claim is that discourses should be treated as comprising autonomous systems of statements. However, he soon came to revise this view and to argue that discursive formations are far from autonomous but are closely tied to power and domination. This marks a key shift in his thinking and it is at this point that 'genealogy' appears as his characteristic method of inquiry.

The change in direction is usually attributed to two key factors. The first is his response to the changing political context. The failure of the May 1968 uprisings in France to produce lasting social transformations and the discovery of the crimes committed by the Stalinist regimes in the USSR, China, Cambodia and Eastern Europe prompted Foucault, like many French intellectuals, to view history as a succession of forms of domination. The second factor is the explosion of social movements based around feminism, the environment and civil rights for minority groups, each suffering differing forms of oppression that could not be explained by historical materialism and its totalizing focus on class exploitation. Foucault himself became increasingly active in these social movements in the 1970s, and he campaigned on behalf of prisoners, immigrants and for gay rights on numerous occasions.

In his effort to understand these various forms of domination Foucault turned to the work of the philosopher Friedrich Nietzsche. This shift is registered in his landmark essay 'Nietzsche, Genealogy, History' (originally published in 1971). One of the central themes he took is Nietzsche's notion of the 'will to power', which criticizes the idea of progress and insists that humanity inevitably proceeds from one form of domination to another. Nietzsche's philosophy is also completely opposed to the search for the origins or causes that drive history; instead he argues that history is composed of competing forces, accidents and 'discontinuity'.

These themes were explored in Foucault's next major work, and perhaps his greatest achievement, *Discipline and Punish*. This book is far more than a history of punishment. It is, rather, a wide-ranging account of how power operates in modernity. The genealogical approach is firmly in place by this point and he insists that the book is a 'history of the present'. This can be seen in the opening pages, where he contrasts the graphic and brutal torture of a criminal in the mid-eighteenth century with the bland listing of an institutional timetable some eighty years later that is recognizable to the modern reader as an acceptable form of punishment. The juxtaposition immediately highlights the importance of discontinuity. In what is now a familiar tactic, he uses the strangeness of past practices to call into question the supposed rationality and legitimacy of the present. Foucault's overall argument is that the disappearance of the public spectacle of torture and its replacement by the prison is not a sign of progress and enlightenment. It is instead a sign of changing techniques of power, which aim to punish more deeply into the social body through discipline and surveillance.

Foucault's thinking on power and knowledge was refined further in the first volume of *The History of Sexuality*. Here he argued not only that the Victorian period was the opposite of what we suppose it to have been, that is, a period when talk about sexuality was repressed, but also that our popular modern view that talking about sex is a form of liberation is wrong. Instead he argues that the Victorian period was one in which a number of disciplines, such as medicine and psychiatry, developed their interrogations of sexuality. Moreover, this process of bringing sexuality under control through classification has continued to grow ever since. Before discussing Foucault's last work it is worthwhile to pause and draw out some of the key themes in relation to a critique of Marxism and a de-centring of the subject, which have come to be regarded as crucial to the development of poststructuralism.

There are a number of ways in which Foucault's work constitutes a major challenge to Marxist accounts of power, understood as an instrument of class domination originating from economic interests. Foucault argued that power operates in a diverse range of settings that cannot be reduced to a single, all-embracing explanatory concept like the mode of production. For instance, in *Discipline and Punish* he unpacks the 'microphysics of power' that operates on the bodies of individuals. The crucial implication is that if power is localized and fragmented, then any effort to transform power relationships must make an effort to address everyday practices. Another aspect of his critique is directed against ideology. This concept is central to Marxist accounts of power, which he likens to the 'economics of untruth' as opposed to his own preoccupation with the 'politics of truth'.

The phrase 'de-centring the subject' is used to criticize humanism — which maintains that human consciousness should lie at the centre of social analysis — by examining the way in which the individual creates meaning in the world. The main target was Jean-Paul Sartre's theory of existentialism. This was then an influential strand of Left humanism and emphasized the freedom of the individual to resist forms of oppression. For Foucault and structuralists like Althusser, this was a mistake. They argued that the subject is not free but is hedged in on all sides by social determinations. Indeed, Foucault argued that the very idea of a subject is a social construction, produced through discourses that position subjects in a field of power relations. A further error is to view individual consciousness as the centre of meaning. Foucault contended that this ignores how meaning is distributed through discourses. He also objected to the idea of a coherent and unified subject. Not only does this vastly exaggerate the degree of control that we have over our destinies, but it also mistakenly implies that human beings are unaffected by irrational and contradictory feelings over which they have little control.

As might be expected, these arguments have provoked fierce debate. Marxist critics reacted by pointing out how he has completely ignored the macro-physics of power. Partly in response to this, Foucault introduced another type of power that has come to the fore in modernity. This is 'bio-power', which focuses on the body and targets whole populations instead of particular individuals. It is this concern with the management of populations that introduces Foucault's later work on governmentality, loosely defined as 'the conduct of conduct': an activity aimed at shaping, guiding or affecting the conduct of an individual or populations. This later writing is also important as it goes some way to acknowledging the significance of human agency. It qualifies his argument that disciplinary power tames, suppresses and reduces individuals to 'docile bodies', by stressing the presence of active subjects in the processes of their own government of conduct. In the final writing on sexuality, Foucault offered 'technologies of the self', which can be adopted by individuals who become involved in the programme of 'subjectification' or who contest governmental practice through 'counter-conducts'.

Historians continue to find fault not only with his overall approach but with what John Braithwaite has referred to as his 'appalling' historical inaccuracies. **Edward Said**, whose own work has drawn heavily on Foucault's ideas, has criticized his Eurocentrism, which does not recognize 'the fact that history is not a homogenous French territory' while remaining silent on how 'discipline was also used to administer, study and reconstruct – then subsequently to occupy, rule and exploit – almost the whole of the non-European world'. Foucault's thinking has had an uneven impact on feminism. Some, like **Judith Butler** and **Dorothy Smith**, find his concepts useful for challenging distinctions between sex and gender. Others have emphasized how Foucault failed to explore the gendered character of discipline. **Jürgen Habermas** takes Foucault to task for preferring 'ascetic description' over normative analysis. Steven Lukes even complains that with the voluntarism of the later writings 'the ultra-radicalism of Foucault's view of power dissolves'. Clearly these are multifaceted criticisms, but it is unlikely that he will be dislodged from his place in the pantheon of modern thought by these objections.

See also: Louis Althusser, Roland Barthes, Judith Butler, Gilles Deleuze, Claude Lévi-Strauss, Edward Said.

See also in *Fifty Key Sociologists: The Formative Theorists*: Emile Durkheim, Karl Marx, Max Weber.

Major works

Madness and Civilization: A History of Insanity in the Age of Reason. 1961. London: Routledge, 2001.
The Birth of the Clinic: An Archaeology of Medical Perception. 1963. New York: Vintage Books, 1975.
The Order of Things: An Archaeology of the Human Sciences. 1966. New York: Vintage Books, 1994.
The Archaeology of Knowledge. 1969. London: Routledge, 2000.
Discipline and Punish: The Birth of the Prison. 1975. London: Penguin, 1991.
The History of Sexuality, Volume 1: An Introduction. 1976. London: Penguin, 1990.
Power/Knowledge: Selected Interviews and Other Writings 1972–1977. Ed. by Colin Gordon. New York: Pantheon Books, 1980.
Society Must Be Defended. 1975–6. Harmondsworth: Penguin, 2003.
'Governmentality'. 1978. In Graham Burchell, Colin Gordon and Peter Miller, eds. *The Foucault Effect: Studies in Governmentality.* London: Harvester Wheatsheaf, 1991.
'The Subject and Power'. 1982. In Hubert Dreyfus and Paul Rabinow, eds. *Michel Foucault: Beyond Structuralism and Hermeneutics.* Chicago: University of Chicago Press.
The Use of Pleasure: Volume 2 of the History of Sexuality. 1984. London: Penguin, 1992.
The Care of the Self: Volume 3 of the History of Sexuality. 1984. London: Penguin, 1990.
P. Rabinow, ed. 1984. *The Foucault Reader.* London: Penguin. A selection of important essays, including the crucial 'Nietzsche, Genealogy, History'.

Further reading

Gordon Burchell, Colin Gordon and Peter Miller, eds. 1991. *The Foucault Effect: Studies in Governmentality.* Hemel Hempstead: Harvester Wheatsheaf.
Hubert Dreyfus and Paul Rabinow. 1983. *Michel Foucault: Beyond Structuralism and Hermeneutics.* Chicago: University of Chicago Press.
Didier Eribon. 1992. *Michel Foucault.* London: Faber and Faber.
Barry Smart. 1985. *Michel Foucault.* London: Routledge. Revised edn 2002.

EAMONN CARRABINE

HAROLD GARFINKEL

Harold Garfinkel, born in 1917, studied under **Talcott Parsons** at Harvard and was awarded his PhD in 1952. He has worked at the University of California since 1954. In his PhD he sought to demonstrate that phenomenology, as applied to the human sciences by Alfred Schutz and Aron Gurwitsch, could offer a very different conception of sociology to that then being developed by Talcott Parsons, despite their common aim of building a systematic, consistent and rigorous approach to sociology on the basis of Max Weber's definition of sociology as the study of social action. Since 1954, Garfinkel has been developing and revising those initial ideas into an empirically researchable form. Garfinkel calls his programme 'ethnomethodology', which he describes as an 'alternate, incommensurable, and asymmetric sociology' to emphasize that it *is* a sociology, though one that is discontinuous with the larger enterprise of sociology as currently practised.

Ethnomethodology focuses on social order, but in a distinctive way. The prevailing concern with 'social order' is with the conditions for the establishment and perpetuation of stabilized regimes of social relationships: how are arrangements of social organization held together? The shift in sociology since the mid-twentieth century was from Parsonian doctrines of social solidarity through value consensus to the now widespread conviction that social organization is effected through power, very broadly construed. The traditional problem of order seemed to Garfinkel to presuppose a prior question: if its deepest roots are to be explored, then how are intelligibly ordered courses of action possible? That is, in any action situation, how can participants know what is going on and how to respond; how can they build up the serially connected doings that make up a course of action? This argument shifts the focus of attention to the relationship between current and next action: given someone now performing a current action, how are they to generate the next action? Generically, how is any *course of action* built up? The problem of social order is subsumed within this question for, of course, it is plain that the actions of others and the need to relate one's actions to those others are part of any action situation.

Setting things out this way could make it appear that Garfinkel's ethnomethodology conceives of social order as the order of face-to-face interaction (and thus does not recognize the large, encompassing arrangements of stabilized structures that comprise real societies and circumstance social interaction). Such a conclusion would be premature and misguided.

Garfinkel is no less sensitive to sociology's methodological problems than its theoretical ones, and empirical objectification has been another preoccupation: how are the (claimed) properties of social order to be evidenced and made available to sociological observers as reportable occurrences? For Garfinkel, social reality is an incessant flow of activities, of innumerable persons engaged in inter-involved doings, and all claims about the properties of society must, sooner or later, be cashed in by reference to observable features of witnessable courses of action in some documentable form. This is Garfinkel's take on the perennially troubled relationship within sociology between theory and research. The former normally dwells in the land of very large abstractions, and it is commonly acknowledged that it is generally difficult to tell what the abstractions of theory are talking about. This has never seemed to Garfinkel a tolerable or manageable situation, and he persistently asks how the phenomena identified in sociology's general schemes are to be identified in localizable instances in the society. Whereabouts are persons engaged in, for example, enforcing compliance with norms, or operating a discourse, and so on, and what exactly are they doing that counts as doing that?

Thus, a central precept of Garfinkel's 'studies of work' programme is to find, for any sociological problem, a place where someone has the practical task of dealing with that problem to see how they organize its practical and everyday solutions. Insofar as the abstractions of social theory can be anchored in witnessable doings and events in social life, the capacity of social theory to speak of them relies on their identity in the 'vernacular', identifying them in terms already in use in the society itself: 'suicide', 'dangerous driving', 'giving therapy' and so on. Thus, the question usually asked by sociologists – 'How can we, as observers, tell that they are doing this, that or the other?' – turns into the question of 'How do they tell?' How do they tell that this person died as a result of suicide, that this patient is making therapeutic progress and so on? Garfinkel commends a thorough substitution of this latter query for the former as his way of exploring how social activities are organized so that they can be talked about in the ways that they are ordinarily spoken of.

Garfinkel does not regard his questions as theoretical ones that need general answers, but as ones that call for studies. His are not problems for the sociologist to solve, but ones that already have solutions: people in the society already have ways of answering them, of finding out whether someone died as a result of suicide and so on. Those studies are ones that identify the ways, whatever these may be, in which members of the society make these determinations, which is just the same as examining the way courses of action are organized. Thus, those who investigate suicide have ways of establishing that someone's death was a result of suicide. Their job involves figuring out their own courses of action, of deciding which thing to do first and which next, of how to do whatever needs to be done first and so on, such that the things they decide to do fit together to make up an effective investigation determining for 'this case' whether the death was suicide. These investigations involve the investigator in reconstructing the actions leading up to the individual's death to determine whether these actions are organized so as to result in the individual taking his or her own life.

Action, for Garfinkel, is practical action, subject to all-practical-purposes and 'custom fitted' to its circumstances: it is organized as it is being done so as to achieve whatever needs to be done. His strategy is the obverse of that usually followed in studies of social action, which is to identify general features of action sequences that can be extricated from the particulars of the specific kind of action it is. Garfinkel insists that it is in the nature of action for it to be done in specific circumstances, addressed to and shaped by those circumstances – thus his emphasis is on just this status of what is done on each occasion. Equally, an insistence that even the most generic topics – order, reason, logic and so on – do not speak of genuinely equivalent occasions in which strictly identical things are done, but speak inclusively and indefinitely of diverse and heterogeneous occasions where the real content of these terms is defined in and for their respective occasions: what counts as reason in the courtroom is not the same as what counts as reason in the classroom or in the laboratory or on the factory shop floor or elsewhere. The studies tell us what, as matters of real engagement in activities-in-situations, professional theoretical abstractions bid to talk about, showing what it is, sociologically speaking, for someone to respect the order of the traffic, to construct an impeccably reasoned courtroom presentation, to produce securely computed company accounts and so on.

Garfinkel does not doubt that societies exhibit large-scale 'Durkheimian properties' of stability, continuity and extended cooperation, but he is concerned with how these properties are somehow actualized, are made to happen as massively standardized features of conduct. For Garfinkel, however, the 'somehow' is the very matter of inquiry: how do people organize their actions to produce a standardized course of conduct? The weight shifts to the organization of courses of action as, so to speak, a 'technical' concern for members of a society. How can any specific course of action be organized such that it can be done over and over again in standard ways? How can a course of action be organized so that it can be done by almost anyone and without preparation? Garfinkel's colleague Melinda Baccus studied the problem of achieving, through regulation, standardization in practices of tyre fitting on trucks. Unless a strict procedure is meticulously followed in refitting certain tyres these are apt to decompress explosively and lethally. How is one to get truck drivers, out on the road, to respect the strict procedure? How is one to represent that procedure to them in instructional form that they will be able to follow in practical circumstances, and to draw their attention to the imperative need to do this? Equally, with the reproducibility of scientific procedures, how do scientists convert the ways they did their original research into an intelligible methodological formula that any other competent scientist in their field can use to reproduce their results? The 'technical' interest is then in finding identities and interdependences that are constituent of an effective course of action: what combination of feet and hand positions, of eye direction and of attention can be identified as part of a teachable formula for safe control of an automobile on the public highways that can be taught to any driver, for example?

Ethnomethodology is no less concerned with the workings of Durkheim's 'immortal society' than any other sociology, but it is unresponsive to the requirements that demand and shape such schemes of theory and method. 'The problem of social order' is no longer conceived as resolved through theoretical debate amongst sociologists, but as being solved within society itself, in and through the unremittingly practical conduct of everyday affairs. Equally, problems of method are 'transferred' to the members of society themselves: the question 'How shall professional sociologists ensure the objectivity of their enquiries?' gives way to that of 'How do members of society practically provide objectified exhibits of the order of their affairs (make records, charts, diagrams, files and so on) that withstand potential challenge as adequate records of "what was done"?' An alternative conception, and incommensurable too, on occasion formulated by Garfinkel as a contrast between the views that there is no order in the concrete and ethnomethodology's commitment to investigating order in the concrete. This effects a differentiation between

- a conviction that the orderliness of social structures becomes evident only by processing the ordinarily observable phenomena of daily life through a professionally contrived theoretical and methodological matrix to extricate generic properties from their localized, exigent circumstances; and

- the opposing idea that such operations strip those phenomena of indispensable organizational essentials.

Any sociological problem is amenable to reformulation as a study in ethnomethodology, as a matter of inquiring where in society that problem is someone's practical task. However, the reverse operation is not possible: the very things that ethnomethodology pays intense attention to 'get in the way' of sound professional inquiry.

See also: Erving Goffman, Talcott Parsons.

See also in *Fifty Key Sociologists: The Formative Theorists*: Alfred Schutz.

Major works

The Perception of the Other: A Study in Social Order. 1952. PhD. thesis. Cambridge, MA: Harvard University.
Studies in Ethnomethodology. 1967. Englewood Cliffs, NJ: Prentice Hall.
'The Work of a Discovering Science Construed with Materials from the Optically Discovered Pulsar'. 1981. With Michael Lynch and Eric Livingston. *Philosophy of the Social Sciences* 11.
Ethnomethodological Studies of Work. 1986. Ed. London: Routledge & Kegan Paul.
'The Curious Seriousness of Professional Sociology'. 1990. In Bernard Conein, M. de Fornel and L. Quéré, eds. *Les Formes de la conversation*. vol. 1. Paris: CNET.
'Respecification'. 1991. In Graham Button, ed. *Ethnomethodology and the Human Sciences*. Cambridge: Cambridge University Press.
'Two Incommensurable, Asymmetrically Alternate Technologies of Social Analysis'. 1992. With D. Lawrence Wieder. In Graham Watson and R.M. Seiler, eds. *Text in Context: Studies in Ethnomethodology*. Beverly Hills, CA: Sage.
'An Overview of Ethnomethodology's Program'. 1996. *Social Psychology Quarterly* 59.
Ethnomethodology's Program: Working through Durkheim's Aphorism. 2002. Oxford: Rowman and Littlefield.

Further reading

Wes Sharrock and Bob Anderson. 1985. *The Ethnomethodologists*. Chichester: Ellis Horwood.
Michael Lynch and Wes Sharrock, eds. 2003. *Harold Garfinkel* 4 vols. London: Sage.

WES SHARROCK

CLIFFORD GEERTZ

Clifford Geertz was born in 1926. After war service in the United States Navy he attended Antioch College, Ohio, under the provisions of the GI Bill. One of his teachers, George Geiger, was a former student of John Dewey, and it was through him that Geertz encountered not only the New England pragmatist tradition but also the new philosophy of language then emerging at Oxford in the work of Gilbert Ryle and John Austin. Geertz was, in addition, introduced to the literary criticism of figures such as Kenneth Burke in the United States and William Empson and F. R. Leavis in Britain.

In 1950, Geertz met Geiger's friend Clyde Kluckhohn, one of the leading anthropologists of his generation and a member of the Harvard Department of Social Relations, led by **Talcott Parsons**. A further meeting with Margaret Mead convinced Geertz that his future lay in anthropology, and in particular in field research. After two years of study he set out, with his wife Hildred, for the newly independent republic of Indonesia. Their stay in the town of Pare resulted in no less than four books: *The Religion of Java*, *Agricultural Involution*, *Peddlers and Princes* and *The Social History of an Indonesian Town*.

On their return, Geertz worked for several years at the University of Chicago. The University was then engaged in a major project analysing current conditions in the so-called 'emerging' states of the post-war, postcolonial Third World, with a view to assisting them to a modern, democratic way of life, albeit under the auspices of the United States. Geertz found this uncongenial and was anxious to return to fieldwork, and after three years, in 1963, he and Hildred settled in Sefrou, twenty miles south of Fez, in Morocco. An Arab town, colonized by the French and with a strong Jewish community, its mix of cultures offered intriguing possibilities for detailed study and cross-cultural comparisons. As with his time in the Far East, Geertz's years in Morocco proved equally productive. On his return, he became a professor in Harvard's School of Social Science, guiding new generations of social anthropologists and students of culture.

When Geertz entered anthropology, a number of traditions conjoined to form the basis of his working method. The first of these was the classical anthropology of Alfred Radcliffe-Brown and Sir Edward Evans-Pritchard. Their concerns were with the functional aspects of such systems and practices as kinship, ceremonies (for example rites of passage), taboos such as incest, and beliefs. The work of Parsons was a second, contrasting influence that emphasized an overarching, quasi-scientific theory of society that focused on the conditions for social order. Such a positivistic approach is markedly unfashionable today, but in the optimistic years after the Second World War it seemed a plausible way both to maintain the status quo in the advanced western democracies and to bring the newly independent former colonial nations into line behind the United States. Kluckhohn's work was more forward-looking, especially in terms of his theory that concepts and judgements are notoriously difficult to translate from one language to another, and hence from one culture to another. This, in turn, connected with Wittgenstein's concept of language as a means of communication, for which there must be agreement not only as to definitions, but also as to judgements.

The final figure to influence the young Geertz was Kenneth Burke. Two concepts are central here. First, Burke was concerned with the rhetorical function of language: language as doing rather than describing. At much the same time, Austin was making a similar distinction between locutionary or propositional language, perlocutionary or performative language, and illocutionary or effective language. The last two of these corresponded roughly to Burke's notion of rhetoric. The interaction of human beings, whether through language or otherwise, was seen by Burke as the social drama, the second idea that Geertz took from Burke. The latter coined the term 'dramatism' to describe how language seeks to induce cooperation within social action. Geertz 's anthropology set out to apply the idea of describing what happens within each 'dramatic' interaction in terms of what it means for the participants in that particular time and place.

Geertz explored this composite, inter-disciplinary method in the four books that emerged from his first spell of fieldwork in Java. *The Social History of an Indonesian Town* describes the way in which Pare had developed against the background of Dutch occupation, Japanese invasion, the short-lived return of the Dutch in 1945 and the upheaval of independence, when four different factions vied for power. It is really an analysis of how communities develop despite, rather than because of, the changes and decisions that take place at a higher, more remote level. The book sets out the background against which the other studies are played out, as well as describing the principal actors. *Agricultural Involution* offers a geographical perspective, grounded on the historiography already provided. In many ways, it is a pioneering work of ecology, warning that political science is no substitute for imperial indifference.

Peddlers and Princes is a class analysis, on Weberian lines, in which Geertz examined the view that the various Muslim factions in

Indonesia might act as catalysts for economic progress, much as the Protestants of sixteenth-century Europe once had. The very fact that the Muslims were divided into progressive and traditionalist factions seemed to anticipate and endorse Geertz's equivocal conclusion. Finally, *The Religion of Java* (Geertz's request for a plural title was rejected by his publisher) attempts to describe the diversity of Islamic and pagan beliefs, and how they inform the actions of those involved.

Perhaps the most famous product of the Geertzs' time in Indonesia is his essay 'Deep Play: Notes on the Balinese Cockfight', included in the volume *The Interpretation of Cultures*. The idea that a sporting event (and a blood-thirsty, illegal one at that) could tell anyone something about a culture and its meanings was (and indeed still is) startling and even controversial. The cockfight is described in vivid terms, and is a superb piece of writing in itself. Geertz's cultural interpretation is that cockfighting reveals something of an alternative, underground culture. Fights present wild, abandoned emotions far removed from the polite, ordered life of the Balinese people in most other surroundings. The vulgarity of the event is, of course, conveyed in the *double entendre* of the word 'cock', such events being a male preserve. The individuals present take on the epic trappings of dramatic personages, those who bet and lose big-time being equated with tragic figures such as Lear or Raskolnikov. Of course, such comparisons should not blind us to the disquieting nature of the event itself. Geertz neither condones nor condemns what is taking place: he places the facts and his interpretation before the reader.

The various aspects of life in Sefrou were divided between Geertz and his team. His own work centred on the market (*suq*) and its complex subdivisions. The sheer exuberant hubbub is described as a kind of mosaic, which he documents, especially with regard to its linguistic practices (for example techniques of bargaining) in amazing detail that goes far beyond the daily round observed by the mere tourist. The rigid hierarchies of shopkeepers by product, seniority, honesty, even devoutness, help Moroccan society to maintain some sort of order or structure in the face of its own diversity.

Having studied two Muslim communities (Java and Morocco), Geertz next produced a study of their forms of religious experience in *Islam Observed*. In order to understand the diversity of Islam, he invoked four key figures in their respective cultures' histories, beginning with Sunan Kalidjaga, an Indonesian convert to Islam noted for his contemplativeness. He was contrasted with the

Moroccan itinerant preacher Sidi Lahsen Lyusi, the scourge of the seventeenth-century Sultans. His explosive character and independent spirit are anything but still and contemplative. These narratives led to Geertz's formulation of the 'theatre-state', in which rulers strive to combine private devotion with public show. Again, Geertz used two figures to exemplify this. Sukarno, the first president of an independent Indonesia, fused his own brand of socialism with elements of Islamic belief to produce an artificial conglomeration of ideas with which to inspire his new nation. The 'theatre-state' took the form of the world's largest mosque, a huge stadium in which to host the ASEAN Olympics, and a 'crusading' army. In contrast, Muhammed V of Morocco used his image as a strong military leader as well as a devout follower of the Prophet to gain independence for his country in 1955. This notion of the theatre-state is examined further in *Negara*, a study of the Balinese court in the nineteenth century.

Geertz's view of a social science is that it is both observational and interpretative. Researchers living within a community record what they observe and try to interpret what they have seen. These interpretations and the conclusions drawn from them are, of course, provisional. We must at all times seek to keep our personal subjectivity at arm's length, whilst (at the other extreme) not being afraid to draw large, general conclusions from our observations, if they can be warranted. The great exemplar in this respect is Charles Darwin, whose minute observations of the species that he encountered enabled him to deduce a 'big' theory. Interpretations (and hence theories) tend to be relative, rather than absolute. The old certainties of anthropologists like Radcliffe-Brown and Evans-Pritchard are those of an earlier age, but Geertz avoids the trap of so much postmodern thought which veers instead towards an extreme relativism, limiting any enquiry to minute observations of one's own culture. Geertz teaches us that we must not be afraid to examine (and criticize where appropriate) other cultures, providing our conclusions are based on detailed, in-depth observation. This same data can also provide us with the basis to construct general theories that connect the local with the global. Lastly, he shows us that culture (as everyday life) is just as significant as (on the one hand) social structures, systems and institutions, or (on the other) each person's character and psychology, in defining the relationship between the individual and the species as a whole.

See also in *Fifty Key Sociologists: The Formative Theorists*: Max Weber.

Major works

The Religion of Java. 1960. Glencoe, IL: The Free Press.
Pedlars and Princes. 1963. Chicago: University of Chicago Press.
Agricultural Innovation. 1964. Berkeley, CA: University of California Press.
Islam Observed. 1968. Chicago: University of Chicago Press.
The Interpretation of Cultures. 1973. New York: Basic Books.
Negara: The Theater State in Nineteenth Century Bali. 1980. Princeton, NJ: Princeton University Press.
Local Knowledge. 1983. New York: Basic Books.
Works and Lives: The Anthropologist as Author. 1988. Stanford, CA: Stanford University Press.

Further reading

Fred Inglis. 2000. *Clifford Geertz: Culture, Custom, and Ethics*. Cambridge: Polity Press.

PAUL TERRY

ERNEST GELLNER

Ernest Gellner, born in 1925, was brought up in Prague until 1939. In that year his family, being Jewish, decided to move to England, where, a few years later, Gellner won a place at Balliol College, Oxford. He served in the Czech army towards the end of the Second World War and then returned to finish his education at Oxford, where he obtained a first in philosophy, politics and economics. Following a brief period in Edinburgh, he obtained an appointment in 1949 to teach moral and social philosophy in the sociology department at the London School of Economics (LSE). Gellner remained at the LSE for thirty-five years, becoming professor of philosophy, logic and scientific method in 1962. His time at the LSE was followed by a nine-year stint as professor of social anthropology at Cambridge. Following his retirement from Cambridge in 1993, he became head of the Centre for the Study of Nationalism in the Central European University at Prague. He died in 1995.

Gellner made his name in three overlapping disciplines: sociology, social anthropology and philosophy. In all three areas, he was critical of contemporary orthodoxies, and especially of those rooted in relativism and idealism. His criticisms were both witty and effective and, despite his institutional eminence (Oxford, Cambridge, LSE), he remained something of an outsider in all three disciplines. During a talk in 1992, Gellner described himself as one of the 'Enlightenment Puritans', an intellectual who accepted the uneasy relationship between faith, indifference and seriousness. He drew inspiration from Hume, Kant, Weber, Durkheim and Karl Popper. In practice this meant that he attacked proponents of closed systems in all fields – his targets included linguistic philosophy, psychoanalysis, Islam, socialism and neo-liberalism. A colleague once declared that he was not sure whether the next revolution would be from the Left or the Right but, whichever it was, Gellner was sure to be the first person to be shot.

Gellner first made his name through his assault on the linguistic idealism of Oxford philosophers in the 1950s in *Words and Things*. By the time this book appeared, he had already turned his attention to social anthropology and had carried out fieldwork in tribal Morocco. In *Saints of the Atlas*, he showed how Berber holy men kept peace amongst the nomadic shepherds who moved their flocks through the passes of the Atlas Mountains. Throughout his career, Gellner maintained an interest in Morocco and Islam. This led him into fierce controversy with **Edward Said** over the significance of imperialism, and Gellner was organizing a conference on Orientalism at the time of his death.

His ideas poured out in a steady stream of books, articles and reviews. Three books, taken together, provide an overview of the backbone of his thought: *Thought and Change*, *Plough, Sword and Book* and *Nations and Nationalism*. In *Thought and Change*, the earliest of the three, Gellner dismissed the idea that social change is an all-embracing process that moves from an undesirable to a desirable state through a series of predictable transitions. There are, indeed, specific historical transitions, such as that from agrarian to industrial society, but they are not explained by their location within a developmental series of several stages. Marxism is a methodologically sound theory insofar as it provides explanations for specific mechanisms of transition, but this is in spite of, not because of, its evolutionist façade of determinate phases.

Gellner saw no need for a resort to schemes encompassing the whole of history. He favoured neo-episodic theories that focus on explaining specific kinds of transition. He saw history as a succession of plateaux that are interrupted by steep cliffs, dramatic transformations such as the Neolithic or Industrial Revolutions. To explain human societies we need two kinds of sociology. One kind is mainly concerned with the way societies that exist on the plateaux maintain themselves in relative stability. This kind of sociology will have a functionalist bias. The other kind of sociology focuses upon how societies confront and deal with the steep cliffs when they are encountered. This second kind of sociology, concerned with profound transformations, must accept that specific explanations of particular kinds of transition (for example industrialization) cannot be generalized into explanations of all kinds of societal transition – the mistake made by Marx and his followers.

Gellner dismissed entelechy, the idea that social progress unfolds in a predetermined way, like an oak from an acorn. In *Plough, Sword and Book*, however, he accepted that, empirically, humankind has indeed passed through a number of stages in a specific order. These stages are: (1) hunting and gathering society; (2) agrarian society; and (3) industrial society. In other words, human history exhibits a structure. Transition directly from (1) to (3) is not conceivable, and regressions from (3) to (2) or from (2) to (1) are rare. His key point is that the switch from agrarian to industrial society entails such an enormous transformation that the likelihood of it occurring spontaneously within a society is very low. Once it has happened in one society, through a near miracle, imitation elsewhere becomes possible and the way back for human kind is effectively blocked.

Explaining this key transition from agrarian to industrial society entails distinguishing between production (the power of technology and the plough), coercion (the power of the sword), and cognition (the power of ideas and the book). None of these has theoretical priority, but Gellner focused on cognition. In simple hunter-gatherer societies, the low division of labour was expressed in multi-stranded cognitive and linguistic styles. Using language meant enacting several roles simultaneously, both affirming one's place in the natural, social and cosmic order and responding in a pragmatically effective way to the challenge of physical survival.

The increase in the level of material surplus that occurred with the transition to agrarian production allowed the appearance of a coercive ruling class and a class of ritual specialists able to codify culture and cognition. The centralization of state power and the codification of culture separated a small and dominant minority from the village peasant communities with their specific local dialects and inward-looking cultures. The literacy and scripturalism of the elite enabled meaning to be given authority through sacred texts rather than communal ritual. Printing allowed the text to become almost universally available, helping priests to codify doctrine and proscribe heresy. These 'Platonic' religious systems provided a pattern for the development of universalistic frameworks of knowledge in government, the professions and trade also.

The leap from agrarian to industrial societies was a complex event, aided by and, in its turn, fostering the spirit of instrumental rationality. The influence of Protestantism, a concept Gellner generalizes beyond any specific religious group, strengthened the impulse to investigate the created world in a systematic way. The systematizing impulse was directed towards nature and, eventually, detached from religious belief. Meanwhile, through the extension of literacy, the majority gained access to a codified high culture.

Gellner's analysis in *Nations and Nationalism* is built within this framework. Nationalism is to be understood in terms of the radical structural and cultural transformations associated with the development of industrial societies. Within such societies, social rank is assigned on the basis of occupational positions that are allocated on the basis of educational credentials. The sense of belonging increasingly derives not from membership of a particular village, lineage or corporate group, but from being part of a shared literate culture broadly co-extensive with the boundaries of the nation-state. Nationalism is rooted in the complex, ever-changing division of labour within an industrial society, which is serviced by a large and expensive education system providing standardized generic training. This ensures that all citizens share the same basic skills and understandings. It represents the victory of high culture over rival low cultures.

Nationalism engenders nations, not *vice versa*, according to Gellner. Successful nationalist movements select and transform a pre-existing culture, working to ensure that this culture is fused with a single polity. People who, in the early phases of industrialization, find they are excluded and deprived may seize on whatever linguistic, genetic or cultural symbols they can as a way of marking themselves out as a people whose demands must be met. Sometimes a localized low culture may be used and sometimes a high culture: Arab nationalism draws on Islam, while some African nationalist movements have adapted European high culture to their own purposes.

These processes perhaps stood out more clearly in the mind of a man such as Gellner who was familiar with many cultures and who declared that he had no faith and belonged to no community. All three of his key books illustrate Gellner's capacity for building simple models of social systems and social processes and explaining them with clarity and wit. He used these skills to identify patterns and sequences on a vast historical scale, quite consciously placing himself in an Enlightenment tradition that includes both David Hume and Max Weber.

See also in *Fifty Key Sociologists: The Formative Theorists*: Emile Durkheim, Max Weber.

Major works

A full bibliography can be found at http://members.tripod.com/Gellner-Page/Biblio.html.

Thought and Change. 1964. London: Weidenfeld and Nicolson.
Saints of the Atlas. 1969. London: Weidenfeld and Nicolson.
Cause and Meaning in the Social Sciences. Essays of various dates. London: Routledge & Kegan Paul, 1973.
Legitimation of Belief. 1975. Cambridge: Cambridge University Press.
Spectacles and Predicaments; Essays in Social Theory. Various dates. Cambridge: Cambridge University Press, 1980.
Muslim Society. 1981. Cambridge: Cambridge University Press.
Nations and Nationalism. 1983. Oxford: Blackwell.
Relativism and the Social Sciences. Essays of various dates. Cambridge: Cambridge University Press, 1985.
The Psychoanalytic Movement. 1985. London: Paladin.
Culture, Identity and Politics. Essays of various dates. Cambridge: Cambridge University Press, 1987.
Plough, Sword and Book. The Structure of Human History. 1988. Chicago: University of Chicago Press.
Reason and Culture, the Historic Role of Rationality and Rationalism. 1992. Oxford: Blackwell.
Encounters with Nationalism. 1994. Oxford: Blackwell.
Language and Solitude. Wittgenstein, Malinowski and the Hapsburg Dilemma. 1998. Cambridge: Cambridge University Press.

Further reading

John A. Hall. 1998. *The State of the Nation: Ernest Gellner and the Theory of Nationalism*. Cambridge: Cambridge University Press.
Michael Lessnoff, ed. 2002. *Ernest Gellner and Modernity*. Cardiff: University of Wales Press.

DENNIS SMITH

ANTHONY GIDDENS

Giddens is perhaps Britain's leading sociologist, renowned especially for his theories of structuration and late modernity and his championing of 'Third Way' politics. Born in London in 1938, he attended the

University of Hull and graduated in 1959 in sociology and psychology. He studied for a master's degree in sociology at the London School of Economics (LSE), and in 1961 became a lecturer in the Department of Sociology at Leicester University. He held positions at Simon Fraser University and the University of California at Los Angeles before moving to King's College, Cambridge. He formed Polity Press in 1985 and became director of the LSE in 1997. His growing status as the most visible intellectual proponent of 'Third Way' politics drew him into the inner circle of British prime minister Tony Blair, and in 2004 he was given a life peerage as Lord Giddens of Southgate.

Giddens' intellectual career is best understood in terms of four overlapping periods, each marked by a distinctive set of theoretical concerns. His early work, 1970–5, focused on the exposition of the classical tradition of European sociology and Giddens was influential in establishing the canonical trilogy of Marx, Weber and Durkheim as the basis of social theory. Subsequently, until 1989, he focused on the possibility of transcending a series of perceived dualisms within social theory, most significantly that between agency and structure. The resulting theory of structuration led to an attempted rewriting and re-periodizing of human history. The third phase of his career, 1990–3, developed these theoretical and temporal insights into a more substantive analysis of the contours of modernity and the contemporary stage of what he referred to as 'late modernity'. This prepared the way for the most recent phase in his work, in which he moved from sociology to more directly political-theoretical concerns. Giddens' presentation of the 'Third Way' can be seen as an application of his earlier theoretical work on 'dualisms': an attempt to transcend the dichotomy between left- and right-wing political ideologies.

His first major book, *Capitalism and Modern Social Theory*, not only set out a comprehensive exposition of the sociological ideas of Marx, Weber and Durkheim, but also re-examined significant areas of convergence and divergence. Rather than converging around an implicit, if abstract, Hobbesian 'problem of order', these three were instead concerned with the substantive historical-sociological problem of the profound rupture separating capitalism from prior feudal or traditional social formations. Their politics sought to synthesize liberalism and revolutionary or radical forms of thought in different ways. Giddens developed some of these ideas in *The Class Structure of Advanced Societies*, synthesizing Weberian and Marxist views of class.

His most significant contribution to social theory, the theory of structuration, was an attempt to overcome the division between sociological approaches that emphasize agency and those that emphasize structural constraints. The former focus on self-conscious agents – their intentionality, knowledgeability and ability to construct, create or make the social world they find themselves in. Advocates have included phenomenology, ethnomethodology, symbolic interactionism and rational choice theory. Structural theories, on the other hand, place more emphasis on the social determination of the self and the invisible forces and emergent dynamics that shape the actions, perceptions and 'second nature' of individuals. These have included functionalism, structuralism and the many varieties of Marxism. The agency/structure dualism that informs these two traditions runs through a series of related perspectival and methodological tensions that plague the discipline: individual versus society, micro versus macro and subjective versus objective.

In his theory of structuration, Giddens argues that the agency/ structure dualism can be overcome only by synthesizing insights from a variety of otherwise flawed perspectives. This involves a reformulation of the lexicon of sociological concepts. For Giddens, prior theoretical applications of the term 'structure' – most significantly those found in functionalism and Marxism – tended to define structure as causally efficacious patterned social relationships that are not only external to human agency but also constraining upon it. He discerns a very different understanding of 'structure' in Lévi-Strauss's structuralism. Structure here refers to abstract models in the form of binary oppositions and dual relations, existing in and through human beings and that do not exist in time and space but as relations of presence and absence. Utilizing this latter approach, Giddens offers his own novel definition of structure. Structures, like languages, are 'virtual' since they exist 'outside time and space', are 'subject-less' and are, for the most part, unintentionally reproduced in practices. By identifying structure with language, he hoped to effect a dynamic juxtaposition between the speech or action implemented by an agent and the structure that forms the condition of possibility for generating this speech and action. This had two effects. First, there is what Giddens refers to as a 'duality of structure': structure is no longer understood as simply constraining but also as enabling. Structure not only limits action through rules of 'syntax'; it also makes possible the generation of action. Second, structure is both the medium and the outcome of action. Hence, the 'instantiation' of structure in individual action recursively draws upon and reproduces structure in a manner akin to a speech act drawing upon and reproducing the totality of language. Every act of social production is therefore simultaneously an act of reproduction.

For Giddens, structure and agency form two sides of the same coin and are connected through social practices. They are inseparable dimensions of the flow of activities in which individuals participate during the course of their day-to-day lives. Specifically, he sees structures as comprised of rules and resources. Rules may be explicit or tacit, intensive or shallow, formal or informal, strongly or weakly sanctioned, but should generally be understood, in Wittgenstein's sense, as practical forms of knowledge that 'allow us to go on' in novel circumstances. Resources are 'authoritative' capabilities that generate command over persons or 'allocative' capabilities that generate command over objects or other material phenomena.

In addition to rethinking the concept of structure, Giddens also reconceptualizes the concept of agency. In his stratification model of action, he draws upon and modifies the Freudian schema of agency to argue that an actor's consciousness has three aspects: discursive consciousness, practical consciousness and unconsciousness. Loosely corresponding to this threefold division of the consciousness, he refers to reflexive monitoring, rationalization and the deep motivations for action. Practical consciousness and its rationalization as the tacit or 'mutual' knowledge that provides agents with the ability to 'go on' in relation to rule-bound social life are most significant for understanding social life.

Although free to choose, agents follow routines in order to avoid ontological insecurity and any disruption of the basic security system internalized during childhood. Drawing on Merton's classic essay on the unintended effects of purposive action, however, Giddens argues that an individual's intentional acts often produce unintended consequences. These unintended consequences then become the future unacknowledged conditions that structure the subsequent action of the agent (see Figure 1).

A second aspect of Giddens' structuration theory relates agency to power, arguing that an agent ceases to be such if she or he loses the

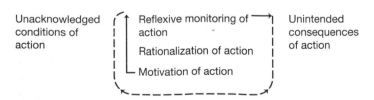

Figure 1: Giddens' model.
Source: Central Problems in Social Theory

ability to 'act otherwise'. However, given that there exists a 'dialectic of control' built into the very nature of agency and involving the interplay of autonomy and dependence, a total loss of agency is rare.

In parallel with the development of the theory of structuration, Giddens produced his own historical sociology as a 'positive critique' of Marx's historical materialism, which he considered as economically reductionist and methodologically suspect. In *A Contemporary Critique of Historical Materialism*, he elaborates a non-functionalist, non-evolutionary, non-teleological, multidimensional and historically contingent view of social change. His historical schema incorporates a tripartite societal typology that distinguishes tribal, class-divided societies from class societies. These societies are defined according to their level of social and system integration and time–space distanciation. In *Nation-state and Violence* he developed and modified this framework, exploring the complex symbiotic co-development of capitalism, industrialism and the nation-state. For Giddens these three spheres provide the basis for the four irreducible, though connected, 'institutional clusterings' that characterize modern society: capitalistic enterprise, industrial production, heightened surveillance and centralized control of the means of violence. This characterization of modernity is developed further in the third phase of his work. In *The Consequences of Modernity*, Giddens argues that the critical feature of the dynamic social formation that began to develop in Europe from about the seventeenth century was its sharp, qualitative discontinuity from the previous, traditional social order. This break involved a profound transformation that is both global and personal.

Underlying modernity are three sources of dynamism: distanciation, disembedding and reflexivity. The 'separation and recombination of time and space' facilitate and promote an increased 'zoning' of social life. Everyday encounters and interactions become less tied to fixed locales and less dependent on the co-presence of the individuals involved. This, in turn, facilitates the development of modern rationalized organizations and permits the emergence of a radical historicity in which the past can be appropriated with the aim of shaping the future. More importantly, it facilitates the 'disembedding' of social systems. Disembedding refers to the 'lifting out' of social relations from their local contexts of interaction, which permits their restructuring across larger spans of time–space. Modernity is inherently globalizing, so that time–space distanciation links the local with the global through disembedding, although there may also be processes of 're-embedding' in which disembedded social relations are again pinned down. The two major types of disembedding mechanism are 'symbolic tokens' and 'expert systems'. Symbolic tokens are media such as money that can be exchanged, regardless of who uses them, while expert systems are systems of technical accomplishment and professional expertise such as those of doctors, lawyers, architects and scientists.

Fundamental to both mechanisms, as well as to the reflexivity of modernity more generally, is the concept of trust. A sense of trust in processes, people and things is a crucial factor in maintaining a sense of ontological security in the modern world, since its absence results in existential angst or dread. By contrast with pre-modern societies, where trust and risk were anchored in the local circumstances of place, rooted in nature and characterized by hazards from the physical world or violence in social life, modernity offers a new 'risk profile' characterized by 'manufactured risk'. Here the pervasiveness of socially organized knowledge in the form of abstract systems means that risk becomes the defining parameter of modern culture and life, even replacing the preoccupation with wealth. As Giddens notes, '[t]he possibility of nuclear war, ecological calamity, uncontainable population explosion, the collapse of global economic exchange, and other potential global catastrophes provide an unnerving horizon of dangers for everyone'. Giddens' analysis of modernity leads to the conclusion that in place of the two classic sociological accounts of the experience of modernity – Marx's theory of alienation and Weber's 'iron cage' of bureaucracy – the discipline would be better served by his own image of modernity as a careering juggernaut.

Although in his structuration theory reflexivity is a fundamental feature of social action, it takes on a special meaning in Giddens' theory of modernity. Under emerging conditions of 'wholesale reflexivity' everything (including both individuals and institutions) becomes open to reflection and self-monitoring, including reflexivity itself. Social practices are continually examined and re-examined in the light of incoming information and processes of self-evaluation.

This leads Giddens to consider the transformation of the intimate and personal features of day-to-day existence in modernity. Increasingly, the pressures of work and domestic life push individuals towards the continual reconstruction of self-identities as part of a reflexive project. In this increasingly unavoidable autobiographical project, individual choices are made in the context of an array of trajectories and options engendered by abstract systems. Modernity involves both a transformation of lifestyle and a 'transformation of intimacy' in which personal and erotic ties are formed as 'pure relationships'. According to Giddens, 'pure relationships' involve 'commitment' and demands for intimacy, such that trust develops through mutual disclosure alone, rather than (as in more traditional societies) through criteria – such as kinship ties, social duty or traditional obligations – that exist outside the relationship itself.

Building on this theory of modernity, Giddens set out a general political programme. In *Beyond Left and Right* and *The Third Way* he considered how radical politics might be rethought, both theoretically and in practice, in the context of a changing modern world. What he refers to as 'Third Way' politics involves a re-evaluation of socialism, social democracy and conservatism in the light of the altered social conditions of modernity that ultimately renders them inoperable. He argues that the collapse of communism has made the distinction between the political 'Left' and 'Right' superfluous. Consequently, the idea of a fixed left/right binary for Giddens needs to be supplanted by the notion of a radical centre or 'active middle' embodying a 'utopian realist' position.

The fostering of an active civil society became a central focus for Third Way politics. This involves the state and civil society acting in partnership with one another to provide material and social support for local groups to engage in 'generative politics' oriented towards empowerment. Echoing **Beck**'s discussion of the importance of 'sub-politics' in an era of risk society, Giddens also argues that increasing individualization and reflexivity have led to new forms of democratization or 'dialogic democracy'. In some ways following **Habermas**' theory of communicative action, this 'democratization of democracy' presupposes un-coerced discussion as a basis for agreement. Rather than referring to the extension of social and civil rights, dialogic democracy points towards a 'deliberative democracy' where forms of social interchange, social solidarity and cultural cosmopolitanism can be established. Widening democracy also requires a decentralization of the state, or what he calls 'double democratization', and a move away from the paternalism of the welfare state.

A further consequence of 'reflexive individualization' has been the re-evaluation of traditional left-wing understandings of emancipation as pertaining to 'life chances' and freedom. Such emancipatory politics must now be supplemented with a 'life politics' that breaks out of the restrictive cast of class politics. Concerning rich and poor groups alike, this life politics addresses universal issues, less driven by the polarities of social class, that is, issues pertaining to lifestyle, leisure, consumption and identity. Giddens also argues for a 'new mixed economy' that would correspond to the realities of 'post-scarcity society' and in which a production orientation is replaced by ideals of self-actualization.

Giddens has often provided unique insights into the nature of the social world. He has been criticized, however, for his eclecticism, inconsistency and lack of empirical utility. More specifically, he has been criticized for placing an excessive emphasis on individual agency, and it has been argued that **Norbert Elias** and **Pierre Bourdieu** provide more fruitful approaches for transcending sociological dualisms. It has also been noted that his politics evidences a strong idealism, most evident in the sweeping prescriptions of the putative 'Third Way', which leads him to ignore the entrenched and unequal distribution of power and capital and the persistence of ethno-national conflict at both the national and global level.

See also: Zygmunt Bauman, Ülrich Beck, Harold Garfinkel, Jürgen Habermas.

See also in *Fifty Key Sociologists: The Formative Theorists*: Emile Durkheim, Karl Marx, Max Weber.

Major works

Capitalism and Modern Social Theory. 1971. Cambridge: Cambridge University Press.
The Class Structure of the Advanced Societies. 1973. London: Hutchinson.
Studies in Social and Political Theory. Essays 1966–76. London: Hutchinson, 1977.
The New Rules of Sociological Method. 1976. London: Macmillan.
A Contemporary Critique of Historical Materialism. 1981. London: Macmillan.
Profiles and Critiques in Social Theory. Essays 1975–82. London: Macmillan, 1982.
The Constitution of Society. 1984. Cambridge: Polity Press.
Social Theory and Modern Sociology. Essays 1982–6. Cambridge: Polity Press.
The Nation-State and Violence. 1985. Cambridge: Polity Press.
The Consequences of Modernity. 1990. Cambridge: Polity Press.
Modernity and Self-Identity. 1991. Cambridge: Polity Press.
The Transformation of Intimacy. 1992. Cambridge: Polity Press.
Beyond Left and Right. 1994. Cambridge: Polity Press.
The Third Way: The Renewal of Social Democracy. 1998. Cambridge: Polity Press.

Further reading

Chris Bryant and David Jary. 1991. *Giddens' Theory of Structuration*. London: Routledge.
L. B. Kasperson. 2000. *Anthony Giddens: An Introduction to a Social Theorist*. Oxford: Blackwell.

David Held and John Thompson, eds. 1989. *Social Theory of Modern Societies: Anthony Giddens and His Critics*. Cambridge: Cambridge University Press.
Steven Loyal. 2003. *The Sociology of Anthony Giddens*. London: Pluto.

STEVEN LOYAL

PAUL GILROY

Paul Gilroy's writing highlights the ways in which our attempts to understand the social world are damaged by the legacy of slavery, empire and racism. One of his enduring warnings is that sociology and social science should not be racism's accomplice. For him the sociological imagination must avoid being annexed to the project of classifying, scrutinizing and controlling those who come under racism's heel. Contained within his writings is an alternative set of protocols and conceptual tools to bring to bear on the understanding of the mutual implication of racism and modernity.

Gilroy was born in London in 1956 and studied for his PhD at the Centre for Contemporary Cultural Studies (CCCS), University of Birmingham. He has taught at the University of Essex and Yale University, and is currently professor of sociology at the London School of Economics. His work moves between sociology, literary criticism, critical historiography, cultural studies and musicology. One of the uniting themes of all his books is the importance of understanding how cultures and traditions are made through and across national borders. Yet it is precisely through the figure of the 'immigrant' that racism holds us hostage and where the presence of so-called immigrants is used in public debates to explain the nation's ills and its lack of cohesion and ultimately a loss of identity. He has intervened in contemporary sociology in four major areas: the sociology of law and order and black pathology; the relationship between modernity, empire and nationalism; movement and culture; and rejecting the absolutism of racial and cultural difference.

Birmingham – Britain's second largest city – is both a heartland of British racism and an important centre for black cultural politics and anti-racist struggle. It was at the CCCS that he began his investigations into law and order and black pathology. Gilroy formed the race and politics group along with fellow graduate students including Hazel Carby, John Solomos, Valerie Amos, Errol Lawrence and Simon Jones. In 1982 the group published *The Empire Strikes Back*, a book which provided an analysis of racism in 1970s Britain but also a political and epistemological challenge to the sociology of race and ethnic relations. Many of its contributors were young intellectuals who had been born in Britain of colonial citizen migrants. One of its key arguments was that sociology, rather than providing a solution, had become part of the problem of racism. In particular, academic accounts produced pathological images of black family life and culture and these communities were cast as experiencing social problems that were essentially of their own making. This line of critique was further developed in 1987 in Gilroy's first single-authored book – based on his doctoral thesis – *Ain't No Black in the Union Jack*. Here Gilroy argued that black communities are regulated through being constructed as either 'victims' or 'problems' and this couplet worked alongside more coercive forms of policing and criminalization.

Gilroy has also analysed the relationship between modernity, empire and nationalism. One of his key contributions is his fore-grounding of the limits of the nation-state as a unit of analysis. Here his work challenges the parochialism of British sociology but also key figures in cultural studies such as Raymond Williams. The history of racism in Britain does not begin with the mid-twentieth-century movement of colonial migrants to the 'motherland'. Rather, the legacy of empire is integral to the development of British society and not an 'other story' that can be treated separately. Taking its title from a racist football song, *Ain't No Black in the Union Jack* identifies the ways in which ideas about race are folded into nation with racially exclusive consequences. As a result, the insistence on being both black and British challenges the logic of race at the heart of the construction of national identity. Through the analysis of the emergence of black British sporting figures, musicians and other public figures, Gilroy brings the cultural politics of race and nation to life.

Gilroy's approach to movement and culture is explored through the investigation of diaspora. For him the descendants of slaves are both inside modernity yet excluded from it. In this sense Gilroy's work illustrates the ways in which complex mutable cultures are made and remade within a condition of exile and itinerancy. It is here that the notion of diaspora – literally meaning scattering – becomes a key conceptual tool in understanding the relationship between culture, time and place. Diaspora cultures develop a non-traditional tradition in which the memory of the past is constantly being carried and yet cannot be reduced or fossilized. In Gilroy's use, the notion of diaspora is always connected to violent realities or a flight from persecution, that is, the brutal theft of human beings as chattel or the escape from domination. The traces of violence are also carried within the culture and experiences of those people who have scattered.

The word 'globalization' does not appear in Gilroy's prose but he does provide an alternative understanding of global interconnection. His book *Black Atlantic* offered new ways of conceptualizing the relationship between culture, movement and racial technologies. Here the Atlantic itself and the spaces between nations are conceived as a cultural system and the ship provides a key emblem of both the forces of slavery and imperial domination and a community in which compound traditions are composed. It is the presence of death within this historical experience, and sometimes choosing death over indentured life, that is carried within what Gilroy calls the 'slave sublime' registered in the aesthetics of black music and literature. This theme is also in his earlier writing but the essential point is that what is at stake within the music and arts of the African diaspora is the development of countercultures of modernity.

Gilroy questions absolute forms of racial and cultural difference. This is a strong theme in all his work and in particular his contention that racially dominated communities can be drawn by the allure of claiming exclusive forms of ownership over cultures or identities. In his early work Gilroy calls this 'ethnic absolutism', but he has been resolutely critical of essentialist claims to the ownership of black cultural forms or bounded notions of racial culture. 'Camp mentalities' are the product of both the echo of fascism and the hardened racial distinctions produced in the commercialization of black popular culture. Novel forms of race thinking or 'raciology' emerge in tune with twenty-first-century corporate multiculture. The black body is coded either as superhuman in the figure of the black athlete or as less than human in the violent black criminal. In *Between Camps*, Gilroy makes a utopian move to break with the legacy of racial thinking and introduces the notion of planetary humanism into social science vocabulary. This is a reinvigorated humanism that acknowledges the damage done to it by the legacy of slavery and racism while emphasizing a worldly scope in which to 'planet' (here used as a verb meaning to revolve or move) indicates a restless, moving and unfinished quality.

Paul Gilroy's work challenges the myopia of nationalism and the pervasive yet shifting nature of colonial and neo-colonial power. Yet he is a vigilant and sharp critic of that legacy and at the same time oriented to future utopian possibilities. In his most recent book, *After Empire*, he returns to the concerns of his early work and the lingering ghosts of empire, race and nation in Britain under Tony Blair and New Labour. Drawing on a Freudian inspired sociology, he suggests that Britain's national identity, cast by turns as melancholic and euphoric, can be characterized as a form of group psychosis that is unable to mourn the passing of empire or embrace a multicultural present. This diagnosis aligned with the 'special relationship' or association with US geopolitical power inhibits mourning but also exposes the colonial antecedents of the current 'war on terror'. Gilroy is also alert to the banal and everyday ways in which people live together in multicultural cities, which he names through the notion 'convivial culture'. This underworld of untidy interaction produces open and spontaneous forms of tolerance where racism is acknowledged and reckoned with.

This work provides the tools to dissect the mutual implication of the metropolis and colony, the unfinished legacy of New World slavery and the coexistence of racism and forms of conviviality beyond its reach. Gilroy challenges his readers to confront the damaged nature of our world society without taking refuge in false comforts, be they the repression of historical memory and imperial amnesia or the purity seeking racial culture of the homelands. His sociology remains critical of the globalization of American racial technologies while struggling for the intellectual and cultural capital necessary to address the pressing questions our time. His work is more committed than ever before to a sociology that provides the information necessary for world citizens to live with the uncertainties of the present and yet imagine a future beyond racism.

See also: Frantz Fanon, Stuart Hall.

Major works

Centre for Contemporary Cultural Studies. *The Empire Strikes Back: Race and Racism in Seventies Britain*. 1982. London: Hutchinson in Association with the Centre for Contemporary Cultural Studies.
There Ain't No Black in the Union Jack: The Cultural Politics of Nation and Race. 1987. London: Unwin Hyman.
The Black Atlantic: Modernity and Double Consciousness. 1993. London: Verso.
Small Acts: Thoughts on the Politics of Black Cultures. 1993. London: Serpent's Tail.
Between Camps: Nations, Cultures and the Allure of Race. 2000. London: Allen Lane The Penguin Press.
After Empire: Melancholia or Convivial Culture. 2004. London: Routledge.

LES BACK

ERVING GOFFMAN

Goffman is one of the most famous proponents of 'microsociology', a term he used to describe his interest in social interaction and its effects on the self. He is often regarded as a figurehead of the symbolic interactionist tradition, although he preferred to think of himself as a mere observer of everyday life: an 'urban ethnographer' or 'human ethologist'. Goffman's work has a great popular appeal beyond sociology because of his unique writing style, which combines meticulous theoretical insights with a dry, witty humour. It is often noted that readers feel a delighted shock of recognition at the quirks of human behaviour that Goffman identifies and explains. Throughout his numerous books and papers, Goffman employed the metaphor of social life as a theatre, drawing on Kenneth Burke's approach to social drama to forge what he called a *dramaturgical* perspective. This allowed him to analyse the ways in which individuals present different 'characters' and perform within teams of 'actors' in everyday life.

Erving Manual Goffman was born in Manville, Alberta, Canada, on 11 June 1922. His family were Ukrainian Jews who later moved to Dauphin, near Winnipeg in Manitoba, where Erving grew up. After leaving school, he first studied chemistry and then worked for the National Film Board in Ottawa before finally deciding to begin a sociology degree at Toronto University. He graduated in 1945 and moved to the University of Chicago, whose thriving sociology department meant that he was taught by Everett Hughes and others working in the tradition of such figures as Robert Park, Edward Burgess and Clifford Shaw. Goffman was encouraged to pursue his interest in social anthropology by his supervisor, Lloyd Warner, and went to the Shetland Isles to study 'the social structure of an island community'. He found, however, that he was more interested in the patterns of interaction and coded communication that went on between the islanders. Goffman's first published paper concerned social class and status, but he soon moved on to a more interactionist analysis of the procedures people use to deal with the loss of a social role, in his paper 'On Cooling the Mark Out'. The copious field-notes he took here would later form the basis of his most celebrated book, *The Presentation of Self in Everyday Life*.

This book was first published in 1959 and established Goffman's reputation as a dramaturgical sociologist. Its argument is that social life is accomplished through everyday actions, rituals and routines that are analogous to a theatrical performance. When people meet in social situations, they cooperate like teams of actors to 'keep the show running' and uphold a certain definition of reality. Meanwhile, individuals are concerned to present particular characters or versions of themselves to the audiences they meet; this involves techniques of 'self-presentation' and 'impression management'. The success of these performances, however, also depends upon audience perceptions. Goffman thought that it was important to study not only the impressions people 'give' deliberately but also those they 'give off' unintentionally. Thus we might detect an actor who does not really believe in the part he or she is playing, giving a 'cynical' rather than a 'sincere' performance.

The physical context in which individual and team performances are given is very important, and Goffman suggested that this is divided into two main parts that correspond to areas of a theatre. The 'frontstage' region is where we present our public identities to an audience and where we are recognized within certain roles. The 'front' of a performance consists of its 'setting' (its location, scenery and décor), typically fixed in one place, together with the 'personal front' that we bring to a situation (items of identity equipment such as clothes, props and facial expressions). The 'backstage' region, on the other hand, is where actors relax out of role and may knowingly contradict their public identities: it is a private space in which to rehearse and reflect upon one's performance and recharge one's batteries before going back onstage. To illustrate this distinction, Goffman gave the example of the rooms in a house: whereas the lounge and dining room may serve as frontstage regions into which we invite guests, the bedrooms and bathroom are deemed more private, backstage areas, into which members of the household can retreat to 'be themselves' and attend to bodily needs. Goffman pointed to the embarrassment that can result if the boundary between these two regions is transgressed – if, for example, someone enters a bedroom without knocking. In his Shetland Isles hotel, he also noted that the staff behaved very differently backstage in the kitchen (where they would chatter and laugh, insult the customers and spit in their food) and frontstage in the restaurant (where they would politely attend to the guests). Making the transition from backstage to frontstage can be dramaturgically quite stressful, as it requires putting on one's public face and preparing to be scrutinized; this can be a particular problem for shy people.

Leaving Chicago in the mid-1950s, Goffman moved with his first wife, Angelica Choate, and their baby son to Washington, DC, where he began to conduct the research for his next book, *Asylums*.

Working at St Elizabeth's Hospital in various positions – as a ward orderly, hospital porter and assistant athletics director – he observed and recorded what was going on. Goffman identified the psychiatric hospital as a 'total institution', a term introduced by his mentor Everett Hughes to describe places in which inmates were confined day and night and controlled by timetabled activities. To Goffman, it seemed that the structure of the hospital, as expressed through the ward rules and routines, treatment procedures and interactions between staff and patients, profoundly changed the self-identities of the inmates. He argued that patients progress through a 'moral career' with three phases: pre-patient, inpatient and ex-patient. Focusing on the first two phases, Goffman explained how patients are gradually stripped of all the possessions, relationships and rights that they had previously used to display their identities in a process he called the 'mortification of the self'. Having lost the identities they had in the outside world, they are forced to comply with the requirements of the hospital's regime. Goffman implicitly sided with the patients and championed their subculture of resistance through the hospital 'underlife', demonstrating that he did not ignore issues of power, as some critics have argued.

Goffman joined the sociology department at the University of California at Berkeley in 1957, rising through the ranks to become a full professor in 1962. Here he published three key books. *Stigma* continued the theme of how relatively powerless groups experience interaction. Goffman defined stigma as a discrepancy between one's 'virtual' and 'actual' identities – that is, between the self we present to others and the self we think we 'really' are, backstage. These 'blemishes of character' could be either potentially discredit*able* (for example a criminal record, which can be kept a secret but might inadvertently be revealed) or actually discredit*ing* (for example a physical disability that cannot be hidden). Goffman was not suggesting that these attributes were inherently undesirable, but simply that they might discredit the actor's claims to be a particular sort of person or to be able to join in with certain activities. Consequently, actors engage in techniques of impression management – called 'information control' – which aim to conceal the stigmatizing attribute from the audience's view. They may also be helped by the groups of sympathetic others that Goffman called the 'own' (those who share the same stigma) and the 'wise' (those who recognize the actor's stigma but do not expect them to hide it). Thus Goffman reminded us that many of the characteristics we see in others are not simply personality traits but rather role performances, which are negotiated in social interaction.

The subsequent two books, *Behavior in Public Places* and *Interaction Ritual*, catalogued the more general self-presentational strategies used in everyday life, complementing an earlier collection of essays called *Encounters*. A social encounter is an example of focused interaction, occurring between people who come together with a common purpose in mind, whereas unfocused interaction occurs when people just happen to be in each other's presence. In *Behavior in Public Places*, Goffman looked at both of these types of interaction, emphasizing in particular the role of the body in 'giving' and 'giving off' communicative gestures. For example, people on the street engage in displays of 'civil inattention', which involve glancing at people to acknowledge their presence but then looking away so as not to be thought rude. By contrast, proper engagement in a focused encounter involves a display of our *accessibility* to others: party guests, for example, may use eye contact and position themselves near to those with whom they wish to interact. If one is present in a focused encounter, but seeks to avoid interaction, an 'involvement shield' can be used to create a little backstage space for oneself whilst in the presence of others. Examples might be a woman reading a newspaper at a bus stop or a party guest going outside to smoke. These observations may also have been informed by the time that Goffman spent working as a blackjack dealer in a Las Vegas casino: he was known amongst his colleagues as a keen gambler.

Interaction Ritual is a collection of essays and articles on a similar theme. The essay 'On Facework' refers again to the strategies of self-presentation used in everyday life to create desired impressions upon others. A 'face' is a socially acceptable, public identity that we know will be valued positively, and 'facework' refers to the techniques actors use to maintain this image. Goffman said that as well as the 'defensive facework' that we use to keep ourselves in face there is also a tendency to provide 'protective facework' for others whom we see as team-mates. In his essay on embarrassment, Goffman explained how people tend to react to displays of abashment with supportive gestures that 'repair' the situation: rather than leaving the actor looking flustered on the stage, they will gloss over the mistake and show that it was not important. This, in turn, helps the actor to regain composure and restore the situation to 'normal appearances' so that the show can go on.

Goffman moved to the University of Pennsylvania in 1968 and published two more books on the minutiae of everyday life. *Strategic Interaction* considered the various 'moves' that actors make when performing before others. There is, for example, the 'control move' that is intended to enhance one's perceived identity and the 'uncovering move' that exposes another actor's secrets. Goffman had been studying game theory during a sabbatical year, and its influence upon this book is evident. *Relations in Public* was published a little later and reflected Goffman's growing interest in ethology, the study of animal behaviour. This book examined the way people use their bodies and social space to display and control their relationships with others. For example, we protect the 'territories of the self' by making claims to personal space and controlling the amount of private information that we disclose to others. Goffman said that these territorial rules only become evident when they are broken, and went on to discuss some of the rituals that people use to repair such awkward interaction. 'Remedial interchanges' such as accounts, apologies and requests for permission serve to demonstrate the actor's distance from any offence and, if accepted, absolve them of moral responsibility.

Goffman's last three books marked a shift in his research interests towards linguistics, phenomenology and hermeneutics. *Frame Analysis* examined the ways in which people interpret situations by projecting 'frames' or definitions of reality on to them. Echoing Schutz, Goffman argued that the sociologist adds another layer of interpretation by theoretically framing these social worlds. *Gender and Advertising* looked at the ways in which people perform and display their gender identities through ritualized gestures, which are interpreted by others according to shared frames of reference. Finally, *Forms of Talk* focused on the styles of discourse used in different communications media, for example the radio play. This was also the year in which Goffman married the linguist Gillian Sankoff, and they had a daughter together.

Goffman's work has met with some criticism over the years, even from those who admire him greatly. **Gouldner**, for example, famously criticized the neglect of power and wider structural inequalities in Goffman's micro-level theory and said that this was a sociology for the American college-educated middle class. Similar remarks might be made about the way he talked about 'people' in general without considering the effects of gender, class, ethnicity and so on. Lofland (1980) also complains about the way in which Goffman wrote, starting each book as if it were the first and jumping about between concepts without linking them together. Nevertheless, some would say that this is what makes his work such a pleasure to read, as one can dip into any book at random and immediately become immersed in his ideas.

Goffman died in November 1982, shortly before he was due to deliver his presidential address to the American Sociological Association in the form of a paper called 'The Interaction Order'. This title reminds us that Goffman did not simply ignore questions of power and structure, but rather saw them as expressed through everyday interaction. By examining the ritualized processes through which people perform identities and manage social encounters, Goffman revealed how even the most private aspects of our lives are socially organized. In this respect, his dramaturgical approach bridges the gap between micro and macro analyses, suggesting possible links between interactionism and structural theories such as functionalism. Goffman's ideas have been enormously influential in shaping the work of sociologists across the world, and he remains one of the most entertaining, creative and insightful figures in modern sociology.

See also: Howard S. Becker, Judith Butler, Randall Collins.

See also in Fifty Key Sociologists: The Formative Theorists: Alfred Radcliffe-Brown, Charles Cooley, George Herbert Mead, Lloyd Warner.

Major works

'The Nature of Deference and Demeanor'. 1956. American Anthropologist 53.
The Presentation of Self in Everyday Life. 1959. Harmondsworth: Penguin.
Encounters. 1961. Indianapolis: Bobbs-Merrill.
Asylums: Essays on the Social Situation of Mental Patients and Other Inmates. 1961. New York: Doubleday.
Stigma. 1963. Englewood Cliffs, NJ: Prentice-Hall.
Behaviour in Public Places. 1963. New York: Free Press.
Interaction Ritual: Essays on Face-to-Face Behaviour. 1967. New York: Doubleday.
Relations in Public. 1971. New York: Free Press.
Frame Analysis. 1974. New York: Harper and Row.
Gender Advertisements. 1979. London: Macmillan.
Forms of Talk. 1981. Pittsburgh: University of Pennsylvania Press.
'The Interaction Order'. 1983. American Sociological Review 48.

Further reading

Kenneth Burke. 1945. A Grammar of Motives. New York: Prentice-Hall.
Tom Burns. 1992. Erving Goffman. London: Routledge.
Alvin Gouldner. 1970. The Coming Crisis of Western Sociology. New York: Basic Books.
Jon Lofland. 1980. 'Early Goffman: Style, Structure, Substance, Soul'. In Jason Ditton, ed. The View from Goffman. London: Macmillan.
Philip Manning. 2003. 'Erving Goffman'. In G. Ritzer, ed. Encyclopaedia of Social Theory. London: Sage.

Susie Scott. 2005. 'The Red, Shaking Fool: Dramaturgical Dilemmas in Shyness'. *Symbolic Interaction* 28.

SUSIE SCOTT

ALVIN W. GOULDNER

Alvin Ward Gouldner, born in 1920, was an American sociologist who contributed to a number of areas of sociological thought. It is interesting to note that 'Ward' was not Gouldner's given middle name. Gouldner adopted it in honour of the great early American sociologist Lester F. Ward. Although Gouldner engaged in empirical research early in his career, primarily for the Columbia dissertation that was subsequently published as *Patterns of Industrial Bureaucracy* in 1954, he is best known as a sociological theorist and social critic.

Gouldner's earliest writings in industrial sociology were influenced by his mentor at Columbia University, **Robert Merton**. In pushing a middle-range theoretical agenda for functionalism, Merton emphasized the importance of keeping the empirical level in sight, rather than engaging in the sort of grand theorizing for which **Talcott Parsons** was best known. This meant that Columbia students writing dissertations under the supervision of Merton during the 1940s and 1950s in the field of organizational or industrial sociology – Gouldner, Peter Blau, Seymour Martin Lipset and Philip Selznick to name a few – engaged in empirical research so as to test extant theories (such as those of Weber and Michels) rather than accepting them as gospel. This orientation towards scientific work taught by Merton, namely organized scepticism or sociological ambivalence, was employed by Gouldner in all his writings.

Gouldner's 'The Norm of Reciprocity', published in 1960, still stands today as one of the most often cited papers ever written by a sociologist. The paper was and remains influential because it was the first systematic explanation and summary of how the concept of reciprocity has been used in sociological and anthropological analysis. Under functionalist usage, reciprocity implies that A provides something of value to B and B does likewise for A, as in the notion of the 'gift', where a good turn is expected to be returned at some unspecified future point. But this often tacit understanding of reciprocity underplays, and is even blind to, the possibility that A may benefit B with no expectation on the part of A that he or she will be compensated. In other words, in conditions of unequal power A may be forced to benefit B, so that what appears as a consensual example of reciprocity may in fact be better characterized as conflictual. Gouldner wrote this, as much as anything, to alert functionalists to the tacit and often unexamined assumptions they make about human social relations, especially in the specific case of the norm of reciprocity.

After 1962 Gouldner pretty much left the field of industrial sociology behind, turning more of his attention to social criticism and the development of a reflexive sociology. Gouldner was also becoming increasingly difficult and combative, and this aspect of his interpersonal style began affecting his ability to do sociology. One of the better-known incidents occurred at Washington University, where Gouldner assaulted and sent to hospital a graduate student of his, Laud Humphreys. Humphreys was conducting research on anonymous lavatory sex between consenting adult males – the so-called 'tearoom trade' that gave Humphreys' book its title. Posing as a 'watch queen', he aimed to get as close to the action as possible for purposes of data collection. The aspect of the methodology that infuriated Gouldner was that Humphreys recorded the license plate numbers of the men engaged in the trade and then tracked down their home addresses through the St Louis Directorate of Motor Vehicles. Another clever methodological twist was that Humphreys then showed up at their houses several months later posing as a researcher conducting a health survey. In this way, Humphreys was able to collect socio-demographic data on the men that otherwise would not have been possible. Although it was methodologically ingenious, Gouldner nevertheless felt that the research was highly unethical and confronted Humphreys to tell him about it. Shortly thereafter the two came to blows, with Gouldner getting the better of the exchange. Humphreys eventually sued the university and Gouldner was banished to the Netherlands. The Washington University sociology department eventually closed because of this and other matters relating either directly or indirectly to Gouldner.

The Humphreys incident has been covered to underscore the fact that had Gouldner not become increasingly hostile, bitter, aggressive, angry and malicious during the 1960s and 1970s he might have gone on to become one of the greatest sociologists ever, American or otherwise. Gouldner was the possessor of a deeply analytical mind, and at his best very few could match his prowess with words and ideas. Through the 1970s until his death in 1980, Gouldner poured his creative energies into the construction of a reflexive sociology.

In Gouldner's version of reflexive sociology, sociology becomes self-conscious of its own domain assumptions about the world, about knowledge and about reality. Just as Gouldner had earlier criticized functionalists for not being reflexive enough concerning their own tacit assumptions of social order and the importance of the norm of reciprocity in contributing to that order, so Marxists and critical theorists were insufficiently self-reflexive. One of the most fitful anomalies stirring within the infrastructure of Marxism was the inability to locate its own theorists within the explanatory schema, especially with regard to the argument that consciousness arises from social location, and most importantly from class background. How could radical intellectuals, most of whom come from privileged backgrounds, become sympathetic with the plight of the down-trodden and the dispossessed, with those oppressed at the hands of the dominant class?

This question was vigorously pursued from *The Coming Crisis of Western Sociology*, published in 1970, until *The Two Marxisms*, published in the year of his death. There was no good answer for this, at least in terms of the internal logic of Marxism. The anomaly had to be explained as resulting from the inadequate levels of reflexivity of Marxism and other strands of critical and conflict theories. Like the vast majority of theoretical programmes in sociology and other subjects, too much time was spent developing the theory's technical level without enough attention being given over to the infrastructural level, that is, the tacit domain assumptions in the areas of ontology, epistemology and axiology that are rarely reflected on or consciously understood.

In the end, Gouldner's reflexive sociology becomes pessimistic in an almost Schopenhauerian or Nietzschean way, and Gouldner himself becomes a tragic hero in an ancient Greek play. Reflexive sociology becomes hyper-pessimistic because it discovers Hegel's 'bad infinity' – no theory lives up to the ideals of reflexivity, and critique becomes an infinite regress of critiques of itself – while Gouldner's own deep and dark character flaws keep him from attaining the greatness that he perhaps was destined to achieve. Yet Gouldner's struggles are our struggles, and that is perhaps his greatest legacy of all.

See also: Robert Merton.

See also in *Fifty Key Sociologists: The Formative Theorists*: Lester Ward, Max Weber.

Major works

Patterns of Industrial Bureaucracy. 1954. Glencoe, IL: Free Press.
Wildcat Strike. 1954. Yellow Springs, OH: Antioch Press.
'Reciprocity and Autonomy in Functional Theory'. 1959. In Llewelyn Gross, ed. *Symposium on Sociological Theory.* New York: Harper and Row.
'The Norm of Reciprocity: A Preliminary Statement'. 1960. *American Sociological Review* 25.
The Coming Crisis of Western Sociology. 1970. New York: Avon.
For Sociology: Renewal and Critique in Sociology Today. 1973. New York: Basic Books.
The Dialectic of Ideology and Technology. 1976. New York: Oxford University Press.
The Future of Intellectuals and the Rise of the New Class. 1979. New York: Seabury Press.
The Two Marxisms. 1980. New York: Oxford University Press.

Further reading

James J. Chriss. 1999. *Alvin W. Gouldner: Sociologist and Outlaw Marxist.* Aldershot, UK: Ashgate.
James J. Chriss. 2002. 'Gouldner's Tragic Vision'. *Sociological Quarterly* 43.

JAMES J. CHRISS

GEORGES GURVITCH

Even the briefest acquaintance with the rise and fall of Gurvitch's reputation is enough to make the reader suspicious of the vagaries attendant on what counts for progress in sociological theorizing. At one time he was an acknowledged leader in sociology, bringing together previously diverse intellectual streams of thought, founding journals and international collaborations. Soon afterwards, his work disappeared from view and his reputation sank almost without trace. Even today, there are only tentative efforts to recuperate his ideas and to recognize their originality and relevance. And yet those who do take a fresh look at his work are often convinced that it was prematurely disregarded and still has much to offer.

Certainly, no one was better equipped to develop sociology in a relevant and intellectually coherent way. Born in November 1894 in Noworossisk, Russia, Gyorgy (Georges) Gurvitch was already a rising university intellectual and radical political activist when the Bolshevik Revolution took place. He was a critical participant in it for several years until 1920: he met Lenin, knew Trotsky and observed with growing mistrust the centralizing direction being taken. He was steeped in Marxist thought, but came to reject its economic determinism. His political involvements did not interrupt his academic career. In 1915 his first dissertation was published, dealing with the doctrines of the Russian political theorist Prokopovitch and in 1917 his study of 'Rousseau and the Declaration of Rights' appeared. He received his doctorate and gave a course at the University of Leningrad–Petrograd in 1920, but a few months later he emigrated to Czechoslovakia and in 1925 to France, where he became a citizen in 1929. Already, before he left Russia, he had travelled widely, becoming acquainted with the thought of the leading French and German social and legal theorists, including Durkheim, Bergson, Weber, Fichte, the neo-Kantian philosophers, dialectical philosophers and the social psychologist Wilhelm Wundt. When he left Russia he took with him the outlines of three books: one on Fichte's dialectical realism applied to ethics, another on the idea of social law (law or regulation arising out of social groups, rather than from the state) and the third on the various strata or levels of social reality. These three strands of his thought remained prominent throughout his life, together with a political commitment to a decentralized socialism that included workers' self-management.

Most of the rest of Gurvitch's career was spent in Paris at the Sorbonne and the Ecole Pratique des Hautes Etudes, apart from a period in New York during the Second World War, when he enjoyed a brief American fame, editing, with Wilbert E. Moore, *Twentieth Century Sociology* (1947). This volume featured articles by many of the leading American sociologists, with a second section composed of articles on sociology in other countries. Taken together with the articles in English written by Gurvitch during this period, it really looked as if he was set to occupy a position in the mainstream of sociology. He had already established himself as a leading figure in French sociology, initially due to the lectures that he was invited to give at the Sorbonne, from 1927 to 1929, on *Contemporary Trends in German Philosophy* (published in 1930), which drew especially on his familiarity with the phenomenological thought of Husserl and Scheler. Although he took a critical stance towards phenomenology, he added some of its insights to his own emerging theoretical and methodological synthesis. In particular, it was the phenomenological concepts of 'intentionality' and the 'open consciousness' that enabled him to develop a dialectical theory of the relationship between society and individual consciousness. He termed his approach 'dialectical hyper-empiricism'. It offered the possibility of bridging the gap between those theorists who have been concerned with the relationship between, on the one hand, society and individual consciousness (such as George Herbert Mead, American symbolic interactionists and phenomenological analyses of the lifeworld and everyday culture as begun by Schutz and continued in part by ethnomethodologists) and, on the other, the dialectical theories of structure provided by many Marxist scholars who lacked a theoretical grasp of the mediations between structural processes and individual consciousness. It has been argued by Stark that Gurvitch's approach subsequently shaped Sartre's description of the social dialectic. In addition, Gurvitch rejected rigid sociological notions of structure (whether **Talcott Parsons**' structural-functionalism or **Claude Lévi-Strauss**' version of structuralism) and emphasized the fluidity of structuration processes (an idea later reintroduced by Giddens).

Gurvitch followed Marcel Mauss in taking as the subject matter of sociology the 'total social phenomenon', which demands that any aspect of social life be viewed in the context of social reality as a whole, so as to avoid the reductive dangers of 'abstract culturalism', sociologism or psychologism. The two precepts of Gurvitch's sociology are that it should take into account all the levels of social reality and that it should apply the typological method. On this basis, social reality, or the total social phenomenon, is differentiated along two main axes, one horizontal and one vertical, corresponding to the 'social types' and the 'depth levels' of social reality. The types differentiate social frameworks (*cadres sociaux*), which is the generic term for categories along the horizontal axis. Gurvitch distinguished three main types: forms of sociality (ways of being bound together in a collectivity), different types of groups and several types of global societies. Each of these is then further differentiated into sub-types; for example, the main forms of sociality are those of mass, community and communion. The depth levels, which constitute the vertical axis of the conceptualized total social phenomenon, can be related in part to degrees of spontaneity or rigidity of different elements of social reality – ranging from the surface level of social morphology and ecology to the deepest level of collective mentalities (or collective consciousness). Essentially, Gurvitch was further elaborating Durkheim's five such levels into ten: the morphological and ecological surface; social organizations; social patterns or models; regular collective behaviour not confined to social organizations; the web of social rules; collective attitudes; social symbols; spontaneous, innovative and creative collective behaviour; collective ideas and values; collective mentalities or collective consciousness.

Although these two axes, the horizontal and the vertical, along with their various typologies, may seem like an extremely elaborate framework, they are part of his ambitious project to solve the problem of linking together microsociology and macrosociology. His theory is perhaps most original and daring where the interactions between the horizontal and vertical axes concern the deepest of the depth levels (those layers of social reality that are least rigid and most spontaneous) and the least structured social frameworks (the forms of sociality – mass, community and communion – which are the subject matter of microsociology). The applicability of this framework to the sociology of knowledge is demonstrated in his most mature work, *The Social Frameworks of Knowledge*, published a year after his death in 1966, and especially the research report on the everyday knowledge of different groups. Other areas in which there has been a recent revival of Gurvitch's theoretical concerns and ideas are the sociology of law, the sociology of religion and the sociology of time.

See also in *Fifty Key Sociologists: The Formative Theorists*: Emile Durkheim, Karl Marx, Marcel Mauss.

Major works

Les Tendencies actuelles de la philosophie allemande. 1930. Paris: Vrin.
L'Idée du droit social. 1932. Paris: Sirey.
Essais de sociologie. 1938. Paris: Sirey.
Sociology of Law. 1942. New York: Philosophical Library.
The Bill of Social Rights. 1946. New York: International Universities Press.
Twentieth Century Sociology. 1946. Ed. with Wilbert E. Moore. New York: Philosophical Library.
La Vocation actuelle de la sociologie. 1950. Paris: Presses Universitaires de France.
Determinismes sociaux et liberté humaine. 1955. Paris: Presses Universitaires de France.
Traité de sociologie, ed. 2 vols. 1957 and 1960. Paris: Presses Universitaires de France.
Dialectique et sociologie. 1962. Paris: Flammarion.
The Spectrum of Social Time. 1964. Dordrecht, Netherlands: D. Reidel.
The Social Frameworks of Knowledge. 1966. Oxford: Basil Blackwell, 1971.

Further reading

Georges Balandier. 1975. *Gurvitch*. Oxford: Blackwell.

R. Banakar. 2001. 'Integrating Reciprocal Perspectives: On Georges Gur-
vitch's Theory of Immediate Jural Experience'. *Canadian Journal of Law
and Society* 16.
A. J. Blasi. 2001. 'Marginality as a Societal Position of Religion'. Presidential
Address, Association for the Sociology of Religion, Anaheim, California.
Philip Bosserman. 1968. *Dialectical Sociology.* Boston, MA: Porter Sargent,
1968.
G. J. Stark. 1975. 'Gurvitch and Sartre's Dialectic'. *Modern Schoolman* 52.
Richard Swedberg. 1982. *Sociology as Disenchantment: The Evolution of the
Work of Georges Gurvitch.* Atlantic Highlands, NJ: Humanities Press.

KEN THOMPSON

JÜRGEN HABERMAS

Social and political theorist, philosopher and critic, Jürgen Habermas
is known for his contributions to critical theory. Some of his most
important contributions centre on language and language use. Originally trained at the Institut für Sozialforschung in Frankfurt,
Habermas belongs to the second generation of the Frankfurt school.
Like his mentors Max Horkheimer and Theodor Adorno, Habermas
initially set out to construct a critical theory within the German tradition of Hegel and Marx, but he soon followed a different intellectual trajectory. In contrast with the early Frankfurt school, he has
been keen to emphasize the positive features of the Enlightenment
tradition, and he has drawn on a wide variety of intellectual sources,
ranging from hermeneutics and system theory to American pragmatism and speech act theory. He has inspired various social and political theorists, not just his former students such as Hans Joas, Axel
Honneth, Thomas McCarthy and Claus Offe, but also many others
such as Craig Calhoun, Jean-Marc Ferry, William Outhwaite and
David Rasmussen.

Born in Düsseldorf in 1929, Habermas studied at the Universities
of Göttingen, Zurich, Bonn and Frankfurt, where he was an assistant
to Adorno. His wrote a doctoral dissertation on Friedrich Schelling's
philosophy and a *Habilitationsschrift* on the historical development of
the public sphere in modern society. He taught in Heidelberg and
Frankfurt before becoming co-director of the Max Planck Institute in
Starnberg in 1971. From 1983 until his retirement in 1993, he was
director of the Institut für Sozialforschung and professor of philosophy at the University of Frankfurt. Habermas became involved in

various public debates: for instance with Popper and positivist philosophers of science (in the *Positivismusstreit*); acolytes of the German philosopher Martin Heidegger; the sociologist **Niklas Luhmann**; the hermeneutic philosopher Hans-Georg Gadamer; French postmodern thinkers; and revisionist German historians. His writings range from highly philosophical works to critical reflections on the workings of contemporary society. An example of the former is his *magnum opus The Theory of Communicative Action*, which proposes a critical theory of society centred round interaction and language use. An example of the latter is *Legitimation Crisis*, which argues that governments today draw their legitimacy from sound economic management (not from ideological stances), but that this legitimacy becomes increasingly precarious given the recurrent economic crises in advanced capitalism.

Habermas' first book, *The Structural Transformation in the Public Sphere*, appeared in 1962. It was a historical account of the emergence, rise and decline of the 'public sphere' between the eighteenth and the twentieth centuries. By public sphere, Habermas refers to a free debate amongst equals. Underlying the bourgeois society of the eighteenth and early nineteenth century was the potential for an open, non-coerced debate, epitomized as it was in the discussions about contemporary social and political issues that took place regularly in the salons and cafés of European urban centres. Initially, the media played a central role in the development of a culture of open debate – articles in newspapers often precipitated the discussions – but their later commercialization and trivialization brought about the rapid decline and 'refeudalization' of the public sphere. The general gist of Habermas' account of this historical trajectory of the public sphere has been widely acclaimed, but critics have pointed out that large sections of the population, notably women and working-class men, were excluded from these salon and café gatherings. Furthermore, feminists have argued that the relocation of women in a private sphere was constitutive of the emergence of the public sphere. Finally, some sociologists have argued that the internet has led to a revival of the public sphere.

In the second half of the 1960s Habermas turned his attention to the philosophy of the social sciences. This research culminated in *Theory and Practice, Knowledge and Human Interests* and *On the Logic of the Social Sciences*. Underlying these works was his discomfort with the reigning positivist orthodoxy in the social sciences. Habermas had already taken sides in the *Positivismusstreit* – the 'positivist dispute' – but by now his epistemological reflections had matured into a coherent pragmatist-inspired framework. Influenced by Charles Peirce's writings, Habermas explored the intricate relationship between types of knowledge and what he called 'a priori interests'. By interests, Habermas referred to fundamental orientations, which are tied to the conditions of reproduction and self-constitution of the human species. Habermas distinguished three such interests: control (and, related, prediction), understanding and emancipation. Three types of knowledge correspond to these interests. Habermas referred to the type of knowledge that aims at steering and prediction as the 'empirical analytical type of knowledge'. Knowledge that pursues understanding is referred to as 'hermeneutics', while knowledge concerned with emancipation is referred to as 'critical theory'. For Habermas, the problem with positivist-inclined philosophers is that they fail to recognize that aims other than prediction can be pursued, thereby mistakenly treating empirical-analytical knowledge as the only valid type of knowledge. Other aims, such as understanding and emancipation, are worth pursuing.

Critical theory aims at emancipation, hence Habermas' attempt to explain what this cognitive interest means precisely. Emancipation takes place whenever individuals become aware and confront past societal restrictions. Critical theory, then, utilizes a combination of empirical-analytical and hermeneutic knowledge to bring about the removal of these restrictions. Psychoanalysis is a case in point. The analyst guides the analysand towards a reconstruction of repressed memories and experiences, which consequently emancipates the analysand from the repression and the associated symptoms. Likewise, historical materialism brings about emancipation, but at a collective – not individual – level, increasing people's critical awareness of the repressive societal conditions of contemporary capitalism.

Critics appreciated Habermas' attention to the pragmatic relationship between knowledge and interests, but they were less enamoured with his view that psychoanalysis is a solid basis for a critical theory of society. They were also quick to point out that Habermas conflated two types of reflection: a Hegelian type of reflection upon socially created constraints and a Kantian type of reflection upon conditions of possibilities of knowing and acting. Habermas agreed, and he subsequently called the latter 'rational reconstruction' and the former 'self-criticism'. Rational reconstruction would play a central part in his theory of communicative action. This theory draws upon 'reconstructive sciences', such as Noam Chomsky's generative grammar, Jean Piaget's theory of cognitive development and Lawrence Kohlberg's theory of moral development, which help to uncover the underlying rules of our pre-theoretical 'knowing how'. Contrary to these earlier epistemological writings, which were still caught in a solipsistic Cartesian 'philosophy of consciousness', with the theory of communicative action Habermas took a decisively *social* turn, emphasizing the social nature of communicative practices and knowledge production.

In the early 1980s, Habermas published the two volumes of *The Theory of Communicative Action*. This theory deals, at its core, with rationality. Habermas' concept of rationality is a procedural one. It does not refer to absolute foundations of knowledge, but to *procedures* of obtaining knowledge. Contrary to Max Weber, Adorno and Horkheimer, who portrayed the transition towards modernity in terms of increasing '*instrumental* rationality', Habermas stressed the intricate connection between modernity and '*communicative* rationality'. By communicative rationality, Habermas refers to the implementation of procedures of open, non-coerced debate amongst equals. This is a positive legacy of the Enlightenment, worth defending, and Habermas made it central to his theory of 'universal pragmatics'. Following Austin's speech act theory, this theory distinguishes between *communicating*, on the one hand, and *doing* something by communicating, on the other. According to Habermas, when individuals communicate, four 'validity claims' are presupposed; these are 'intelligibility', 'truth', 'moral rightness' and 'sincerity'. Implicit in any act of communication is the assumption that the content of what is being said (or written) is comprehensible, that it is true, that the people who say or write it have the right to do so and that they are not trying to deceive anyone by saying (or writing) it. Communicative rationality comes into play whenever procedures are in place, which guarantee an open debate concerning these validity claims. The epitome of communicative rationality is the 'ideal speech situation', in which all barriers to a non-coerced debate have been lifted and only the 'force of the better argument' reigns. The ideal speech situation can operate as a 'counterfactual' ideal – a yardstick to criticize 'systematically distorted communication'.

Habermas used the theory of communicative action for various purposes. First, in *The Philosophical Discourse of Modernity* he attempted to show that contemporary critics of the Enlightenment, such as **Michel Foucault** and Jean-François Lyotard, drew an impoverished picture of the Enlightenment tradition, failing to grasp its truly emancipatory potential. He agreed with the critics that the paradigm of consciousness had run its course, but disagreed with the new direction to take. For Habermas, the Enlightenment project should not be abandoned, but rediscovered. Second, in *Justification and Application: Remarks on Discourse Ethics* he proposed 'discourse ethics', an application of the theory of universal pragmatics to the domain of ethics. In discourse ethics, the grounding of normative claims requires dialogue. As such, discourse ethics avoids both 'formal' and 'communitarian' perspectives on ethics: moral judgements are not simply the product of private deliberation; nor do they just reflect social codes. Instead, Habermas' proposal is a procedural one, specifying the conditions of open dialogue, which allow individuals to examine normative propositions. This dialogical structure implies that individuals are encouraged to adopt the perspectives of all other individuals affected before deciding upon the validity of a given norm. Third, in *Between Facts and Norms; Contributions to a Discourse Theory of Law and Democracy* Habermas argued against the view that society today had become so complex that legal and political decisions should be left to experts. Habermas argued in favour of 'discursive democracy': norms are valid only if they have been accepted by the individuals who are potentially affected by these norms and if this acceptance is based upon rational discourse. That is, they are not produced through systematically distorted communication. In short, we should try to inform as many people as possible and include them in the debate.

Amongst Habermas' contributions to social theory, his theory of communicative action has been the most influential, but this does not mean that it has been devoid of criticism. The 'reconstructive sciences' that inspired Habermas − those of Piaget, Kohlberg and **Lévi-Strauss** − are now treated with more suspicion, relying, as they now appear to do, on inadequate empirical bases. Habermas' claim that communicative action is action oriented to '*Verständigung*' is problematic, because *Verständigung* means both understanding and agreement, and whilst it is true that an open, unconstrained debate may lead to greater understanding between the different parties involved, it does not necessarily lead to consensus. Likewise, Habermas' appeal to 'the force of the better argument' is not straightforward because it assumes that individuals will come to an agreement on what counts as a superior (or inferior) argument, and, unfortunately, there are very few cases where people disagree about significant issues whilst concurring on what counts as a proper way of arguing. This problem is particularly striking when the individuals involved do not share a common framework or culture.

See also: Anthony Giddens.

STUART HALL

See also in *Fifty Key Sociologists: The Formative Theorists*: Theodor Adorno, Karl Marx, Max Weber.

Major works

The Structural Transformation of the Public Sphere: An Inquiry into a Category of Bourgeois Society. 1962. Cambridge: Polity Press, 1989.
Knowledge and Human Interests. 1968. Cambridge: Polity Press, 1986.
Legitimation Crisis. 1973. Cambridge: Polity Press, 1988.
Theory of Communicative Action, vols 1–2. 1981. Cambridge: Polity Press, 1984–7.
The Philosophical Discourse of Modernity: Twelve Lectures. 1985. Cambridge, MA: MIT Press.
Justification and Application: Remarks on Discourse Ethics. 1991. Cambridge: Polity Press, 1993.
Between Facts and Norms. Contributions to a Discourse Theory of Law and Democracy. 1992. Cambridge: Polity Press, 1996.
The Postnational Constellation. 1998. Cambridge: Polity Press, 2001.

Further reading

Craig Calhoun, ed. 1993. *Habermas and the Public Sphere*. Cambridge, MA: MIT Press.
Axel Honneth and Hans Joas, eds. 1991. *Communicative Action: Essays on Jürgen Habermas's Theory of Communicative Action*. Cambridge: Polity Press.
William Outhwaite. 1994. *Habermas: A Critical Introduction*. Cambridge: Polity Press.
M. Rosenfeld and A. Arato, eds. 1998. *Habermas on Law and Democracy: Critical Exchanges*. Berkeley, CA: University of California Press.

PATRICK BAERT

STUART HALL

Stuart Hall is one of the founding figures in cultural studies, yet his influence stretches far beyond academic boundaries. He is best known to the public as the political commentator who coined the term 'Thatcherism' to describe the radical social transformations in British society during the 1970s and 1980s under the Thatcher government. His more recent interventions in public life include his significant contributions to the Commission on the Future of Multi-Ethnic Britain (the Parekh Report of 2000), which examined racism and multiculturalism to controversially demand a rethinking of British

131

national identity. Hall himself would maintain that he is first and foremost a teacher, but he remains an intellectual prepared to present unsettling arguments in the public sphere.

Born in Kingston, Jamaica, in 1932, Hall was raised in what he later described as 'a lower-middle class family that was trying to be an upper-middle class family trying to be an English Victorian family'. As the youngest and 'blackest' of three children, Hall experienced otherness and difference from an early age. Negotiating the tensions produced by class, colour and colonialism is part of his personal history and subsequent intellectual development. In 1951 he moved to Britain as a Rhodes scholar to study English at Oxford University, where he continued to be involved in anti-colonial politics and helped form the 'New Left' in Britain in the 1950s. He abandoned plans to write a doctoral thesis on the novelist Henry James during the tumultuous year of 1956, following the Soviet invasion of Hungary and the British invasion of Suez. Hall strongly felt that these political upheavals meant that it was no longer possible to 'go on thinking cultural questions in "pure" literary terms'.

Hall left Oxford for London to be a supply teacher by day and, by night, to edit the *Universities and Left Review*, a journal that eventually, in 1960, became the *New Left Review*. Following some intense editorial disagreements, Hall took up what was then an undoubtedly unique post teaching media studies at Chelsea College in the University of London. He combined this teaching with some research with Paddy Whannel on film that was published as *The Popular Arts* in 1964. In the same year he was appointed research fellow at the newly established Centre for Contemporary Cultural Studies (CCCS) at the University of Birmingham. He became director in 1968 and guided the CCCS through a hectic period that saw the introduction of innovative approaches to culture, politics and society. With never more than three staff members, two research fellows and forty postgraduate students, the work produced here, much of it collectively, was crucial to the development of cultural studies. In another auspicious year, 1979, Hall was appointed professor of sociology at the Open University in order to reach a much broader range of students. In doing so he, along with others, revitalized the core of the subject by making such matters as representation, identity and modernity central to the curriculum.

Hall's thinking has developed in distinct phases. In his discussion of the origins of cultural studies, Hall identifies 'two paradigms' that have been especially important to his own intellectual formation. The first he terms 'culturalism' and is a distinctly British tradition that has its roots in the New Left. It is associated with the approach pioneered by Richard Hoggart in his *The Uses of Literacy*, a nostalgic account of how working-class culture had been undermined by the advent of a 'new mass culture'. Another key influence was the socialist literary critic Raymond Williams, who crucially regarded 'culture', in contrast to the elitist 'selective tradition', as 'a particular way of life', a view that he set out in such books as *Culture and Society* and *The Long Revolution*. Also pivotal was the Marxist social historian Edward (E. P.) Thompson. In particular, his *Making of the English Working Class* provided a 'history from below' that clearly understood culture as 'a way of struggle'. The combined contributions of Hoggart, Williams and Thompson enabled a more democratic understanding of culture and emphasized the creativity of individuals in making history.

Hall's early work is clearly influenced by culturalism, but by the end of the 1960s he and others at the CCCS were dissatisfied with it and turned to a new body of theory emerging across the Channel. This was 'structuralism', the second paradigm identified by Hall. It is a product of European thinkers and was incorporated into the CCCS as a way of overcoming the defects in culturalism. Culturalism, as a form of analysis, was seen as theoretically naïve and regressively humanistic through its concentration on individual experience and a broader failure to understand the 'cultural totality'. To overcome these limitations, those at CCCS turned to a number of Continental theorists, including the structuralist anthropologist **Claude Lévi-Strauss**, who had adopted methods used in the study of language to understand the practices of 'primitive' societies. The structuralist philosopher **Louis Althusser** played a central role in renewing Marxism through advocating an 'anti-humanist' and 'rigorously scientific' form that could effectively challenge the Stalinist distortion of Marxism. Behind the influence of Althusser was the earlier work of the Italian communist Antonio Gramsci, whose concept of hegemony – the uneven process by which ruling classes secure the consent of the dominated – perhaps had the greatest influence on Hall's work.

A clear indication of this shift is in Hall's work on the media in the early 1970s, which displays the influences of structuralism and semiotics. His analysis of news photographs, for instance, draws on **Roland Barthes** to explain how 'the rhetoric of connotation saturates the world of events with ideological meanings' and to signal a break with the orthodox mass-communication approaches then common in sociology. Hall's seminal paper on 'Encoding/Decoding', which was originally published in 1973, is indebted to Althusser and Gramsci in its attempt to grasp the systematic distortion of media representation. Hall emphasized that the production and consumption of media messages are structurally overdetermined by a range of powerful influences – including the medium used, discursive conventions, signifying codes and institutional constraints. He also highlights the cultural struggle over meaning in classifying different types of audience reading (which he defines as 'preferred', 'negotiated' and 'oppositional' positions that viewers can adopt in relation to the media text).

The most sustained application of the CCCS approach is *Policing the Crisis*, which analyses the hegemonic crisis in Britain that began in the late 1960s and anticipates the victory of Margaret Thatcher's authoritarian 'law and order' programme in the 1979 general election. The book particularly explores the moral panic that developed in Britain during the early 1970s over the phenomenon of mugging. Hall and his colleagues demonstrate how the police, media and judiciary interact to produce ideological closure around the issue. Black youth are cast as the folk devil in police and media portrayals of the archetypal mugger – a scapegoat for all social anxieties produced by the changes to an affluent but destabilized society. The book thereby returned Hall to issues of race in similar ways to his colleague **Paul Gilroy**, who was criticizing the implicit nationalism, ethnic absolutism and 'morbid celebration of England' in the cultural studies project. *Policing the Crisis* also led Hall into a confrontation with the politics of Thatcherism, which was taken up in much of the next decade in a series of articles in the magazine *Marxism Today*. Hall coined the influential term 'authoritarian populism' to describe the distinctive combination of popular social conservatism and free-market economics that the Thatcher project aggressively invoked. Hall argued that it is only by understanding the deep shift to authoritarianism at a popular level that the political Left could begin to think about contesting Thatcherism in these 'new times'.

It is clear that by the mid-1980s Hall had once again rethought his theoretical position. Although continuing to insist on the relevance of hegemony, representation and signification, he turned from a preoccupation with class and ideology to the 'politics of difference' and 'hyphenated identity'. A vocabulary borrowed from Jacques Derrida, **Michel Foucault**, Jacques Lacan and **Edward Said** looms large in this more recent work, albeit articulated from a Gramscian standpoint. In his account of 'new ethnicities' he argues for 'an awareness of the black experience as a *diaspora* experience, and the consequences which this carries for the process of unsettling, recombination, hybridization and "cut and mix" – in short, the process of cultural *diaspora-ization*'. Hall's account of 'hybridity' is critical of claims that forms of national identity are unified and integrated; hence his insistence that the category of 'black subject' can no longer serve as the basis of identity politics under these fragmented circumstances.

In the years since his retirement in 1997, Hall has continued to produce insightful articles, including a penetrating critique of the Blair government that recalls his earlier formidable analyses of Thatcherism. Ironically, some have argued that New Labour has learned the lessons of Hall's critique only too well. Given their provocative stature, Hall's ideas have been subjected to some fierce objections over the years. E. P. Thompson's *The Poverty of Theory* attacked the abstract, rigid and mechanical formulations of structuralist analysis. Bob Jessop argued that Hall's characterization of authoritarian populism over-emphasized ideology at the expense of economy. The most serious criticism of Hall's work overall is what Chris Rojek calls 'slippage': how he tends to take up new and fashionable positions that then leave gaping holes in his own conceptual framework that he conveniently ignores by his sophistry. However, this charge does not bear close scrutiny, as the longstanding attachment to Gramsci makes plain. Yet there is a sense in which his movement from positions is a response to recognizing the limits of established ways of thinking and attempting to forge links between them as a model of innovative theoretical practice.

See also: Louis Althusser, Roland Barthes, Michel Foucault, Paul Gilroy, Ernesto Laclau, Claude Lévi-Strauss, Edward Said.

See also in *Fifty Key Sociologists: The Formative Theorists*: Antonio Gramsci, Karl Marx, Ferdinand de Saussure.

Major works

The Popular Arts. 1964. With Paddy Whannel. London: Hutchinson.
'Encoding/Decoding'. 1973. In Stuart Hall, Dorothy Hobson, Andre Lowe and Paul Willis, eds. *Culture, Media, Language: Working Papers in Cultural Studies (1972–1979)*. London: Hutchinson, 1980.
'The Determination of News Photographs'. 1973. In Stan Cohen and Jock Young, eds. *The Manufacture of News*. London: Constable.
Resistance through Rituals: Youth Subcultures in Post-war Britain. 1976. Ed. with Tony Jefferson. London: Routledge.

Policing the Crisis: Mugging, the State and Law and Order. 1978. With Chas Critcher, Tony Jefferson, John Clarke and Brian Roberts. London: Macmillan.

'Cultural Studies: Two Paradigms'. 1980. *Media, Culture and Society* 2.

'Popular Democratic Versus Authoritarian Populism'. 1980. In Alan Hunt, ed. *Marxism and Democracy.* London: Lawrence and Wishart.

The Hard Road to Renewal: Thatcherism and the Crisis of the Left. 1988. London: Verso.

'Minimal Selves'. 1993. In Ann Gray and Jim McGuigan, eds. *Studying Culture.* London: Arnold.

'New Ethnicities'. 1996. In David Morley and Kuan-Hsing Chen, eds. *Stuart Hall: Critical Dialogues in Cultural Studies.* London: Routledge.

'New Labour's Double Shuffle'. 2003. *Soundings*, November.

Some important essays and commentaries can be found in David Morley and Kuan-Hsing Chen, eds. 1996. *Stuart Hall: Critical Dialogues in Cultural Studies.* London: Routledge.

Further reading

'The Formation of a Diasporic Intellectual: An Interview with Stuart Hall by Kuan-Hsing Chen'. 1996. In David Morley and Kuan-Hsing Chen, eds. *Stuart Hall: Critical Dialogues in Cultural Studies.* London: Routledge.

Helen Davis. 2004. *Understanding Stuart Hall.* London: Sage.

James Proctor. 2004. *Stuart Hall.* London: Routledge.

Chris Rojek. 2003. *Stuart Hall.* Cambridge: Polity Press.

EAMONN CARRABINE

DONNA HARAWAY

Donna Jeanne Haraway was born 6 September 1944 and grew up in Denver, Colorado, in a white middle-class Irish-Catholic family. She went to Catholic schools and during her teens remained a committed Catholic. Haraway studied at Colorado College, graduating in 1966. Her educational background is interdisciplinary, as is her academic career. She majored in zoology, with minors in philosophy and English literature. In 1972, she was awarded a PhD in biology from Yale University for her dissertation on *Crystals, Fabrics, and Fields: Metaphors of Organicism in 20th Century Developmental Biology* – a result of her shift in focus from biology as experimental practice to the history and philosophy of biology. In 1974, Haraway became an assistant professor in the Department of the History of Science at Johns

Hopkins University, where she stayed for six years until she was headhunted for the new interdisciplinary and experimental unit at the University of California, Santa Cruz, called the Board in the History of Consciousness.

The unit was at that time in the making under the leadership of literary historian and philosopher Hayden White. White was looking for young scholars who were intellectually prepared to transgress disciplinary borders. He hired Haraway to teach feminist theory and science studies, impressed by her dissertation and by her provocative articles on primatology, sex, gender and race that were published in the renowned feminist journal *Signs*. According to a recent biography by Joseph Schneider, the position Haraway took up at the University of California was the first to be explicitly defined for feminist theory in the USA. Haraway has been part of the Board in the History of Consciousness since then, and from 1984 as a full professor.

As is the case for many of her generation, Haraway has combined political activism, an academic career and a commitment to alternative ways of living. She took part in the anti-Vietnam War movement, and she became a socialist and anti-racist feminist activist in the 1970s; while at Johns Hopkins University she joined the Marxist-feminist Women's Union. Together with a deep interest in the diversity of lifeforms, Marxist feminism and later a critically leftist version of postmodern feminism have been major inspirations for Haraway's scholarly work, political commitments and personal life. How the personal, the theoretical and the political are intertwined for Haraway is highlighted in the interview book *How Like a Leaf*, in which her former PhD student Thyrza Nichols Goodeve interviews her about her life and ideas. Haraway's scholarly work has a wide interdisciplinary scope and is internationally very influential. It has had a major impact, in particular, within the fields of feminist theory, techno-science studies and cultural studies of gender, bodies and technology. Moreover, Haraway has a broad readership outside academia. In particular, her 'cyborg theory' has caught the attention of many readers all over the world.

Her article 'A Cyborg Manifesto' has attained cult status. 'Cyborg' is an abbreviation of '*cyb*ernetic *org*anism' and refers to an organism (human or animal) that is fused with technology, a machine-human or a machine-animal. The term was coined in 1960 as part of early US space research in the context of speculations about the radical redesign of bodies that would make humans and animals fit for life in outer space. The cyborg is also a figure in science fiction such as the protagonist of the *Terminator* films. In 'A Cyborg Manifesto', Haraway appropriates the figure for critical feminist and anti-racist politics and techno-culture studies. She emphasizes that the cyborg should be seen from a multiple perspective. It is, on the one hand, an accomplice of both capitalism and social relations pervaded by all kinds of gendered, racialized, sexualized, class-related inequalities. But, on the other hand, the figure has critical potentials. To expose these potentials, Haraway points out that the figure is neither purely natural nor purely cultural, and neither purely factual nor purely fictional. She underlines its position as a boundary-figure that transgresses borders of nature/culture, body/mind, sex/gender, fact/fiction. In so doing, the cyborg challenges hegemonies and inequalities that have been legitimized by the keeping up of these boundaries. Seen from a feminist point of view, it is, for example, important that the cyborg's boundary position may erode any kind of theoretical foundation for arguments about biological sex as a determinant for unequal gendered positions in culture and society. According to Haraway's cyborg theory, bodies cannot be understood as fixed entities and never legitimize any kinds of socio-cultural constructions of stereotypes. When sexed/gendered bodies are considered as cyborg bodies, they are instead to be seen as fluid networks of words and matter engaged in continuous processes of reconfiguration. To characterize the complex reconfigurations of cyborg bodies, Haraway uses the term 'material-semiotic'. In this way, she underlines that the materiality of bodies and the meanings ascribed to them are intertwined; materiality and meaning-making should not be separated.

Besides the cyborg figure and cyborg feminism, another red thread through Haraway's works is her interest in human–animal relationships. Animals, like the cyborgs, act as boundary-figures between the world of humans and that of non-humans (a category that comprises both animals and machines). An important example is her groundbreaking study of primates, *Primate Visions. Gender, Race, and Nature in the World of Modern Science*. Here she critically scrutinizes how the history of biology can be read as a practice of telling stories of sex, gender and race. Another example is the onco-mouse, the genetically engineered laboratory mouse that was developed for breast cancer research and became the world's first patented animal. OncoMouse appears as a prominent key figure in *Modest_Witness@ Second_Millennium. Female-man _Meets_OncoMouse™*, a book that explores the interplay of such things as stories, dreams, theories and advertising practices. One more example is Haraway's present work on dog–human relationships, on which she recently published yet another 'manifesto', *The Companion Species Manifesto. Dogs, People, and Significant Otherness*.

When a researcher enters into meaningful conversations with boundary-figures, such as cyborgs, primates, OncoMouse and dogs, it is, according to Haraway, necessary to develop new theoretical and methodological approaches, or 'thinking technologies' as she prefers to call them. In so doing, she combines her exquisite skills as a biologist, a literary scholar, a philosopher and a science historian in highly unorthodox and original ways. This makes her texts and her academic writing style very complex and rich in an empirical and theoretical as well as methodological sense.

Haraway is internationally well known for her methodological reflections and for her contributions to epistemological debates within feminism and postmodernism. In particular, her article 'Situated Knowledge: The Science Question in Feminism and the Privilege of Partial Perspective' has been crucial for reflections on the politics of location of knowledge production. Haraway argues forcefully that knowledge production is not universal. It should instead be reflected as part of specific local contexts and always seen as carried out by embodied subjects with only partial access to reality. Contrary to a classic relativist postmodernism, Haraway also makes a plea for a reclaiming of objectivity. Based in a reflection on her or his situatedness and on the specific view it opens, the researcher should commit her- or himself to give as objective an account of reality as it is possible from her or his always partial position.

See also: Judith Butler, Shulamith Firestone.

Major works

Crystals, Fabrics, and Fields: Metaphors of Organicism in 20th Century Developmental Biology. 1976. New Haven, CT: Yale University Press. Republished under the title Crystals, Fabrics, and Fields: Metaphors that Shape Embryos. Berkeley, CA: North Atlantic Press, 2004.

'A Cyborg Manifesto: Science, Technology, and Socialist-Feminism in the Late Twentieth Century'. 1985. Socialist Review 80.

'Situated Knowledge: The Science Question in Feminism and the Privilege of Partial Perspective'. 1988. Feminist Studies 14.

Primate Visions. Gender, Race, and Nature in the World of Modern Science. 1989. London: Routledge.

Simians, Cyborgs, and Women. The Reinvention of Nature. (Essays from 1978–89). London: Free Association Books, 1991.

'The Promises of Monsters: A Regenerative Politics for Inappropriate/d Others'. In Lawrence Grossberg, Cary Nelson and Paula A. Treichler, eds. Cultural Studies. London and New York: Routledge, 1992.

Modest_Witness@Second_Millennium. FemaleMan_Meets_OncoMouse^{TM}. 1996. London: Routledge.

The Companion Species Manifesto. Dogs, People, and Significant Otherness. 2003. Chicago: Prickly Paradigm Press.

Various extracts are reprinted in *The Haraway Reader.* London: Routledge, 2004.

Further reading

'Cyborgs, Coyotes and Dogs: A Kinship of Feminist Figurations, and There Are Always More Things Going on Than You Thought! Methodologies as Thinking Technologies. An Interview with Donna Haraway by Nina Lykke, Randi Markussen and Finn Olesen'. 2004. In Donna Haraway, *The Haraway Reader.* London: Routledge.

Donna J. Haraway and Thyrza N. Goodeve. 2000. *How Like a Leaf. Donna J. Haraway. An Interview with Thyrza Nichols Goodeve.* London: Routledge.

Joseph Schneider. 2005. *Donna Haraway: Live Theory.* London: Continuum.

NINA LYKKE

GEORGE HOMANS

George Homans was born in 1910 into a family of 'Boston Brahmins' – the long-established and highly educated Boston families of British descent. His ancestors arrived in America in colonial times and established themselves as successful East Coast professionals. Many generations of his male ancestors attended Harvard and two had been presidents of the United States. As Homans makes clear in his autobiography, his attitudes and sympathies tended to be those of the upper class. He had little time for romantic, wishful-thinking liberals or radicals, but on the other hand he volunteered for service before America joined the Second World War and spent much of the war on active service in command of smaller naval vessels.

Like his father, and his father before him, Homans was a Harvard undergraduate. Apart from war service (and a period of unemployment after graduating during the Great Depression), he spent the whole of his adult career at Harvard as fellow, instructor and professor. A career at Harvard for a Boston Brahmin was scarcely exceptional, but a career as a sociologist was more surprising. It was largely accidental. He had majored in English literature as an undergraduate and had aspirations to be a poet but, while unemployed, was asked by Lawrence Henderson (professor of biological chemistry but with wide-ranging intellectual interests, including system theory) to help him organize a seminar series on the great Italian sociologist Vilfredo Pareto. Elton Mayo, Fritz Roethlisberger, **Talcott Parsons**, **Robert Merton** and (briefly) Pitirim Sorokin were also participants in the seminar. Homans subsequently was asked to help Charles Curtis to write an introduction to Pareto's work for an American audience, and duly obliged. Henderson next suggested that he apply for election to the newly formed Society of Fellows as a sociologist, and his career as a sociologist was thus established.

The main intellectual influence on Homans at this stage of his career was neither Sorokin nor Parsons but Elton Mayo. Mayo was a psychologist at the Harvard Graduate School of Business Administration and directed what was to become the classic 'Hawthorne Study', with its famous studies of the Relay Assembly Test Room and the Bank Wiring Observation Room. Mayo was a founder of the human relations school of industrial psychology and was particularly interested in the social relationships that developed in small groups. He encouraged Homans to carry out fieldwork in this kind of setting himself and stimulated the interests (reinforced by his experiences of small groups on board ship in the navy) that were to culminate in Homans' first major book, *The Human Group*.

In *The Human Group* Homans took five existing case studies of small groups, such as Roethlisberger and Dickson's report of the Bank Wiring Observation Room and William F. Whyte's study of street corner society, and reanalysed them using his own conceptual framework of actions, sentiments, interactions and norms. From these reanalyses he developed generalizations (or, as he terms them, analytical hypotheses) that broadly apply to all the groups studied. Thus, for example, he suggested that the frequency of interaction between people strengthens their sentiments of liking for one another and that the more nearly equal in social rank a number of people are, the more frequently they will interact with one another. What Homans was attempting to establish was that, while the content of behaviour may vary from one context to another (reflecting the nature of the particular constraints provided by the external environment), there were nonetheless regularities in the form of relationships between variables that were common across all settings. In this respect there are strong similarities between his programme and that of Georg Simmel and the latter's analysis of the common features of interaction in small groups.

Homans' work on the human group also led him to embrace a particular account of the nature of scientific explanation and a distinctive programme for (his) sociology. His view, described in his short book on *The Nature of Social Science*, was that the 'covering law' view of scientific explanation, by Hempel and others, applied to sociology as much as to the other sciences and social sciences. A sociological explanation should therefore utilize general propositions (such as the regularities suggested in *The Human Group*) plus specific conditions to derive logically the explanandum (that which is to be explained). More controversially he saw these general propositions as primarily psychological. He owned up to being a psychological reductionist: human behaviour was to be explained by psychological regularities that were, he held, largely invariant across cultures and societies.

It should be noted in passing that Homans' view of sociological explanation was fundamentally different from that of his Harvard colleague Talcott Parsons, whose work he regarded as in essence classificatory rather than explanatory and which he did not regard as warranting the title theory. He also had fundamental intellectual objections to the teleological functionalism that Parsons advocated.

Homans' programme, then, was a scientific one which we might now describe as one looking for the micro-foundations of social behaviour or for the explanatory mechanisms that underlie sociological regularities. The fullest exemplification of this programme came in *Social Behaviour: Its Elementary Forms*. In this work he revisited many of the themes first addressed in *The Human Group* — influence, conformity to norms, esteem and liking — but he also added distributive justice. He suggested that propositions about justice, such as proportionality of rewards and costs, could be derived from the more fundamental propositions of behavioural psychology. Homans recognized that many of these fundamental propositions had strong similarities with the rational choice propositions of micro-economics, and the language he used to describe these fundamental propositions is couched in terms of rewards and costs, much as in economics. However, drawing on behavioural psychology gave him access to a wider range of propositions that enabled him to include sentiments and emotions (such as the anger that arises when principles of justice are violated) as well as behaviour.

Homans' approach came to be known as exchange theory (a label he had himself given it in his article 'Social Behaviour as Exchange', although he later regretted this). The term 'exchange' was correct in signalling that the theory was, in part, about social interaction conceived as an exchange of services broadly defined. However, 'exchange' suggests an economic analogy, and while the economic analogy was strong in Peter Blau's contemporary version of exchange theory, it played a somewhat lesser role in Homans' version.

In practice, the economic analogy has proved to be more influential in sociology since Homans' death in 1989 than has been Homans' own version of behavioural psychology. Economists such as Gary Becker have straightforwardly applied economic models to sociological topics such as fertility choices and the household division of labour, and sociologists such as James Coleman have used rational choice as the micro-foundations for sociological theory. In one sense Homans was an important forerunner of Coleman's work by insisting on the need for a rigorous and explanatory micro-sociology and by resisting the tide of grand abstract typologizing characteristic of Talcott Parsons' work. Homans would, however, have been disappointed by the rather narrow conception of rational action that Coleman and his followers have adopted as their foundation for social theory. He would have reminded us about the large range of social phenomena, such as sentiments of liking, esteem and patriotism, and principles of social justice that economic modelling cannot explain. Homans' greatest impact in fact has probably been in social psychology and on the empirical study of social justice, rather than on mainstream sociology.

See also: Talcott Parsons.

See also in *Fifty Key Sociologists: The Formative Theorists*: Vilfredo Pareto, Georg Simmel, Lloyd Warner.

Major works

An Introduction to Pareto. 1934. With Charles Curtis. New York: Alfred A. Knopf.
English Villagers of the Thirteenth Century. 1941. Cambridge, MA: Harvard University Press.
The Human Group. 1950. New York: Harcourt Brace.
Marriage, Authority, and Final Causes: A Study of Unilateral Cross-Cousin Marriage. 1955. Glencoe, IL: Free Press.
Sentiments and Activities: Essays in Social Science. (Essays of 1946–59.) New York: Free Press of Glencoe, 1962.
Social Behaviour: Its Elementary Forms. 1961. New York: Harcourt Brace & World. Revised edn New York: Harcourt Brace Jovanovich, 1974.
The Nature of Social Science. 1967. New York: Harcourt Brace.
Coming to My Senses: Autobiography of a Sociologist. 1985. New Brunswick, NJ: Transaction.
Certainties and Doubts. (Essays of 1962–85.) New Brunswick, NJ: Transaction, 1987.

Further reading

James S. Coleman. 1990. *Foundations of Social Theory.* Cambridge, MA: The Belknap Press of Harvard University Press.

J. Greenberg and Ronald L. Cohen, eds. 1982. *Equity and Justice in Social Behaviour.* New York: Academic Press.

Robert L. Hamblin and John H. Kunkel, eds. 1977. *Behavioural Theory in Sociology: Essays in Honor of George C Homans.* New Brunswick, NJ: Transaction Books.

A. F. Heath. 1976. *Rational Choice and Social Exchange: A Critique of Exchange Theory.* Cambridge: Cambridge University Press.

Charles Tilly. 1990. 'George Caspar Homans and the Rest of Us'. *Theory and Society* 19.

ANTHONY HEATH

C. L. R. JAMES

The race question is subsidiary to the class question in politics, and to think of imperialism in terms of race is disastrous. But to neglect the racial factor as merely incidental is an error only less grave than to make it fundamental.

(*Black Jacobins*)

What James meant by this statement is that while a phenomenon such as slavery is best explained primarily in economic terms (the enslavement of Africans was a solution to the labour needs of the European capitalists who conquered the territories of the so-called New World) racism is also crucially important. Racist ideologies were developed and articulated more systematically during slavery and continue to have a powerful influence upon people's thinking that can be more significant than economics: think of stereotypes of black sexuality and sport. In all his work, he tackled profound and enduring constraints upon the efforts of humans to realize their full potential.

Cyril Lionel Robert James (generally known as C. L. R. James) was a man of letters, a social and cultural critic, historian, sports writer and journalist, playwright and novelist, and a labour organizer and political activist. Many said that he was obsessed with English literature and with cricket. His knowledge drew upon a vast array of literature, including Shakespeare and Melville, Marx and Trotsky, DuBois and Garvey. All who met him were disarmed by his incredible knowledge of the European literary classics and by the ease with which he moved between them, the political writings of Marx and the pan-Africanist writings of W. E. B. DuBois. He had an uncanny ability to reconcile the traditional and the radical. His writing style reflected his keen perception and incredible memory, his sense of the dramatic and his ability to craft his prose with the deft hand of a novelist – most notably in the metaphors and images that he conjured up to communicate his ideas. His work on history and on Marxism and pan-Africanism drew upon sociology and contributed much to its development. His central concerns were with inequality and class relations, colonialism and capitalism and race relations. Underlying all his work was a concern with the relationship between individual freedom and social life. Marxism, pan-Africanism and culture were the domains in which he explored this relationship.

Reading James' biography is fascinating. It is more like an adventure story than a typical academic biography. He interacted with communists in the United States and anti-colonial nationalists in Britain, moved between continents with ease, was arrested, imprisoned and deported, visited the Soviet Union and China, and debated with Trotsky. His friends were imprisoned for anti-colonial insurrection. When they got out of jail they became presidents of independent African nations and turned to him for advice.

James was born in the eastern Caribbean island of Trinidad in 1901, when Trinidad and Tobago was still a colony of Great Britain. Benefiting from a public school education, he began as an English teacher in a school and then became an emerging novelist. His first publication was a short story – *La Divina Pastora* – published in 1927. He went to England in the 1930s to pursue a writing career, but one of his first jobs was as a cricket correspondent in Lancashire. His first political book, *The Life of Captain Cipriani*, was published in 1932 and concerned the nature of colonialism. At the end of the book, James called for West Indian independence. During this decade he immersed himself in both Marxism and pan-Africanism, and was politically active in both arenas. At the end of the 1930s he went to the United States on a speaking tour and he continued his writing and political organizing. On this occasion he stayed there until 1952, when he was expelled.

His most important works are *The Black Jacobins* and *Beyond a Boundary*. *The Black Jacobins* is a history of the slave revolt in the nineteenth century on the Caribbean island of San Domingo, which established the independent republic of Haiti in 1803. James began the prologue to the book in his characteristic concise and compelling manner: 'Christopher Columbus landed first in the New World at the island of San Salvador, and after praising God enquired urgently for gold'. He described the various racial power groups on the island, the relations between them, and the circumstances and unfolding of the revolt. Led by Toussaint L'Ouverture, this was the most successful slave revolt in the history of the New World and the only one to set up an independent black nation. In this book, James turned his attention to a topic typically neglected by mainstream analysts of social change, who usually kept their eyes focused resolutely on Europe and white people, and he showed the ways in which marginalized peoples – in this instance, black people on the periphery of the French Empire – could directly shape the fortunes of the Empire itself. More than this, he also demonstrated how black human agency – black people acting on their own behalf to achieve goals – can create wide-reaching and long-lasting effects. The consequences of an independent Haiti reverberated throughout France, the British Empire and the USA.

In *Beyond a Boundary* his distinctive contribution lies in the way in which he brought popular cultural phenomena usually ignored by academics, such as cricket and calypso music, to the forefront of his social and cultural analysis, providing histories and demonstrating their importance in the construction and growth of social institutions and ideologies. Most notably, he took cricket – which to the non-British world was, and is, an idiosyncratic and inscrutable form of upper-class sport – and articulated its role in colonial and postcolonial cultural relations. Contemporary analysts of other forms of popular culture, such as music, television, sport and fashion, would gain greatly from his conceptual and theoretical contributions.

James wrote on many other topics, including Marxism, pan-Africanism and black studies, as well as art, aesthetics and American civilization. He published essays or books on dialectical materialism, world revolution and class struggle. He was a member of a small but significant group of Marxist writers in the United States in the 1930s and beyond who criticized the Stalinist Soviet Union and were much influenced by Trotskyite writings. He envisaged a future organization of society based on socialist values, but he also saw the communitarian values of African societies, and the numerical superiority of Africans, as basic constituents of such a society. His writings revealed many attempts to link Marxist analyses of the struggles of working-class people with pan-African analyses of blacks in the West and the colonies. He also published plays, wrote novels and was a sports reporter. His publications on American civilization examined American writers like Whitman and Melville, and took up the issues of individualism, freedom and the struggle for happiness.

James worked hard as a pan-Africanist. He campaigned in anti-colonial struggles and independence movements, for example, and quickly established an organization called the International Friends of Abyssinia after that country (now Ethiopia) was invaded by Mussolini in the 1930s. In the United States he helped organize African-American sharecroppers – farmers subordinated and exploited through a farming system that left them in greater and greater debt each year. He also worked towards West Indian independence and the creation of a West Indian Federation – a Federation that would join the many West Indians islands into one political, economic and social organization. The former was eventually realized during his lifetime; the latter is yet to happen. Like other prominent black intellectuals of his time, he travelled ceaselessly, exploring the African diaspora and visiting capitalist and communist countries for concrete experience of the theoretical issues about which he had read. He spent more than forty years in the Caribbean, a total of twenty-five in the United States and at least twenty-five in Britain, with extensive travelling from wherever he lived.

He interacted with the soon-to-be presidents of many British colonies: Jomo Kenyatta in Kenya, Kwame Nkrumah in Ghana and Eric Williams in Trinidad and Tobago were colleagues or friends. When Nkrumah went to England in the 1940s on his quest to liberate Ghana (then named the Gold Coast) from colonial rule, it was James who provided him with a letter of introduction to prominent black nationalists living there. Few scholars can claim such influence outside the academy. This influence did not go unnoticed and he was constantly under threat from the British authorities for his anti-colonial activities and from the American authorities for his socialist ideals. He was arrested and interned on Ellis Island in 1952 by the American government, and was later expelled from the country.

After his expulsion from the United States, James spent time in the Caribbean and lectured in Europe. In the 1970s, he returned to the United States, where he lectured for ten years. James spent his final years in London, living on Railton Road, which was home to the Brixton riots of 1981. Though he had no direct part in these riots, he offered many insights into them. He died in 1989 and was buried in Trinidad and Tobago.

See also: Stuart Hall.

See also in *Fifty Key Sociologists: The Formative Theorists*: W. E. B. DuBois, Karl Marx.

Major works

The Black Jacobins: Toussaint L'Ouverture and the San Domingo Revolution.
1938. Harmondsworth: Penguin, 2001.
Notes on Dialectics: Hegel, Marx and Lenin. 1948. New York: Lexington
Books, 2004
*Mariners, Renegades and Castaways: The Story of Herman Melville and the World
We Live in.* 1953. London: Allison and Busby, 1985.
Beyond a Boundary. 1963. London: Yellow Jersey Press, 2005.

Further reading

Paul Buhle. 1988. *C.L.R. James. The Artist as Revolutionary.* London: Verso.
Kent Worcester. 1996. *C.L.R. James. A Political Biography.* Albany, NY: State
University of New York Press.
James D. Young. 1999. *The World of C.L.R. James. The Unfragmented Vision.*
Glasgow: Clydeside Press.

STEPHEN SMALL

MELANIE KLEIN

A key figure in the psychoanalytic tradition, Melanie Klein is widely
regarded as one of the most influential of the 'post-Freudian' thinkers. She is famously associated with a particular branch of psychoanalysis called object relations, which focuses on the relationships
formed between images, ideas and feelings in the mind and people or
objects in the external world. Klein also pioneered a method of child
psychoanalysis called the play technique, which continues to be used
today. She was born Melanie Riezes in Vienna in 1882, trained in
Budapest and then moved to London, where she remained until her
death in 1960.

Writing in the mid-twentieth century, Klein could not help but be
influenced by the work of Sigmund Freud, but her theories differed
from his in a number of ways. First, whereas Freud had presented a
topographical model of the psyche as divided into id, ego and
superego, Klein believed that the secret of psychoanalysis lay in
understanding the ego. Indeed, her approach is often referred to as
'ego psychology'. Second, Klein disagreed with Freud's assumption
that the unconscious part of the mind was inaccessible to the analyst.
She argued that the unconscious consists of instincts and their associated emotions that are expressed in all forms of human behaviour.

Third, whereas Freud believed that the child progressed through several sequential *stages* of 'psycho-sexual' development, Klein referred to two recurring *positions* that people continue to adopt throughout their lives. Children and adults could be understood in the same way, she said, because the roots of ego development are laid down during early infancy.

It was this latter assertion that led Klein to develop a new technique of psychotherapy based upon play. If children and adults are driven by similar unconscious conflicts, she thought, then each could benefit from psychoanalysis. However, Klein recognized that younger children and those with autistic disorders might have difficulty in expressing themselves verbally, and so she devised an alternative way in which such patients could communicate their thoughts and feelings. In the clinical consultation room, Klein would provide children with generic toys and materials, such as dolls, model cars, pencils, paper and paintbrushes, and she would encourage them to create whatever they liked. She would sit and watch them play, asking occasional questions to find out what kind of symbolic meanings the child was imputing to these objects. Klein believed that play had latent, as well as manifest, content that revealed the child's unconscious feelings. For example, a young girl, 'Trude', played by pretending to attack her analyst and search for doll figures inside her stomach. Klein suggested that this symbolized her jealousy towards a new baby sibling who was demanding her mother's attention.

Much of Klein's work explored the ways in which infants experience and relate to their social environment. She argued that humans are born with a set of basic drives or instincts that shape their perception of other people and objects. In particular, human nature involves a conflict between the life and death instincts, or good and bad, and their associated emotions: love, hate, guilt, anxiety, rage and envy. Klein suggested that infants learn to reconcile these conflicting drives in the inner world through their interactions with the outside world. The process of breastfeeding was significant in this respect, as it gave infants their first encounter with an external object that could be both satisfying and frustrating. The way in which this conflict is resolved shapes a person's approach to future relationships.

Central to this process of relating one's inner and outer worlds is the notion of 'phantasy'. Klein suggested that infants create a phantasy inner world of images and representations of objects in the real world to help relate to them. Unconscious emotional conflicts are first played out on phantasy objects in the inner world and then projected on to real people in the outside world. Toys are important in this regard because they also symbolize real objects, and so during play therapy the child might reveal their unconscious phantasies through the way that they treat their toys.

These emotional conflicts are also expressed throughout later life. Klein argued, for example, that feelings of envy represent an everyday manifestation of the death instinct. In contrast to jealousy, which involves wanting something that you love, envy involves anger and bitterness as the desired object is defensively pushed away. There is a feeling of 'sour grapes' as we tell ourselves that we do not want what we cannot have: the expensive dress is 'not that nice anyway', or the celebrity lifestyle 'must be quite miserable'.

Klein suggested that the process of ego development involved two positions, which emerge first in infancy but also recur throughout an individual's life. In the *paranoid-schizoid* position, a baby fears the consequence of its own destructive impulses and so refuses to acknowledge these feelings as its own. This involves the defence mechanisms of 'splitting' one's good and bad experiences and 'projecting' the latter on to objects in the outside world. For example, a baby might believe that her 'good' mother is a separate object from the 'bad' breast that refuses to feed her.

In the *depressive* position, however, the infant can recognize that the same love object can be both good and bad, and so learns to integrate these experiences into the self. It begins to tolerate deprivation when needs are not satisfied, and can retain an internal image of the mother in the absence of its 'real' equivalent. This is also the point at which infants fear that events they had wished for in their phantasies might affect objects in the real world: rage against the 'bad' part of a parent, for example, might also damage the 'good' parts of that person. Klein saw this creating feelings of guilt and anxiety, and consequent attempts to make reparation for any damage. In later life, this position also helps in the process of mourning, as a lost object can be 'introjected' back into the self through memories and internal images. Nevertheless, adopting this position can involve feelings of disappointment, as people realize that 'no one is perfect' and that 'happiness never lasts'. Learning to live with ambivalent feelings of love and hate, gratitude and envy, anger and guilt is all part of human development, Klein believed, and so the healthy mind is one that can integrate all of these elements.

Klein's theories are also prone to criticism, of course. Neville Symington argues that Klein referred to generic 'objects' in the world without considering the specific nature of these objects. She did not consider, for example, how mothers feel towards the infants they feed and how this might affect the interaction between them. Klein is also guilty of identifying mothers as the main caregivers (although at the time of her writing this was normally the case) and neglecting the role of fathers and other role models. Nevertheless, her work does succeed in developing Freud's work in significant ways: by focusing on ego development rather than infantile sexuality, by recognizing the similarities between the emotional worlds of adults and children, and by pioneering the technique of play therapy. Klein has had an enormous influence upon twentieth-century writers such as Juliet Mitchell, Hanna Segal and Ian Craib, and her ideas continue to hold relevance today.

See also in *Fifty Key Sociologists: The Formative Theorists*: Sigmund Freud.

Major works

Klein's work since the 1920s has been brought together in *The Collected Works of Melanie Klein*. 1975. London: Hogarth Press and Institute of Psychoanalysis:

Vol. I: Love, Guilt and Reparation, and Other Works.
Vol. II: The Psycho-Analysis of Children.
Vol. III: Envy and Gratitude, and Other Works.
Vol. IV: Narrative of a Child Analysis.

Some extracts from her work can be found in Juliet Mitchell, ed. *The Selected Melanie Klein*. London: Penguin, 1986.

Further reading

Ian Craib. *The Importance of Disappointment*. London: Routledge, 1994.
Hanna Segal. *Melanie Klein*. London: Sage, 1992.
Neville Symington. *The Analytic Experience: Lectures from the Tavistock*. London: Free Association Books, 1986.

SUSIE SCOTT

VIOLA KLEIN

Viola Klein, a pioneer in the sociology of women, was one of the many refugees from Europe under Nazi control who contributed to the development of British post-war sociology. Her contribution lay both in her original theoretical work on the social construction of purportedly scientific knowledge about women and in her contribution as social researcher to the development of better empirical knowledge about women's changing position in society and the labour market.

Viola Klein was born in Vienna in 1908 into a progressive Jewish household that valued learning and intellectual independence for women. Political unrest forced her and her family to move to Prague. She studied for a year at the Sorbonne in Paris and for a brief and politically turbulent period at Vienna University. In Czechoslovakia she worked as assistant editor on a political weekly and became a graduate student in languages, psychology and philosophy at Prague University, writing a doctoral dissertation on the linguistic style of the modernist French author Louis-Ferdinand Celine. His dark and stylistically revolutionary novel *Journey to the End of Night* (1932) was a literary sensation in its verbally blunt exposure of French and American working-class life during the First World War and the ensuing Depression. To her thesis Klein brought her knowledge of philosophy and linguistics and, more importantly for her future work, her readings of Karl Mannheim's early works on the sociology of knowledge and the importance of the social context in understanding changing ideologies. She was already, as a young, independent and politically progressive student, interested in the 'woman question', particularly as presented in psychology and psychoanalysis. During this period she visited the Soviet Union, which led to several later articles in the British press on marriage, the family, the persistence of prostitution and the gap between Soviet official egalitarian gender ideology and the day-to-day reality for many women. Around the same time as Klein gained her doctoral award, Celine published the first of a series of aggressively anti-Semitic political pamphlets which led to his post-war exile from France and imprisonment in Denmark in 1945, and she never in her later writings referred to Celine or her thesis again. As the German armies advanced on Prague in 1938, Klein and her brother fled to England, leaving both parents behind to perish in concentration camps.

England was not overly welcoming to Continental refugees and Klein initially found herself working as a domestic servant to support herself. A scholarship by the Czech government-in-exile enabled her to enrol for a second doctorate at the London School of Economics (LSE). Being already familiar with his work, she wrote to Mannheim, by then also a refugee academic working at the LSE, asking him to become her supervisor. He agreed and her second thesis was completed in 1944 and published in 1946 under the title *The Feminine Character: History of an Ideology* as one of the first volumes in the long-running series the 'International Library of Sociology', published by

Routledge and Kegan Paul and edited by Mannheim until his death in 1947.

Klein's second thesis was a theoretically groundbreaking work in the sociology of knowledge and a detailed critical investigation of psychological, biological, psychoanalytical, anthropological and sociological 'scientific' conceptions of 'femininity'. Though it was a theoretical analysis, rather than a political one, Klein's feminist credentials were laid out from the start when she asked what the effects have been on women's personality of persistent inferior social status and what characteristics they have in common with other suppressed or minority groups. One such characteristic, she argued, is that of being socially constructed as a stereotype, in this case of 'femininity', and judged as intellectually and emotionally inferior and dependent by thinkers whose theories about women are more influenced by a male-dominated culture than by the quality of their empirical evidence. Upon publication the book was criticized for its militant feminism, for its 'sternly masculine objectivity' and for encouraging women to go to work and thereby undermine their own sex. Her serious attempt at the sociology of knowledge was, she felt, seriously ignored and misunderstood. In the light of such criticisms, and in the growing competition for academic work generated by men returning from the war, her search for an academic post proved futile until 1964, when, late in life, she gained a lectureship at Reading University. Her continuous search for sources of income led to a succession of posts as a government translator of captured German documents and later as a researcher. She supplemented her income with editorial work and writings for both the British and the German press. As a researching civil servant, retaining her association with the LSE, she became responsible for, amongst other things, major innovative research reports on the changing patterns of female employment in Britain.

By the early 1950s, Klein's reputation as a feminist writer and researcher of women had spread amongst international women's organizations. She was approached by Alva Myrdal, a Swedish social scientist and feminist activist who was internationally known for her contribution, in collaboration with her husband, Gunnar Myrdal, to the early developments of the woman-friendly Swedish welfare state. Alva Myrdal was at the time working in Paris as director of UNESCO's Department of Social Science and sought Klein's collaboration on a book to present a comparative picture of the labour market position and domestic situation of women in Sweden, Germany, France and the US. The ensuing work, *Women's Two Roles: Home and Work*, was published in 1956 and translated into many languages. It became a classic in women's sociology, albeit much criticized by later waves of feminism for its failure to address the problem of the absence of men from the domestic sphere. It was also reviled for its assumptions about children's need for their mothers, and mothers' for their children, during crucial periods their lives. Alva Myrdal contributed her political visions of practical policy solutions to women's dilemmas over how to manage work and family commitments, and Klein contributed her theoretical academic knowledge and her research skills in assembling detailed and complex empirical information into comparative tables. At the time, international databases on women were non-existent and international comparative empirical sociology was in its infancy. Both women shared the desire actively to communicate their thoughts on the rights of women with ordinary readers and to make a difference through popular dissemination of information and ideas. When the book was later republished in Germany, Klein went on lecture tours there and was received in the press as a feminist radical advocating that women leave their husbands and children in their search for work.

In 1960, Viola Klein became active in the International Sociological Association and a founder member of the editorial board of the *International Journal of Comparative Sociology*, for which she wrote on married women in employment, a subject pursued with the support of the Institute of Personnel Management. She also worked for the Organization for Economic Cooperation and Development in Paris, for which she assembled information about women's working hours and services from twenty-one countries, exposing the inequalities and hardships universally experienced by working women. Her various reports on British women were assembled in her book *British Married Women Workers*. Having abandoned her skills as a theorist in favour of income-generating research work, though never abandoning her interest in women, she now faced sociological criticism for her uncritical empiricism.

In her final post as a full-time academic, she embraced teaching and postgraduate supervision with great passion and commitment. She continued to have contacts with German friends and colleagues, and she wrote a major overview for a German sociological audience of post-war developments in British sociology, emphasizing its empirical nature and its closeness to social policy formation. In 1971, *The Feminist Character* was republished in Britain, and in America the year after. To her own surprise and excitement, her original theoretical work on intellectual constructions of women was rediscovered by a new generation of feminists critical of the power of men over knowledge about them. A further edition was published in Britain in 1989, ensuring its reputation as a major sociological work. Tragically, Viola Klein died in 1973, shortly after her retirement, leaving her dreams for more time to pursue further research and writing on women unfulfilled.

See also: Ann Oakley.

See also in *Fifty Key Sociologists: The Formative Theorists*: Karl Mannheim, Gunnar Myrdal.

Major works

Stil und Sprache des Louis Ferdinand Celine. 1937. PhD thesis: University of Prague. Reading University: Viola Klein Archive.
The Feminine Character: History of an Ideology. 1938. London: Routledge & Kegan Paul.
'The Stereotype of Femininity'. 1950. *Journal of Social Issues* 6(3).
'*Women's Two Roles: Home and Work*'. 1956. With Alva Myrdal. London: Routledge & Kegan Paul.
'Married Women in Employment'. 1960. *International Journal of Comparative Sociology* 1, September.
Employing Married Women. 1961 Occasional Papers, No. 17. London: Institute of Personnel Management.
'Industrialisation and the Changing Role of Women'. 1963–4. *Current Sociology* 12.
Britain's Married Women Workers. 1965. London: Routledge & Kegan Paul.
Women Workers: Working Hours and Services: A Survey of 21 Countries. 1965. Paris: Organisation for Economic Cooperation and Development.
'The Demand for Professional Woman Power'. 1966. *British Journal of Sociology* 17(2).
'Die gegenwartige Situation der Soziologie in Grossbrittanien'. 1967. In G. Eisermann, ed. *Die gegenwartige Situation der Soziologie*. Stuttgart: Enke.

Further reading

Mary Jo Deegan, ed. 1991. *Women in Sociology: A Bio-Bibliographical Sourcebook*. New York: Greenwood Press.
Janet Sayers. 1989. 'Introduction'. In V. Klein. *The Feminine Character: History of an Ideology*. London: Routledge.
Dale Spender. 1983. 'On Whose Authority? Viola Klein (?–1973)'. In Dale Spender. *Women of Ideas and What Men Have Done to Them*. London: Arc.

E. STINA LYON

ERNESTO LACLAU

The Argentinean social and political theorist Ernesto Laclau, born in 1936, currently teaches at the University of Essex and at various universities in the United States. He is the foremost exponent of a distinctively 'post-Marxist' approach to social analysis. He has drawn on currents within poststructuralist thought (such as Jacques Derrida and **Michel Foucault**), the post-analytical philosophy of Ludwig Wittgenstein and the psychoanalysis of Jacques Lacan to elaborate a novel political concept of 'discourse'. His work can be divided into three basic phases: first, an attempt to develop a Marxist theory of ideology and politics by drawing upon the work of Antonio Gramsci and Louis Althusser; second, the development of a post-Marxist theory of hegemony that incorporates poststructuralist philosophy and breaks decisively with the residual determinism and essentialism of the Marxist paradigm; third, the further development of this post-Marxist approach through a deeper engagement with Derrida's deconstructionist philosophy and Lacan's interpretation of Freudian psychoanalysis. His work is central to understanding and explaining the emergence and dissolution of political ideologies and, at the normative level, in advocating what he, with Chantal Mouffe, calls a project for a radical and plural democracy.

In *Politics and Ideology in Marxist Theory*, as the title suggests, Laclau seeks to furnish a theory of what Marxists call the political and ideological superstructure, as against an underlying economic base or foundation, by tackling the problems of economic determinism and class reductionism in Marxist theory. As against the reduction of the character and content of political ideologies and different state forms to the interests of the dominant social classes in a society (class reductionism), or the restriction of these forms to mirroring or reflecting underlying material processes (economic determinism), Laclau argues that not all ideological elements have 'a necessary class belonging'. In making this argument, he develops the work of the Greek Althusserian theorist Nicos Poulantzas to stress the relative autonomy of the capitalist state in specific historical circumstances. The 'non-necessary class belonging' of ideological elements is parti- cularly evident in what Laclau calls populist ideologies – such as nationalism or fascism – where appeals to 'the people' or 'the nation' are available for appropriation by opposed class forces.

Hegemony and Socialist Strategy, co-authored with Chantal Mouffe, breaks with any commitment to the role of a 'fundamental social class', whether bourgeois or proletarian, that can articulate the meaning of ideological elements such as 'the people' or 'the nation'. Laclau and Mouffe develop the idea that *all* ideological elements are 'contingent'. This argument widens the sphere of political articulation, understood as the linking together of different political demands and appeals into a unified discourse, and inaugurates the move towards a post-Marxist stance. This contingency, in which ideological 'elements' are conceived as 'floating signifiers' that can be transformed into the 'moments' of a discourse by hegemonic practices, is predicated on a poststructuralist theory of language derived from thinkers such as Derrida, **Roland Barthes** and Foucault. The structuralist theory of language as a system of differential signs without positive terms, formulated by Ferdinand de Saussure, is transformed into an account of discourse whereby the meaning of signs is not fixed by a closed, underlying structure but is produced by articulatory practices. In the discourse of Thatcherism in Britain, for example, signifiers such as 'the free economy', 'the strong state' and 'individual freedom' were welded together into a new political ideology that was able to recruit or 'interpellate' social subjects who were dislocated by the intensified political, economic and ideological crisis of the 1970s (crystallized in the so-called Winter of Discontent of 1973–4) by conferring a new identity. The articulation and partial fixing of the meaning of signifiers is thus a social and political practice, but one that presupposes the ultimate contingency of meaning.

Crucial to fixing the meaning of floating signifiers in this theory of politics and ideology is the way in which political forces draw frontiers between differently positioned agents, thus establishing boundaries between the 'insiders' and 'outsiders' of a discourse. The outsiders in the case of Thatcherite discourse – the welfare scroungers, the trades unions, socialists, deviant social groups such as gays and single parents, overweening bureaucrats and so forth – were thus central to constituting the identities of the insiders, precisely because they were seen to threaten their values. In accounting for the creation of political boundaries which temporarily stabilize and fix the meaning of identities, Laclau develops a conception of antagonism that emphasizes the role of negativity in political life. Social antagonisms occur when the presence of 'an Other' is constructed as blocking or impeding the attainment of identity by a subject. For instance, coal-miners faced with the closure of their pits and an end to their particular way of life were able to construct the Thatcher government and the National Coal Board as a threatening Other that blocked their identities, thus provoking sustained resistance and conflict through their trades union.

One of the main objectives of post-Marxist discourse theory is to explore the way in which social antagonisms are constructed, the precise forms that they take and how they may be accommodated within democratic forms of social life. In doing this, Laclau develops the logics of equivalence and difference, which are derived in part from Saussure's paradigmatic and syntagmatic poles of language. The former refers to the construction of equivalences between different demands and identities, thus dividing social relations into opposed camps, while the latter refers to the process of disarticulating the elements of an equivalent chain and reconfiguring them as mere differences, thus relegating social antagonisms and the division of the social to the margins of society.

In the third phase of his work – represented in books such as *New Reflections on the Revolution of Our Time, Emancipation(s), Contingency, Hegemony, Universality* and *On Populist Reason* – Laclau has responded to important commentaries on his approach by those such as Slavoj Žižek and he develops the deconstructionist and psychoanalytic themes more prominently. In this view, all social relations are built upon a fundamental 'structural undecidability' or 'lack' that can never be fully sutured. At best, these gaps in a symbolic order are rendered visible by dislocatory events that can be symbolized in different ways. One such symbolization is achieved by the construction of social antagonisms that divide the social into opposed camps; other symbolizations may pre-empt or contain such antagonistic constructions. The struggle for hegemony is now conceived as the production of empty signifiers that strive to represent the 'absent fullness' of a social order.

Two additional elements are present in this third phase. First, Laclau introduces the concepts of 'myth' and 'social imaginary' to account for the way in which particular attempts to cover over a dislocated structure are transformed into broad horizons within which many demands and identities can be accommodated. Second, Laclau develops a theory of political subjectivity or agency that emerges in the space opened up by a dislocated structure. If 'subject positions' are available places for identification in a sedimented social structure, then the failure of such structures to stabilize meaning and identity gives rise to new political subjects that seek to reorder social relations in new ways by proposing alternative myths and instituting a different collective social imaginary.

Laclau has continued to extend his post-Marxist theory of discourse to various areas of social and political science. His most recent book accounts for the distinctive logic of populist discourse and practice, and his approach continues to inform a burgeoning research programme, with new books and articles devoted to employing its categories to ever-wider sets of research questions and problems. The latter include analyses of European, Southern African and Latin American politics and society.

See also: Louis Althusser.

See also in *Fifty Key Sociologists: The Formative Theorists*: Karl Marx.

Major works

Politics and Ideology in Marxist Theory. 1977. London: New Left Books.
Hegemony and Socialist Strategy. 1985. With Chantal Mouffe. London: Verso.
New Reflections on the Revolution of Our Time. 1990. London: Verso.
Emancipation(s). 1996. London: Verso.
Contingency, Hegemony, Universality: New Discussions on the Left. 2000. With Judith Butler and Slavoj Žižek. London: Verso.
On Populist Reason. 2005. London: Verso.

Further reading

David Howarth. 2000. *Discourse.* Buckingham: Open University.
David Howarth and Jacob Torfing. 2004. *Discourse Theory in European Politics.* London: Palgrave.
Aletta J. Norval. 1996. *Deconstructing Apartheid Discourse.* London: Verso.
Jacob Torfing. 1999. *New Theories of Discourse.* Oxford: Blackwell.
Yannis Stavrakakis. 1999. *Lacan and the Political.* London: Routledge.

DAVID HOWARTH

CLAUDE LÉVI-STRAUSS

Born of French parents in Brussels in 1908, Claude Lévi-Strauss studied at the Faculty of Law in Paris and at the Sorbonne. He received his *agrégation de philosophie* in 1931. In 1934, when he was twenty-six years old, he decided to teach sociology at the University of Sao Paulo and to become an ethnologist. His book *Tristes Tropiques* is the marvellous story of his travels in Brazil and of his first fieldwork in the Mato Grosso and Amazonia.

Mobilized in 1939–40, Lévi-Strauss – who is Jewish – left his country for the USA. There he taught at the New School for Social

Research in New York and founded, with French colleagues Henri Focillon, Jacques Maritain and J. Perrin, the Ecole Libre des Hautes Etudes. During this period he discovered the work of the linguist Roman Jakobson and he wrote the doctoral thesis that was later published as *The Elementary Structures of Kinship* (1949). In this book, Lévi-Strauss argued that kinship relations – which are fundamental aspects of any culture's organization – represent a specific kind of structure: genealogical charts, with their symbols for father and mothers, sisters and brothers, are an example of kinship systems represented as structures.

The same year, Levi-Strauss was hired as associate director of the Musée de l'Homme and the year after he was nominated as professor (*directeur d'études*) at the Ecole Pratique des Hautes Etudes, where he became the chair of the division on 'Religions comparées des peuples sans écriture'. In 1950, Lévi-Strauss edited Marcel Mauss' *Sociology and Antropology*, a collection of many important essays (including 'The Gift') by the founder of modern French anthropology. Lévi-Strauss had not been a student of Mauss, but Mauss had helped him at the beginning of his career to secure a grant for his travels to Brazil. Lévi-Strauss' intellectual debt to Mauss is great.

In 1959, then fifty-one years old, Lévi-Strauss was elected to the chair of social anthropology at the Collège de France, where he created the Laboratoire d'Anthropologie Sociale. The year before this, he published *Structural Anthropology*, which became the bible of a new school of thought in the human and social sciences: structuralism. Lévi-Strauss has applied his structural perspective to the analysis of mythology in books such as *The Raw and the Cooked*. He explained how the structures of myths provide basic understanding of cultural relations. These relations appear as binary pairs or opposites, as the title of his book implies: what is 'raw' is opposed to what is 'cooked', and the 'raw' is associated with nature while the 'cooked' is associated with culture. These oppositions form the basic structure for all the ideas and concepts of a culture.

Structuralism as a school of thought became an important tool of analysis not only in anthropology but also in diverse fields of the human sciences: in semiology (**Roland Barthes**), philosophy and political sciences (**Louis Althusser**) and psychoanalysis (Jacques Lacan). To be or not to be structuralist was the main debate in the social sciences during the 1970s and 1980s.

Claude Lévi-Strauss was elected as member of the Académie Française in May 1973, the most important honour for a French intellectual who also has the status of a writer.

See also: Louis Althusser, Roland Barthes.

See also in *Fifty Key Sociologists: The Formative Theorists*: Emile Durkheim, Marcel Mauss.

Major works

La Vie familiale et sociale des Indiens Nambikwara. 1948. Paris: Société des Américanistes.
The Elementary Structures of Kinship. 1949. New York: Beacon Press, 1969.
Race and History. 1952. Paris: UNESCO.
Tristes Tropiques. 1955. Harmondsworth: Penguin, 1992.
Structural Anthropology, vol. 1. (Essays of 1944–57.) Harmondsworth: Penguin, 1968.
Totemism. 1962. London: Merlin Press, 1964.
The Savage Mind. 1962. London: George Weidenfeld and Nicholson, 1966.
The Raw and the Cooked (Mythologiques, vol. 1). 1964. London: Cape, 1969.
From Honey to Ashes (Mythologiques, vol. 2). 1967. London: Cape, 1973.
The Origin of Table Manners (Mythologiques, vol. 3). 1968. London: Cape, 1978.
The Naked Man (Mythologiques, vol. 4). 1971. London: Cape, 1981.
Anthropology and Myth. (Lectures of 1951–82.) Oxford: Basil Blackwell, 1987.
Structural Anthropology, vol. 2. (Essays of 1952–73.) Chicago: University of Chicago Press, 1983.
The Way of the Masks. 1975. Washington, DC: University of Washington Press, 1988.
The View from Afar. (Essays of 1956–83.) Chicago: University of Chicago Press, 1992.
The Jealous Potter. 1985. Chicago: University of Chicago Press, 1996.
The Story of Lynx. 1991. Chicago: University of Chicago Press, 1996.
Look, Listen, Read. 1993. New York: Basic Books, 1997.
De Près et de Loin. 1990. Paris: Odile Jacob.

Further reading

Miriam Glucksmann. 1974. *Structuralist Analysis in Contemporary Social Thought*. London: Routledge & Kegan Paul.
Marcel Hénaff. 1998. *Claude Lévi-Strauss and the Making of Modern Anthropology*. Minneapolis, MN: University of Minnesota Press.
Alan Jenkins. 1979. *The Social Theory of Claude Lévi-Strauss*. London: Macmillan.
Edmund Leach. 1974. *Lévi-Strauss*. Chicago: University of Chicago Press, 1989.

MARCEL FOURNIER

DAVID LOCKWOOD

Central to the debates on social stratification and social order that have dominated sociology since the mid-twentieth century, David Lockwood has made a number of conceptual innovations that have now become elements in the standard sociological toolbox: the ideas of system integration, work situation and civic integration, to mention but a few, have resulted from his reflections on the formative work of Durkheim, Marx and Weber, his critical engagement with the ideas of **Talcott Parsons** and normative functionalism, and his exploration of the implications of both affluence and stagnation for social inequality and political order.

David Lockwood was born in Holmfirth, Yorkshire, in 1929. Although he earned a grammar school scholarship, he was forced to leave school early to earn a living in the local textile mill. An army scholarship allowed him to study at the London School of Economics (LSE), where he graduated in 1952 as part of an influential post-war cohort of sociology students. His doctoral research was an investigation into the changing class position of male clerical workers, and he began to engage critically with both Marxist class theory and the then fashionable functionalist theories of Talcott Parsons. Teaching at the LSE, he ran a seminar at which these ideas were explored and that led directly to his first papers on general social theory. Moving to Cambridge University in 1958, he pursued his interests in social class and joined John Goldthorpe in a major project on the 'affluent worker' of the new, technologically advanced industries that were replacing more traditional forms of working-class employment. The results of this study were published in 1968, when Lockwood moved to a chair at the University of Essex. At Essex he worked on the general statement of social theory published as *Solidarity and Schism* in 1992 and he became centrally involved in work producing a new scheme of class classification to replace the registrar general's classification in official investigations.

Lockwood's view of social stratification begins from Weber's distinction between class and status as distinctive causal components in the determination of individual life chances. Lockwood sees class and class situation as comprising the material aspects of social systems, as manifest in their structures of economic relations, and he distinguishes the 'market situations' rooted in property and employment relations from the 'work situations' that emerge in the division of labour and the distribution of authority at work. The task of class analysis, therefore, is not limited to an investigation of the economic relations of the market but must also involve an examination of the changing social relations associated with technological change. Thus, writing in the 1950s, he argued that technology had transformed the work situations in which wage earners were to be found. The non-manual work of clerks had been transformed by the enlargement of the office and the declining authority of clerks *vis-à-vis* the expanding levels of managerial workers. Manual work in the coal mines, ship-yards, steelworks and textile mills was giving way to work on pro-duction lines and in process plants based on the new technologies of the automobile and chemical industries that had expanded through the middle years of the twentieth century. As a result, the status situation and cultural outlook of both groups were altering. Clerical workers no longer enjoyed any status privileges or affinity with their employers; they were no longer the objects of working-class defer-ence and their jobs were no longer the objects of working-class aspiration. Manual workers, for their part, were less likely to experi-ence a sense of collective solidarity and were likely to aspire to the higher wages that they now felt to be within their grasp. The 'afflu-ent worker' project explored these changing class relations, showing that the workers employed in the new industries were adopting fun-damentally new industrial and political attitudes: they were less committed to the collective action of the trades unions, more prag-matic in their voting decisions and more strongly oriented to the improvement of their family and domestic conditions. While they were not pursuing a 'middle-class' social standing – as suggested in theories of '*embourgeoisement*' – status concerns were playing a more important part. Lockwood's more recent work took up T. H. Mar-shall's analysis of citizenship status to show that contemporary socie-ties are increasingly divided by differential citizenship rights (especially as these relate to age, gender and ethnicity) and that pat-terns of class formation and political action are shaped by these as well as by market and work situations.

Lockwood's general theoretical work has drawn out the wider implications of this view. In his critical examination of Parsons' sociology, Lockwood diagnosed an overemphasis on cultural and normative factors that he later traced back to the influence of Dur-kheim. The material factors that were central to Marx's theory were marginalized, though this theory, for its part, marginalized cultural concerns. Parsons' arguments, it followed, had to be complemented by the more materialist analyses of Marx if they were to help in providing a more comprehensive view of social order. Lockwood held that Marxist theory – and the Weberian analysis of class relations that he had himself pursued – provided a way of understanding the material or 'factual substratum' on which the normative institutions and status imagery rested. The material substratum, comprising a distribution of power and resources, formed the bases for social division and schism. This has led Lockwood to be categorized, along with Ralf Dahrendorf and John Rex, as a 'conflict theorist'. Lockwood, however, saw normative factors and value commitments as having the capacity to limit and contain social conflict through the establishment of consensus and social solidarity. It is the interplay of the material and the normative that explains the occurrence of social order and disorder.

Lockwood sees this order as depending on processes at two distinct levels of social systems. The level of 'social integration' refers to the interactions of individuals and groups as they engage in more or less harmonious or conflictual actions on the basis of the norms that they invoke in defining their situations and the resources on which they are able to draw in carrying out their actions. 'System integration', on the other hand, refers to the level of institutions and material relations through which norms and resources are organized. The actions of individuals and groups cannot be applied at the level of social integration alone, but must be seen in relation to the harmonies and contradictions that exist at the level of system integration.

Lockwood's theoretical ideas have been very influential, both **Anthony Giddens** and **Jürgen Habermas** showing the influence of his distinction between social integration and system integration. He has shown how a comprehensive theoretical understanding can be achieved without resort to either an eclecticism or a premature attempt at synthesis.

See also: Alvin Gouldner, Talcott Parsons.

See also in *Fifty Key Sociologists: The Formative Theorists*: Emile Durkheim, Karl Marx, Max Weber.

Major works

'Some Remarks on *The Social System*'. 1956. *British Journal of Sociology* 7.
The Blackcoated Worker. 1958. Second edn. Oxford: Clarendon Press, 1989.
'The New Working Class'. 1960. *European Journal of Sociology* 1(2).
'Affluence and the British Class Structure'. 1963. With John Goldthorpe. *Sociological Review* 11(2).
'System Integration and Social Integration'. 1964. In George K. Zollschan and Walter Hirsch, eds. *Explorations in Social Change*. London: Routledge & Kegan Paul.

'Sources of Variation in Working Class Images of Society'. 1966. In Martin Bulmer, ed. *Working Class Images of Society*. London: Routledge & Kegan Paul, 1975.

The Affluent Worker: Industrial Attitudes and Behaviour. 1968. Cambridge: Cambridge University Press. (First volume of 'The Affluent Worker Study'.)

The Affluent Worker: Political Attitudes and Behaviour. 1968. Cambridge: Cambridge University Press. (Second volume of 'The Affluent Worker Study'.)

The Affluent Worker in the Class Structure. 1968. Cambridge: Cambridge University Press. (Third volume of 'The Affluent Worker Study'.)

Solidarity and Schism. 1992. Oxford: Clarendon Press.

'Civic Integration and Class Formation'. 1996. *British Journal of Sociology* 47(3).

Further reading

David Rose, ed. 1996. *For David Lockwood*. Special issue of *British Journal of Sociology* 47(4).

JOHN SCOTT

NIKLAS LUHMANN

Functionalism seemed to die with **Talcott Parsons**, having already lost much of its influence to 'conflict' and 'interactionist' theories. Within a very few years, however, functionalism was as influential as ever, known variously as 'system theory' or neo-functionalism. A leading figure in this revival was Niklas Luhmann, a long-time functionalist theorist who had developed a distinctive form of system theory that had begun to attract many adherents and to influence theorists such as **Jürgen Habermas**.

Luhmann was born in 1927 in Lüneburg, Germany. He studied law at the University of Freiburg and went into practice as a lawyer, making this a base for his involvement in regional politics. He visited the United States in the early 1960s and, while at Harvard, discovered sociology in the form of the functionalism of Parsons. When he returned to Germany he studied for a doctorate at the University of Münster. In 1968 he became professor of sociology at the University of Bielefeld, where he remained until his death in 1998. He published a series of articles on function and system during the 1960s, applying his developing ideas in books on organizations and law. It was in 1971 that he entered into a famous debate over the uses of system theory with Habermas. A rash of books on power, trust and religion followed. Although some articles began to appear in English translation during the 1970s, it was not until 1982 that his major theoretical articles were brought together into a single English-language volume under the title *The Differentiation of Society*. The appearance of this book established Luhmann's reputation outside Germany and since then his books have appeared regularly in English and German. He has published on such topics as love, religion, welfare, risk, the mass media and modernity, and has produced a general treatise on social systems.

Luhmann sees social systems as symbolically constituted and bounded entities produced through human communication and as constituting the frameworks of meaning within which people live their lives. They exist as clusters of organized activities that are specialized in relation to the specific problems generated by the environments in which they operate. Existing within an environment, a system must 'adapt' to the conditions or requirements set by the system–environment relationship. By organizing the actions of their members, systems allow the 'complexity' – the severity of the adjustment problems – of the environment to be reduced. In the tradition of Spencer, Luhmann sees adaptation as a mechanism of social evolution.

In the earliest forms of society, 'system' and 'environment' can barely be distinguished as elements in the whole social context in which people act. Hunter-gatherers must adapt to the specific physical environment in which they live or they must migrate to preferable environments, but there are few real problems of adaptation. The adoption of agriculture and the building of more complex, and more settled, forms of social life, however, pose far greater problems of adaptation. As social life becomes more complex, particular activities may be 'differentiated' from the overall system and formed into clusters of related activities. This formation of distinct 'subsystems' allows people better to control the conditions under which they live and act. Systems of production, marketing, regulation, religion and so on become established in this way. The driving force in subsystem formation, then, is 'complexity reduction': the differentiation of systems into specialized subsystems allows the complexity or uncertainty inherent in the environment of action to be reduced.

Luhmann recognized three forms of differentiation: segmentation, stratification and functional differentiation. Segmentation is the formation of sub-units, each of which is identical to all the others. In a segmental society, as Durkheim showed, social solidarity is mechanical in character, resting on the similarity and interchangeability of the social segments. Stratification is the formation of vertically differentiated sub-units – social 'strata' – that are unequal in resources and whose members pursue their distinctive way of life. In a stratified society, the subsystems are diverse, rather than identical, and they stand in relations of power and exploitation to each other. Luhmann saw functional differentiation as the most important form of differentiation in complex societies. This begins in traditional, stratified societies as the differentiation of roles and rapidly gains momentum. Roles come to be organized into distinct and specialized subsystems of 'complementary expectations' concerned with specific functions. Within each specialized subsystem, some roles may be particularly concerned with connecting the specialist roles with the wider society – priests, for example, were held to be responsible for connecting a whole array of religious roles with the laity. Subsystems of production, marketing and regulation become established in this way, forming religious systems, economic systems, political systems and so on. Thus, societies become compartmentalized by function but also internally interdependent: systems are specialized around particular functions that are consequential for other systems. A complex society, then, will consist of a number of differentiated subsystems. They must, however, operate interdependently if the society is not to fragment and collapse. As there is no single co-ordinating centre for these differentiated subsystems, they were said to face problems of 'system integration'. Luhmann rejected Parsons' view that normative consensus is the means through which this problem of system integration can be solved. System integration, then, is a problem that all ongoing systems must resolve.

In European societies, Luhmann argued, there was an evolution from stratified to functionally differentiated societies during the seventeenth and eighteenth centuries. The sharp vertical differentiation of closed and cohesive social strata that had formed around differences of wealth and control gave way to more open 'class' divisions that relate to functionally differentiated positions in the division of labour. Within these modern societies, Luhmann argued, the economic system has a functional primacy and so is central to the problem of system integration in society as a whole. The relations of markets, firms and households in a monetary system of exchange are a distinct and autonomous system of action that had no counterpart in pre-modern forms of society. Politics, also, is an important sphere of activity in the modern world, and Luhmann traced the differentiation of political roles and activities such as bureaucratic administration, party politics and citizenship. This differentiated political system first emerged with the rise of the nation-state in modern Europe. Other functionally differentiated systems analysed by Luhmann include the system of modern scientific and technical knowledge and the system of family and kinship.

The differentiation of the economic and political spheres was associated with the development of differentiated 'media' of money and power, which became the principal mechanisms through which system integration could be achieved. Money, power and the other media of communication and association that are generated in the specialized spheres of social life are the means through which each sphere can be integrated and are the only basis on which the system as a whole can be integrated. It was the invention of new media of mass communications that allowed these 'generalized symbolic media' to emerge as potent forces of system integration. Thus, money became the universal means of exchange that allowed economic transactions to be co-ordinated in terms of a common yardstick. Because of the centrality of the economic subsystem within modern societies, it is also the principal steering mechanism for system integration: society as a whole can be integrated if everything can find its price.

See also: Jürgen Habermas, Talcott Parsons.

See also in *Fifty Key Sociologists: The Formative Theorists*: Herbert Spencer.

Major works

Funktionen und Folgen formaler Organisation. 1964. Berlin: Duncker & Humblot.
A Sociological Theory of Law. 1965. London: Routledge & Kegan Paul, 1985.
'Trust'. 1968. In *Trust and Power*. New York: Wiley, 1979.
Theorie der Gesellschaft oder Sozialtechnologie. Was leistet die Systemforschung. 1971–3. 2 vols. Frankfurt am Main: Suhrkamp.
The Differentiation of Society. 1964–79. New York: Columbia University Press, 1982.
'Power'. 1975. In *Trust and Power*. New York: Wiley, 1979.
Religious Dogmatics and the Evolution of Societies. 1977. Lewiston, NY: Edwin Mellen Press, 1984.
Political Theory in the Welfare State. 1981. Berlin: W. de Gruyter, 1990.
Love as Passion. 1982. Cambridge: Polity Press, 1986.
Social Systems. 1984. Stanford, CA: Stanford University Press, 1995.
Essays on Self-Reference. (Essays of various dates.) New York: Columbia University Press, 1990.

Risk. 1991. Berlin: W. de Gruyter, 1993.
Observations on Modernity. 1992. Stanford, CA: Stanford University Press, 1998.
Art as a Social System. 1993. Stanford, CA: Stanford University Press, 2000.
Law as a Social System. 1993. Oxford: Oxford University Press, 2004.
The Reality of the Mass Media. 1994. Cambridge: Polity Press, 2000.
Theories of Distinction: Redescribing the Descriptions of Modernity. (Essays of 1990–96.) Stanford, CA: Stanford University Press, 2002.

Further reading

Michael King and Chris Thornhill. 2005. *Niklas Luhmann's Theory of Politics and Law*. Basingstoke: Palgrave.
William Rasch. 2001. *Niklas Luhmann's Modernity: The Paradoxes of Differentiation*. Stanford, CA: Stanford University Press.

JOHN SCOTT

ROBERT MERTON

Merton belonged to the most influential school of sociologists of the twentieth century. He was the founder of a sophisticated variety of structural-functionalism, the originator of the contemporary sociology of science and a prolific contributor to the conceptual and theoretical resources of several sociological specialisms.

Robert King Merton was born Meyer R. Schkolnick on 4 July 1910 in Philadelphia. He graduated from Temple College in 1931 and went for graduate study to Harvard University, where he worked with Pitirim Sorokin and **Talcott Parsons** and, in 1936, defended his doctoral dissertation on *Science, Technology and Society in Seventeenth-century England*. The 'Merton Thesis' on the influence of puritan, pietist religion on the emergence of experimental natural science, phrased with obvious reference to the classical work of Max Weber, is still vigorously debated among historians of science. The influence of Parsons in steering Merton's interest towards theoretical considerations was immense, but for almost forty years after the memorable meeting of the American Sociological Association in the 1940s Parsons' abstract manner of theorizing was the subject of persistent challenge from Merton, leading him to propose in 1945 the notion of a 'middle-range theory'. Similarly, the static and ahistoric 'structural functionalism' proposed by Parsons was subject to Merton's strong critique and contributed to the birth of his own dynamic 'functional analysis' in 1949.

Merton moved to Columbia University in 1941 and he was to stay on the faculty of the sociology department for thirty-eight years until his retirement. In the 1940s and 1950s he took part in a number of empirical projects carried out in the Bureau of Applied Social Research (established by himself and Paul Lazarsfeld), one of which was the study of a radio campaign known as the 'war-bond drive', summarized in 1946 in a volume on *Mass Persuasion*. Another of his contributions was the reinterpretation of the findings of war-time studies carried out by Samuel Stouffer and his team on *The American Soldier*, which resulted in an influential article on reference groups, published in 1950. In later years Merton turned almost exclusively to theoretical work, but always attempted to link theory with rich empirical data.

He received the highest symbols of academic recognition, among them twenty-four honorary doctoral degrees from universities all around the world. In 1994 the president of the United States granted him the top academic honour of the National Medal of Science. His books have gone through multiple foreign editions, with *Social Theory and Social Structure* appearing in more than twenty languages. In the Books of the Century contest organized in 1998 by the International Sociological Association, this volume finds its place among the top five, together with the classical work of Weber and Durkheim. Merton died on 24 February 2003 in New York.

For two main reasons Merton's work is often referred to as a 'modern sociological classic'. First, he made a lasting substantive contribution to general sociological theory, as well as to some special theories of sociological sub-disciplines. This was particularly great in the sociology of science and the sociology of deviance, where strong Mertonian 'schools' are still operating. Second, he exemplified a certain unique, 'classical' style of sociological theorizing and concept formation.

Merton has elaborated two theoretical orientations: functional analysis and structural analysis (the latter in the sense different from the current usage of 'structuralism' or 'poststructuralism'). For him, functionalism meant the practice of interpreting data by establishing their consequences for the larger structures in which they are implicated. In 1949 he published his famous 'paradigm for functional analysis', outlining a flexible, undogmatic, deeply revised version of functionalism that allowed for the conceptualization of social conflict and social change. He put an emphasis not only on functions, but also on dysfunctions of various components in the social system, together with what he called the variable 'balance of functional consequences':

the components may appear not only in harmonious but also conflictual relations. The effect of a specific balance is not necessarily equilibrium, order and continuity (as in the earlier 'structural-functionalism' of Talcott Parsons), but sometimes disequilibrium, disorder, disorganization and, consequently, social change. A quarter-century later, in 1975, he wrote an important paper on 'Structural Analysis in Sociology' in which he presented a correlative sociological orientation, emphasizing the network of relationships within which components of the system are located. Structural analysis is a natural, complementary outgrowth of functional analysis. Whereas functional analysis specifies the consequences of a social phenomenon for its differentiated structural context, structural analysis searches for the determinants of the phenomenon in its structural milieu.

The best example of Merton's structural-functional analysis is his famous theory of anomie. Understood as a structural condition of dissociation between cultural demands of success and the actual opportunities for success, anomie is shown to generate various forms of deviant conduct – 'innovation', 'ritualism', 'retreatism' or 'rebellion' – depending on the wider structural context within which it appears. In turn, these various ways of departing from established normative order have different effects on the functioning of the whole system, sometimes leading to social change. Obviously, both orientations refer to the different sides of the same coin; they scrutinize two vectors of the same relationship between a social phenomenon and its structural setting.

A particular implementation of the structural orientation is to be found in Merton's sociology of science, the field that comprises the empirical sociology of scientific communities as producing, selecting and distributing scientific knowledge. Apart from mapping the whole field of this new sociological sub-discipline, Merton has contributed influential ideas to its three focal topics: the scientific ethos, the scientific community and the origins of modern science.

The analysis of scientific ethos was introduced in the context of penetrating critique of the fate of science under the totalitarian Nazi regime in Germany. Merton showed that the context functionally indispensable for the proper operation of the system of science is the liberal-democratic order. He believed that the future of science is allied with the spread of the democratic attitude and institutions. The scientific ethos appears as a micro-model of democratic ethos. It is defined as follows: 'The ethos of science is that affectively toned complex of values and norms which is held to be binding on scientists'. The paramount values are objectivity (the commitment to the pursuit of knowledge as adequate and as complete as possible) and originality (the commitment to the pursuit of new knowledge). Norms or 'institutional imperatives' define the acceptable or preferred means for realizing these values. There are four of these: 'universalism' requires science to be impersonal; 'communism' requires that scientific knowledge be treated not as the private property of its creator, but rather as a common good, to be freely communicated and distributed; 'disinterestedness' demands the subordination of extrinsic interests to the intrinsic satisfaction of finding the truth; and 'organized scepticism' requires the scientist to doubt, and then to check whether the doubt is well founded. This is carried out through public criticism by scientists of claimed contributions to scientific knowledge.

Merton was well aware that this idealized picture of scientific ethos is rarely to be found in reality. The most interesting reason for deviance from it is found in the internal ambivalences and anomie inherent in the scientific ethos itself. Anomic conduct in science derives primarily from the great values placed upon originality, and uniformly so for all working scientists, whereas the opportunities and possibilities of achieving original results are most variable owing to personal constraints (talents, abilities, competences), as well as to structural constraints (limited resources, underdeveloped scientific culture, unavailable experimental technologies and so on): 'In this situation of stress, all manner of adaptive behaviors are called into play, some of these being far beyond the mores of science'. Examples would include outright fraud, the fabrication of data, the denouncing of rivals, aggressive self-assertion and plagiarism.

The other aspect of science that Merton vigorously investigates is the scientific community, a specific type of social organization made up of scientists in their role behaviour and mutual, interactive relationships. There are several subsystems that are singled out within the scientific community. The first is the 'system of institutionalized vigilance': the examination, appraisal, criticism and verification of scientific results by academic peers. The second is the 'communication system of science', the complex mechanism of scientific publication that makes the results visible. Here Merton introduces the biblical metaphor and the concept of the 'Matthew Effect', observing that the works published by recognized scholars have much better chances of visibility in the scientific community than equally significant or original contributions by scholars of less renown. Another concept of 'obliteration by incorporation' signifies the situation in which both the original source and the literal formulation of an idea are forgotten, owing to its long and widespread use. The notion of 'cognitive conduits' refers to the spreading and inheriting of ideas over time. Another subsystem of the scientific community is the evaluation and reward system of science, the complex mechanisms of scientific recognition and reward allocation, again biased in favour of already recognized scholars. All these processes lead to the emergence of the stratification system of science, involving the patterned differentiation of scholars according to identifiable criteria. Finally, there is the 'informal influence system of science': the network of personal ties, acquaintanceships, friendships, loyalties that cut across other systems and significantly modify their operation. Merton paid ever-growing attention to this elusive domain, giving new prominence to the seventeenth-century concept of the 'invisible college' (used earlier by Derek de Solla Price) as well as the twentieth-century idea of the 'thought collective' (introduced by Ludwig Fleck).

The third focus of Merton's concern with science, in fact the earliest in his own research biography, was the historical origins of science and its subsequent development. Already in his doctoral dissertation, studying the origins of empirical science in seventeenth-century England, Merton observed a linkage between religious commitments and a sustained interest in science. He noted that English scientists in that period were disproportionately ascetic Protestants or Puritans. The values and attitudes characteristic for Puritanism were seen to have had the effect of stimulating scientific research by inviting the empirical and rational quest for identifying the God-given order in the world and for practical applications – just as they legitimized scientific research through religious justification. Once it had obtained institutional legitimacy, science largely severed its link with religion, finally to become a counterforce, curbing the influence of religion. But, as the first push, religion was seen as crucially important.

Merton's thought was deeply rooted in the classical sociological tradition of the nineteenth century, which he synthesized and extended. He attained balanced, intermediate positions on various traditional issues and unravelled entangled premises to reach their rational core. He had a strong aversion to extremes. The most famous illustration of this is his strategy of 'middle-range theory', based on the rejection of both narrow empiricism and abstract, scholastic theorizing. The systematic quality of his work is emphasized by the repeated use of what he called 'paradigms', long before Thomas Kuhn popularized the word with a different meaning. For Merton, a paradigm is an heuristic scheme designed to introduce a measure of order and lucidity into qualitative and discursive sociological analysis by codifying the results of prior inquiry and specifying the directions of further research. This allowed him to introduce a further measure of order and systematization in the classical heritage: the synthesis becomes much more than a summary of earlier ideas by bringing about their selective and critical reformulation and the accumulation of knowledge.

The thematic range of his empirical interests was very wide: from drug addicts to professionals, from anomie to social time, from friendship formation to role conflicts, from functional analysis to scientific ethos, from medical education to multiple discoveries, from bureaucratic structure to the origins of medieval aphorisms, and so on. He seemed to pick up various topics here and there and then to pursue them methodically and meticulously in depth, sometimes for many years. One of his strongest contributions was insightful concepts. As he identified new aspects of social life that he found sociologically significant, he coined neologisms to designate them. A number of these have entered the vocabularies not only of social science but of the vernacular of everyday life. The list of concepts coined by Merton that have entered the canon of contemporary sociology would include: manifest and latent functions, dysfunctions, self-fulfilling prophecy, homophily and heterophily, status-sets and role-sets, opportunity structures, anticipatory socialization, reference group behaviour, middle-range theories, sociological ambivalence, local and cosmopolitan influentials, obliteration by incorporation and many others.

Merton's most important service to the development of contemporary sociology was the vindication of the classical style of doing sociology and classical heritage of theoretical ideas. In his work, paradigms of classical thought gained new vitality, as they were shown to be fruitful: both in the explanatory sense, as means of solving the puzzles confronting social actors, and in the heuristic sense, as means of raising new questions and suggesting new puzzles for solution.

See also: Talcott Parsons.

See also in *Fifty Key Sociologists: The Formative Theorists*: Emile Durkheim, Max Weber.

Major works

Science, Technology and Society in Seventeenth-century England. 1936. New York: Harper and Row, 1970.
Mass Persuasion. 1946. With Marjorie Fiske and Alberta Curtis. New York: Howard Fertig Publishers, 2004.

Social Theory and Social Structure. 1949. (Essays of various dates.) New York: Free Press. Revised edn 1957; enlarged and revised edn 1968.
The Sociology of Science: Theoretical and Empirical Investigations. 1973. Chicago: University of Chicago Press.
Sociological Ambivalence and Other Essays. 1976. New York: Free Press.

Various extracts can be found in P. Sztompka, ed. *On Social Structure and Science*. Chicago: University of Chicago Press, 1996.

Further reading

Jon Clark, Celia Modgil and Sohan Modgil, eds. 1990. *Robert K. Merton: Consensus and Controversy*. London: The Falmer Press.
Charles Crothers. 1987. *Robert K. Merton*. London: Tavistock.
Piotr Sztompka. 1986. *Robert K. Merton: An Intellectual Profile*. London and New York: Macmillan and St Martin's Press.

PIOTR SZTOMPKA

RALPH MILIBAND

Ralph Miliband was probably the most influential Marxist political sociologist writing in English in the second half of the twentieth century, his output simultaneously contributing both to the academic research agenda and to student protest movements of the era. This was in line with his own thinking, for he always regarded scholarly work as an integral part of political activism.

Miliband was born on 7 January 1924 in Brussels, the son of Polish Jewish immigrants. He escaped to Britain with his father in May 1940, just before the Belgian surrender to Germany. Despite arriving in London with only a rudimentary grasp of English, he gained entry into the London School of Economics (LSE) in the autumn of 1941, studying government until, in June 1943, he joined the navy. He returned to the LSE after the war to complete his degree, and he subsequently pursued the bulk of his academic career there. He was, however, deeply alienated by the repressive response to the student protest movement in the late 1960s, and he moved to Leeds University in 1972, becoming professor of politics and head of department. Yet this did not suit him either and he resigned in 1978, subsequently dividing his time between North America, where he held a series of professorships, and London, where he did most of his research and writing. He died in 1994.

Harold Laski, professor of government at the LSE, was an important early influence. Combining an intense socialist commitment with academic life, Laski became Miliband's mentor and friend, encouraging him to study the history of political ideas. However, Miliband subsequently grew dissatisfied with this mode of analysis in the conviction that social and economic power played the key role in shaping political and institutional behaviour. A second, and still greater, influence was **C. Wright Mills**, with whom he formed a close friendship in 1957. *The Power Elite* had just been published, and Mills' method immediately struck a chord with Miliband, leading him to adopt a more sociological approach. Yet the two also differed in fundamental respects: while Mills stressed the integration of the labour movement and the importance of intellectuals in bringing about change, Miliband regarded class conflict as central and believed that the working class must play the main role in effecting its transformation. His enduring preoccupation, however, was with the complex relationships between politics and other dimensions of power.

These concerns were evident in his first major book, *Parliamentary Socialism: A Study in the Politics of Labour*. This was a highly influential critique of the Labour Party, in which Miliband argued that the failures of Labour governments lay less in leadership betrayals than in the nature of the party itself. The doctrine of 'labourism' papered over the differences between socialists and non-socialists and meant that a preference for parliament and the constitution would always prevail over rank-and-file activism based on working-class demands. Social change would be possible, he argued, only if the party adopted a thoroughgoing commitment to socialism rather than social reform. Although focused on Britain, *Parliamentary Socialism* raised many general issues about power and ideology in an implicit way, and these were discussed more explicitly through a comparative analysis in *The State in Capitalist Society*.

At the time this book was published – 1969 – the dominant paradigm in western political science was pluralism. This is the notion that power is dispersed amongst a large number of competing groups in society. Miliband's major goal was to refute this claim by demonstrating the concentration of power in capitalist societies. And while pluralists argued that the government was open to influence by competing parties and groups, Miliband argued that the competition was always highly unequal, with the dominant class playing a pre-eminent role.

His book led to much discussion within mainstream political sociology, partly because the argument was underpinned by an impressive amount of evidence, but it also provoked intense controversy within Marxist academic circles. Miliband acknowledged the positive contribution of Gramsci, but argued that most Marxists had relied too much on the notion of the state as a coercive instrument of the ruling class, without sufficient analysis of the way it operated in contemporary societies. However, Nicos Poulantzas (1936–79), who was at that time greatly influenced by **Althusser** and his school of Marxist thought, criticized the book for being too empirical and too willing to accept the concepts of orthodox political science. In particular, he attacked Miliband for concentrating upon the social origins and current networks of state personnel. His own argument was that government policies followed from the *structural* position of the state within a capitalist society, rather than from the origins or social relationships of the people who occupied particular political or bureaucratic positions. This led to a much wider debate about the relationships between different forms of power and contributed to a renewal of interest in state theory.

The majority of Miliband's writings concentrated on advanced capitalist societies, but he did not regard existing communist regimes as any kind of 'model' for socialism, and he became increasingly critical of Soviet-style systems after the late 1960s. *Marxism and Politics* was an attempt to explain their weaknesses while simultaneously providing an insight into the possibilities of a socialist transformation that would lead to democracy rather than dictatorship. However, the political climate was now changing fast and his subsequent books reflected this. *Capitalist Democracy in Britain* was published as the first Thatcher government was restructuring the welfare state, and the book attempted to explain how British institutions and political culture constrained the possibilities of protest and change. *Divided Societies: Class Struggles in Contemporary Capitalism* sought to demonstrate that the fundamental cleavages in capitalist society remained rooted in class relationships, despite the rise of new social movements and accompanying ideologies of identity politics. Finally, his posthumous book, *Socialism for a Sceptical Age*, acknowledged failures in twentieth-century Marxism, but reaffirmed his argument that only socialism could provide a basis for equality and democracy.

Miliband never disguised his partisan engagement and he was an important theoretical influence on the New Left. Yet his clarity of analysis, ability to distil complex ideas in a simple style, and independence of thought ensured that his impact extended far beyond such circles. His work has enduring importance both because of its specific insights into underlying power structures and because he challenges readers to look critically into their own political and social assumptions.

See also: C. Wright Mills.

See also in *Fifty Key Sociologists: The Formative Theorists*: Karl Marx.

Major works

Parliamentary Socialism: A Study in the Politics of Labour. 1961. London: Merlin Press. Second edn, with new postscript, 1972.
The State in Capitalist Society. 1969. London: Weidenfeld and Nicolson.
Marxism and Politics. 1977. Oxford: Oxford University Press.
Capitalist Democracy in Britain. 1982. Oxford: Oxford University Press.
Class Power and State Power. (Essays from the 1970s and 1980s.) London: Verso, 1983.
Divided Societies: Class Struggle in Contemporary Capitalism. 1989. Oxford: Oxford University Press.
Socialism for a Sceptical Age. 1994. Cambridge: Polity Press.

Further reading

Stanley Aronowitz and Peter Bratsis, eds. 2002. *Paradigm Lost: State Theory Reconsidered.* London and Minneapolis, MN: University of Minnesota Press.
David Coates and Leo Panitch. 2003. 'The Continuing Relevance of the Milibandian Perspective'. In John Callaghan, Steven Fielding and Steve Ludlam, eds. *Interpreting the Labour Party: Approaches to Labour Politics and History.* Manchester: Manchester University Press.
Michael Newman. 2002. *Ralph Miliband and the Politics of the New Left.* London: Merlin Press.

MICHAEL NEWMAN

C. WRIGHT MILLS

A radical intellectual and a sociologist, writing the bulk of his publications during the Cold War, Mills was very much a controversial figure in the American social science of his time. Born in Waco, Texas, on 28 August 1916 to middle-class parents of Irish-English descent, his full name was Charles Wright Mills. He was always known outside the family as 'Wright'. Of his life he says the following in an unpublished autobiographical manuscript addressed to an imaginary Soviet friend:

> The son of a white collar man who travelled all the time, I grew up under the projections of a [doting] mother, was

accordingly a sissy boy until my first year of college, and so was sent to military academy 'to make a man of me'. It didn't work; it did work; it was a mistake; it was the best; I revolted. Because of certain teachers, the revolt took an intellectual turn. Because of isolation, it made me a kind of spiritual Wobbly. Because of the nature of the epoch, this spiritual condition became political. Because I used to be more or less bright, and because of a high metabolic rate, I've gotten away with it. Also, by chance, circumstance, and instinct, Irishly drunk on words, I've liked it – most of it, so far – immensely.

After high school he attended the Texas Agricultural & Mechanical College in 1934–5. In the following four years he was a student at the University of Texas at Austin, where he obtained both a bachelor's and a master's degree in sociology in the same year, 1939. He got a research fellowship and was accepted onto the doctoral programme in sociology at the University of Wisconsin in Madison, with Howard P. Becker as his supervisor.

His doctoral thesis, 'A Sociological Account of Pragmatism: An Essay on the Sociology of Knowledge', was accepted and he received his PhD in September 1942. The year before his thesis was completed he was appointed associate professor of sociology at the University of Maryland at College Park. In 1945, however, he was offered a position as a research associate at the Bureau of Applied Social Research at Columbia University, New York, where he worked with Paul Lazarsfeld. He accepted an assistant professorship at the University of Columbia in 1946 and resigned from his job in Maryland. His main affiliation for the rest of his life was at Columbia, and in 1956 he was granted a full professorship there. However, he spent much time as a visiting professor at other universities in the United States and Europe, including Chicago, Brandeis and Copenhagen.

In his doctoral thesis, Mills explored the role of American pragmatism for the institutionalization of professionalism in higher education. He focused on the influence of Charles Peirce, William James and John Dewey, later regretting his omission of George Herbert Mead. Pragmatism was his first and main source of theoretical inspiration. In the papers he published while still at Texas, he discussed issues of philosophy of knowledge with reference to the works of Mead and Dewey in particular. As Irving L. Horowitz points out in his biography of Mills, Mead's notion of the self as *social* became an important starting point for Mills' thoughts on the relationship between the individual and social structures, or, as he later put it in

The Sociological Imagination, the relationship between history and biography. In an early paper on 'Language, Logic and Culture', published in 1939, Mills built on Mead's theory of the self and on aspects of Karl Mannheim's sociology of knowledge to develop a more conflict-oriented understanding of social communication than Mead's original thoughts contained.

Mills was also well acquainted with classic and contemporary European sociological thought. The sociology of knowledge in Mannheim's version is an inspiration in much of Mills' writing. One of his first books – produced with Hans Gerth, a former teaching assistant to Karl Mannheim – was a translated and edited volume of Max Weber's work.

In 1948 Mills published *The New Men of Power. America's Labor Leaders*, which was based on a study of trades unions and union leaders in America just before the Cold War set in in earnest. The book is the first in what is regarded as Mills' trilogy of the American class society and the structure of power. The second book – *White Collar. The American Middle Classes* – was published in 1951 and *The Power Elite* in 1956. The first book is based on a study of 500 of the most influential labour leaders in the USA. Undertaken at the Columbia Bureau of Applied Social Research (BASR), it inevitably took the form of a quantitative study. As Miliband pointed out, the other two studies have more originality and sweep but the first study must be seen in the light of the contemporary situation it was set within. Labour leaders can be considered an elite among their peers, but Mills, nevertheless, really thought that trades unions would make a difference for the situation of ordinary people in America. This was, however, before the Cold War and a different political climate took hold.

White Collar represents a continuation of his study into stratification. Its focus is on the emerging American middle class of 'the dependent employee': office workers, nurses, teachers, managers and insurance agents whose values are apolitical but nevertheless conservative and stand in contrast to the independent entrepreneurial spirit of the traditional American middle classes. 'The shift from skills with things to skills with persons', Mills held, implies that the 'white collars' sell their services and a 'personality market' emerges where 'correct' emotional responses are taught in courses. The white-collar jobs therefore involve a different type of alienation from that of production work: estrangement from self and from other people. This book was the one of Mills' publications that received the most unanimously positive reception among reviewers and the wider public.

The third book in this trilogy, *The Power Elite*, focuses on three loci of power in American society: the corporate rich, the military leadership and the political directorate. Whereas the first had traditionally had their power base in regional businesses, they were becoming increasingly national and a managerial elite within corporations had replaced the propertied class who made their profits from ownership. The military had during the Cold War become more autonomous and independent of political control, a trait that Mills was very concerned about. What he termed the political directorate comprised the very powerful few in the executive branch of the state who had strengthened their power in the political sphere in the post-war era. The most powerful political figures were those who were well connected in the corporate world and had close ties within the military. Mills charted the fusion of these three groups into a single 'power elite'.

Together these three books make up the most important publications from Mills' empirical studies. *White Collar* and *The Power Elite* are still widely read, and indeed also inspire contemporary research such as that of Arlie Hochschild in *The Managed Heart* and Richard Sennett in *The Corrosion of Character*.

Mills was not only a thorough and committed empirical researcher. He was also a radical political analyst and writer. When Castro came to power in Cuba in 1959, Mills was, according to his personal letters, rather unaware of the significance of the event for Latin America as well as for the USA itself. He then visited Cuba for two weeks in 1960 and while there he met with Castro and with Che Guevara, among others. What seem to have impressed him most were the health care and the education systems and what he interpreted as an independent socialism. *Listen Yankee: The Cuban Case against the United States* was written from the viewpoint of a Cuban revolutionary who explains the situation in his country and its relationship to the USA to a wider US public. With this book Mills reached a wider readership than he had previously enjoyed: the paperback version sold half a million copies and was translated into Spanish, Greek and Italian. Mills' radical political viewpoints during the height of the Cold War, and especially his passionate defence of the Cuban Revolution, had inevitably brought him to the attention of the Federal Bureau of Investigation, who kept him under surveillance for years. He received anonymous threats of assassination at the hands of American undercover agents on his next visit to Cuba.

The public discussion created by *Listen Yankee* and the attention around Mills' person was, in his own words, exhausting. For years he had been suffering from hypertension. At the beginning of 1961 he was due to appear in a television debate with a conservative senator on the subject of Cuba, but he had a massive heart attack two days prior to the debate. Although he recovered from this, he died from another heart attack fifteen months later, on 20 March 1962. He left three children, a wife and two ex-wives.

Mills was an ardent writer and scholar. Considering his short life and career, the eight single-authored books and the four co-authored ones, plus many articles and papers, demonstrate a productive writer. His viewpoints were distinct and direct. In his day he is said to have made more enemies than friends and was often regarded as a difficult person to be around. The historical period during which he researched and published was characterized by attitudes and values that ran contrary to his. American society in the Cold War period was deeply conservative and suspicious of radical political and social scientific ideas. American sociology was influenced by this climate. Mills consequently found it wanting, and saw the most prominent directions in sociology of his time as concerned with irrelevant problems that were either related to 'The Theory' (grand theory) or 'The Method' (abstracted empiricism). The most prominent representative of the former was **Talcott Parsons**, and Paul Lazarsfeld, Mills' superior at BASR, was a leading figure of the latter. This critique was elaborated in *The Sociological Imagination*, a book that sums up many of Mills' ideas and ideals over his intellectual career. In it he lays out not only his critique of the wrongs of contemporary sociology but also his vision of what he thought sociology should be about: 'the sociological imagination enables us to grasp history and biography and the relations between the two within society'. One of the key insights in this book, and indeed in most of Mills' writing, is that at the core of sociology must be a focus on how 'private troubles' are also 'public issues'. Individual biography can only be made sense of in the context of history; and history cannot be comprehended without understanding people in their contexts. Sociology is about the intersection of the two and one of the discipline's main objectives is to help people make sense of the wider societies in which they live. Any reader, student or scholar will learn something from Mills' thoughts on the practice of research, from the designing of projects to the development of concepts that are outlined in the appendix entitled 'On Intellectual Craftsmanship'.

See also: Ralph Miliband.

See also in *Fifty Key Sociologists: The Formative Theorists*: George Herbert Mead, Karl Marx, Max Weber.

Major works

Sociology and Pragmatism: The Higher Learning in America. 1942. New York: Oxford University Press, 1964.
Power, Politics and People. (Essays of 1930s and 1940s.) New York: Oxford University Press, 1963.
The New Men of Power. America's Labor Leaders. 1948. New York: Harcourt, Brace & Company.
White Collar. The American Middle Classes. 1951. New York: Oxford University Press.
The Power Elite. 1956. New York: Oxford University Press.
The Sociological Imagination. 1959. London: Penguin.
Listen Yankee: The Cuban Case against the United States. 1960. New York: Ballantine.

Further reading

Irving Louis Horowitz, ed. 1964. *The New Sociology. Essays in Social Science and Social Theory in Honor of C. Wright Mills.* New York: Oxford University Press.
Irving Louis Horowitz. 1984. *C. Wright Mills. An American Utopian.* New York: The Free Press.
Kathryn Mills, Pamela Mills and Dan Wakefield Mills, eds. 2000. *C. Wright Mills. Letters and Autobiographical Writings.* Berkeley, CA: University of California Press.

ANN NILSEN

ANN OAKLEY

Ann Oakley was born in 1944, the daughter of Richard and Kay Titmuss. Richard Titmuss was himself an influential social scientist and wrote several significant works on the welfare state, including *The Gift Relationship*, which was republished in an edition co-edited by Oakley in 1997. The influence of both her parents on her own intellectual development can also be found in her double biography of them, *Man and Wife*. Oakley's undergraduate study at Oxford University was followed by a PhD at the University of London, in which she undertook the study of housework; this resulted in two books, *Housewife* and *The Sociology of Housework*, that were to have a major and longstanding influence on sociology. These works reflected her commitment to a feminist social science that remains central to her thought and work. Her subsequent academic career included periods at Bedford College, University of London, and at the National

Perinatal Epidemiology Unit, University of Oxford. In 1985 she took up post at the Institute of Education, University of London, and has remained there since. She set up the Social Science Research Unit in 1990, which she headed until the beginning of 2005, and also established the Evidence for Policy and Practice Information and Co-ordinating Centre (EPPI-Centre) in 1993. Alongside her academic writing she has maintained her early interest in writing fiction; for example, *The Men's Room* was published in 1988 and subsequently televised. She has also written in forms which cross genre boundaries, combining fiction and non-fiction, academic research and creative writing.

In the edited reader of her own work, Oakley partitions her intellectual contribution into four segments: 'sex and gender', 'housework and family life', 'childbirth, motherhood and medicine' and 'doing social science'. While there are obvious overlaps between the sections – for example, her substantive work reflects her approaches to social science methodology and concerns with gender pervade her work – these four areas nevertheless reflect those in which Oakley has made unique and influential contributions to sociology.

Oakley is widely credited as having introduced the concept of 'gender' into the social sciences. She distinguished between the biological 'fact' of sex (itself not a clear, binary distinction) and culturally specific expressions and expectations of 'masculinity' and 'femininity', which are justified by association with biological sex and therefore appear immutable. She exposed the process by which the 'lines are tied between the act of giving birth and the act of cleaning the house' as determined by a form of social ascription unrelated to individual capacities and open to challenge. Oakley has subsequently defended gender as a valuable sociological concept against criticisms from and rejections by postmodernists (including feminist postmodernists) and socio-biologists. And she maintains that the gender/ sex distinction continues to have analytic value, despite recognition of the contingent nature of sex itself. She argues that the sex/gender distinction retains a crucial role in identifying and exploring persisting material inequalities and their ideational causes.

Oakley, according to her biographical note, 'puzzled the academic establishment' by venturing on a study of housework for her PhD. However, both her insights into housework as a form of work that is physically demanding and emotionally draining and her quantification of the hours that women spent on this work in addition to or instead of paid employment created a sociological place for housework and were (and have remained) highly influential. One example of such influence is in Ivan Illich's work *Gender*, in which he explicitly acknowledged the influence of Oakley's investigations of housework on his thought and writing.

In studying housework, a subject that had not previously been considered worthy of sociological scrutiny, Oakley revealed the masculinism of the discipline. Not only have most of the main sociologists been men, but the topics they have studied and the way in which they have studied them have been masculine in their orientation. Therefore topics or aspects of topics that do not accord with a masculine worldview have often been neglected or considered to be outside the domain of sociology. In addition, those subjects which have been considered worthy of study have been treated in ways which reinforce the perspectives of the powerful. Oakley's work can be seen as challenging this hegemony on both fronts.

This is reflected in her work on motherhood, which followed the housework research. Oakley had a long association with medical sociology and studies of health care, which began with a study of sixty-six London women having their first babies. This research demonstrated (and presumably fed) her feminist commitment to the welfare of women and to the role of social science within that. It brought a new bearing to the sociological understanding of motherhood, as with the housework study; challenged the naturalization of highly gendered experiences of medical intervention and care; and questioned the existing relationship between science and women's reproductive experience. Her investigation emphasized the experiences of antenatal contact and of giving birth of the mothers themselves. Accessing the world of her subjects through both interviews and observations of doctor–patient encounters was a critical part of her study; and the stress on appropriate method and the potential impact of investigation, whether social scientific or medical scientific, was also captured in her collection of feedback from the participants of the study on their experience of being research subjects.

Oakley's study of housework had already demonstrated her interest in methodology. It reflected on the appropriateness of her methodology, with a detailed account of her approach and the extent to which inferences could be drawn from her findings. She has consistently argued that it is critical that all research should contribute to knowledge, and to knowledge that can be used in evaluating and challenging myths: anything else, she claims, is unethical. As a feminist, she has continued to assert that well-designed empirical research has an important role to play in documenting the lived realities of women's lives in the service of producing practical truths with emancipatory potential. In this she has offered a means to resist the ultimately futile qualitative versus quantitative paradigm wars and the tendency for feminism to be inseparably associated with qualitative research. Instead, she has argued that it is the fitness for purpose of social science research and its potential for challenging, rather than reinforcing, dominant and oppressive structures and interpersonal power relations that are the issues at stake.

In line with her concern with method and with the production of usable knowledge that can influence policy, she has defended randomized controlled trials as an instrument of feminist research and argued that British social science is unwarrantedly neglectful of experiment. There were, she considered, also lessons to be learned from the medical establishment's attempts to create a firmer evidence base for interventions. The establishment of the EPPI-Centre was intended to bring the principles and benefits of meta-analysis, associated with the Cochrane Collaboration, into social science. In doing this, Oakley attempted to show the potential for combining quantitative approaches with qualitative material. In stressing the potential for synthesizing methodological approaches she has contested the gendering of her own research and also highlighted the extent to which research methods, as well as research domains, can be interrogated in relation to the historical contexts which have produced and shaped them. Consistent with her retention of the utility of the concept of gender, the implication of her methodological argument is that if a condition of feminist research is instead the femininity of its methods, then it will risk naturalizing the very inequalities it is trying to challenge.

See also: Simone de Beauvoir.

Further reading

Sex, Gender and Society. 1972. London: Temple Smith

The Sociology of Housework. 1974. Oxford: Martin Robertson. Also published as *Woman's Work.*

Housewife. 1974. Harmondsworth, Penguin.

Becoming a Mother. 1979. Oxford: Martin Robertson. Also published as *From Here to Maternity.*

Women Confined: Towards a Sociology of Childbirth. 1980. New York: Schoken.

Subject Women. 1981. Oxford: Martin Robertson.

The Captured Womb: A History of the Medical Care of Pregnant Women. 1984. Oxford: Basil Blackwell.

Experiments in Knowing: Gender and Method in the Social Sciences. 2000. Cambridge: Polity Press.

Some extracts from her work can be found in *The Ann Oakley Reader: Gender, Women and Social Science*. Bristol: The Policy Press, 2005.

LUCINDA PLATT

TALCOTT PARSONS

Despite his reputation for impenetrable prose and the coining of unnecessary jargon, Parsons became one of the most influential sociologists of his generation and his ideas continue to inform the work of many other theorists. Parsons' writing style reflects the fact that he was among the first to attempt to move social theory to a more analytical level of general and highly formal theorizing. Such a strategy required a more precise use of concepts and, because of its level of abstraction, was difficult to express in simple, everyday language. These days, formal and abstract theorizing has become far more common and Parsons' language no longer appears so dense and impenetrable – certainly when compared with some of the French and German theorists who have worked in the wake of his ideas. Those turning to Parsons today now tend to be pleasantly surprised by the relative ease with which his principal ideas can be understood.

Talcott Parsons was born in Colorado in 1902, the son of a Congregational minister who became principal of a small college in Ohio. Parsons intended to study biology or medicine and went to Amherst College, Massachusetts, to begin his degree. At Amherst he became interested in economics and sociology and he shifted his academic interests in this direction. Reading Sumner, Cooley, Durkheim and Veblen, Parsons became fascinated by the question of the relationship between economics and sociology and the whole question of the embedding or institutionalizing of economic relations in a larger social context. After graduating from Amherst he took up an opportunity to study in Europe and he spent the year 1924–5 at the London School of Economics, studying with Leonard Hobhouse and the anthropologist Bronislaw Malinowski. He moved on to Heidelberg, where the influence of Max Weber was still strong, and Weber's version of economic sociology became the overriding influence on his own thought. It was European social theory – and especially that of Weber and Durkheim – that became his principal concern, and he sought to work through the implications of their ideas in his doctoral dissertation. In 1927 he obtained a job at Harvard University in the

Department led by Pitirim Sorokin, and he began work on his major study *The Structure of Social Action*, published ten years later.

The argument of *The Structure of Social Action* was that the works of the formative sociologists had laid the foundations for a new departure in social theory. Durkheim and Weber, along with Vilfredo Pareto and the economist Alfred Marshall, were seen as the leading representatives of the formative tradition in sociology and as having converged, from different starting points, on the outlines of a novel and sophisticated approach to social theory. They had, in their varying ways, resolved the 'Hobbesian problem of order', which Parsons saw as inherent in individualistic theories of self-interested action of the kind studied in economics. Conflict and disorder can be avoided, they argued, only where the exercise of individual self-interest is constrained by a moral framework of shared cultural values. Durkheim and Weber, in particular, showed that these moral values – ultimately religious in origin – were the key elements of social order. Individuals are socialized into systems of cultural values and build up normative expectations that are formed into the social institutions through which individual action is regulated.

Parsons saw his own task as the elaboration of this emergent body of theory, furthering the synthesis that had become apparent in their individual works. He described the new social theory as the 'voluntaristic' theory of action. What he meant by this was that individual actors are not determined in their actions by their material conditions or their socialization: they must exercise choice among the alternatives open to them and so must be seen as acting voluntarily. The subjective choices made by actors are based on, but not determined by, the values that they have acquired during their socialization. Voluntaristic action involves a choice among alternative ends or goals and the use of means towards those goals that are appropriate in relation to the conditions under which the individuals find themselves and the moral values to which they are committed.

These ideas were elaborated in an approach to social theory that placed the concept of the 'social system' at the centre of attention. The idea of the social system was being elaborated at Harvard by the physiologist Lawrence Henderson, who drew strongly on the ideas of Pareto and was inspiring the early work of people such as **George Homans**. According to this point of view the actions of individuals and groups were interrelated with the institutions and other structures produced through their actions and could, therefore, be analysed in terms of the systematic relations among these elements. Following the publication of *The Structure of Social Action*, Parsons began to develop this idea in a series of essays in which he set out an approach to what he called 'structural functionalism'.

Structural functionalism was seen by Parsons as a first approximation to a truly general theory of social systems. In the stage at which sociological understanding had arrived, he argued, it would be premature to move directly to a general, perhaps mathematical, theory of the social system. Certain simplifying assumptions had to be made that would allow a realistic, yet cut-down model to be constructed. The aim of a structural functional analysis is to identify certain structural 'parts' of a social system (such as roles and social institutions) that have a 'functional significance' for the system. Functional significance itself involves two distinct problems: the relationship between a system and its environment (termed 'adaptation') and the interconnections among the parts of the system itself (termed 'integration'). Thus, roles and institutions can be classified according to whether they have an adaptive or an integrative significance for the system, and any system is best described by starting out from its adaptive and integrative structures. All processes within a system, according to Parsons, must either contribute to the reproduction and patterned development of the system or be 'dysfunctional'. The dynamic element in structural-functional analysis is provided by the socialization of individuals into the motivational patterns that allow them to reproduce the social structures. Breakdown and disorder result from 'failures' of such socialization.

Parsons developed this model further in his most famous work, *The Social System*. In this book – reputedly his most difficult – he constructed a complex set of analytical categories for the analysis of action, interaction and social structure. All the various elements and structural parts that he identified were systematically related to the functions of adaptation and integration, though Parsons began to move away from this towards a more complex four-function scheme. He made this move by introducing what he called the 'pattern variables'. These were analytical categories for describing the elements involved in individual choices of action. Values and motives, and therefore roles and institutions, could be analysed in terms of a limited set of categories that define the ranges within which they can vary. Drawing on the arguments of such writers as Weber and Tönnies on the contrast between traditionalism and rationalism, Parsons identified a number of pairs of pattern variables: affectivity/neutrality, particularism/universalism, ascription/achievement and diffuseness/specificity. The first item in each pair relates to the traditional or 'emotional' pole, and they are principally involved in defining integrative roles and institutions. The second item in each pair, on the other hand, relates to the rational pole and they are principally involved in defining adaptive roles and institutions. While Parsons' discussion of these ideas in the abstract is very complex, he illustrated their usage in a famous and influential study of doctor–patient relationships and the sick role.

As he developed his account of the pattern variables, Parsons came to recognize that they do not all hang together in a neat way. Instead of just two combinations of variables (adaptive and integrative) he began to identify four combinations. These corresponded to the functional problems that he termed adaptation, goal attainment, integration and latent pattern maintenance. This new conception of the social system was elaborated in two volumes of working papers and in a comprehensive account, written with Neil Smelser, that returned to his analysis of the relationship between economy and society. In these books, Parsons developed his characteristic diagrams of the social system in which each functional 'subsystem' was indicated by a box embedded in a larger box (see Figure 2).

Social processes could be analytically distinguished according to the specific functional problem with which they are primarily concerned. The social structures of a society show a tendency over time to differentiate along functional lines. That is, they tend to become functionally specialized. Thus, economic activities are seen as differentiated from the larger society as they become specialized into roles, organizations and institutions that deal with adaptive matters. Political activities, on the other hand, are those structural elements that have come to be specialized in goal attainment issues. The core of any society comprises its 'communal' features that relate to integrative problems. These are less likely to be differentiated in simpler societies and it is only in modern societies that the tendency to structural differentiation operates in this area, resulting in a relative differentiation of

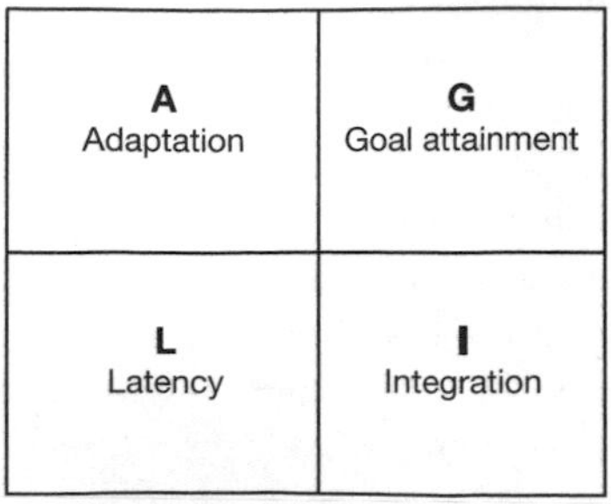

A Adaptation	**G** Goal attainment
L Latency	**I** Integration

Figure 2: The four-function scheme.

institutions concerned with kinship, law and social stratification from other social institutions. Activities involved in latent pattern maintenance through socialization into shared social values remain the most diffuse of all, though religious institutions were an early form of structural differentiation around this problem.

A particularly important feature of Parsons' work was that he saw these functional processes occurring at a number of distinct levels. Social systems were seen as one type of element in larger action systems, which were, in turn, seen as differentiated into personality and cultural systems as well as social systems. Thus, psychology, sociology and anthropology (the science of culture) were seen as academic disciplines focused around specific functional problems of human action. This overarching scheme became the basis of a reorganization of the teaching of the social sciences at Harvard during the 1950s, as Parsons, by then head of department, created an inter-disciplinary Department of Social Relations.

During the 1960s Parsons began to feel that it was possible to move beyond structural functionalism to the more general and analytical approach that he had sought in his early work. His inspiration in moving his intellectual project forward was the development of general system theory. Taking his four-function system as the starting point, Parsons attempted to develop dynamic models of the 'interchanges' between subsystems. According to this model, each subsystem operates in terms of a particular 'medium of exchange' and generates 'outputs' that serve as 'inputs' to other subsystems. The four subsystems, therefore, are connected through a series of 'double interchanges', through which inputs and outputs are exchanged. The economy, for example, is organized around money as its medium of exchange, producing the goods and services required by other subsystems. The political system, on the other hand, is organized around 'power' and produces the mobilization and support required for societal goal attainment and the pursuit of other social activities. The analysis of 'generalized media' became a central part of Parsons' work in the 1960s and 1970s as he took money as his model for such media as power, influence (or prestige) and commitments. He explored the cultural codes through which each medium is structured and the roles, organizations and institutions involved in its generation, accumulation and distribution.

This analysis of interchanges among subsystems became the basis on which he recast his model of the action system to highlight the causal linkages involved in the structure of social action. There is, he argued, a 'cybernetic hierarchy' according to which those subsystems that are high in 'information' are able to guide and control the development of the overall system through the shaping of value choices and subjective patterns of motivation. Subsystems high in 'energy', on the other hand, are able to limit or condition this development through the availability and distribution of resources. The overall development of any action system, then, is an outcome of both controlling and conditioning factors.

The over-generalization of Parsons' scheme and the high level of abstraction on which it was cast led many to reject his whole approach. His emphasis on socialization, shared values and social order was frequently depicted as exhibiting social conservatism and a failure to recognize the importance of social conflict and organized deviance. There was undoubtedly some truth in these criticisms, and Parsons' work was rapidly supplanted by more radical approaches during the 1960s and 1970s. Since his death in 1979, however, the implications of his arguments have been reassessed and have been taken up in the work of neo-functionalists such as Jeffrey Alexander and system theorists such as Niklas Luhmann.

See also: David Lockwood, Niklas Luhmann, Robert Merton.

See also in *Fifty Key Sociologists: The Formative Theorists*: Emile Durkheim, Bronislaw Malinowski, Vilfredo Pareto, Max Weber.

Major works

The Early Essays. (Essays of 1928–37.) Chicago: University of Chicago Press, 1991.
The Structure of Social Action. 1937. New York: McGraw Hill.
The Social System. 1951. New York: Free Press.
Towards A General Theory of Action. 1951. With Edward Shils. Cambridge, MA: Harvard University Press.
Working Papers in the Theory of Action. 1953. With Robert F. Bales and Edward Shils. New York: Free Press.
Essays in Sociological Theory. (Essays of 1938–53.) Revised edn. New York: Free Press, 1954.
Family, Socialization and Interaction Process. 1956. With Robert F. Bales. London: Routledge & Kegan Paul.
Economy and Society. 1956. With Neil J. Smelser. New York: Free Press.
Structure and Process in Modern Society. (Essays of 1956–9.) New York: Free Press, 1960.
Social Structure and Personality. (Essays of 1952–63.) New York: Free Press, 1964.
Sociological Theory and Modern Society. (Essays of 1959–65.) New York: Free Press, 1967.

Societies: Evolutionary and Comparative Perspectives. 1966. Englewood Cliffs, NJ: Prentice-Hall.
Politics and Social Structure. (Essays of 1942–68.) New York: Free Press, 1969.
The System of Modern Societies. 1971. Englewood Cliffs, NJ: Prentice-Hall.
The American University. 1973. With Gerald Platt. Cambridge, MA: Harvard University Press.
Social Systems and the Evolution of Action Theory. (Essays of 1968–75.) New York: Free Press, 1977.
Action Theory and the Human Condition. (Essays of 1968–76.) New York: Free Press, 1978.

Further reading

Uta Gerhardt. 2002. *Talcott Parsons: An Intellectual Biography.* Cambridge: Cambridge University Press.
Peter Hamilton. 1983. *Talcott Parsons.* London: Routledge.
Roland Robertson and Bryan S. Turner, eds. 1991. *Talcott Parsons: Theorist of Modernity.* London: Sage.

JOHN SCOTT

ORLANDO PATTERSON

Orlando Patterson is professor of sociology at Harvard University, where he has taught since 1969. He was born in 1941 and completed his early schooling in Jamaica, receiving his BSc in economics in 1962 from the University College of the West Indies. He earned his PhD in sociology from the London School of Economics in 1965 and he taught briefly at the London School of Economics and at the University of the West Indies before moving to Harvard. While most of his work is primarily sociological – and falls largely within the field of what is now called historical sociology – he has also written three novels and is widely known as a public intellectual through his frequent short pieces and critical essays in well-established newspapers (such as *The New York Times* and *New Republic*) and his television discussions of contemporary issues of significant public interest. Celebrated as a profound thinker of tremendous magnitude and scope – his books on comparative slavery and on freedom tackle massive structures, huge processes and lengthy time periods – he is known for broadening the terms of debates on well-established areas, often highlighting unexamined or under-examined assumptions. He has been awarded numerous prizes for his scholarship, including the

Distinguished Contribution to Scholarship Award of the American Sociological Association (the Sorokin Prize), and the National Book Award. He is a fellow of the American Academy of Arts and Sciences. He worked as special advisor on social policy and development to the prime minister of Jamaica in the 1970s, and he was awarded the Order of Distinction (Commander Class) by the Jamaican government in 1999 for his public service to that nation. While he worked as special advisor to the government of Jamaica he published a number of papers and policy reports.

Patterson's first set of important writings was on Caribbean slave society, with a particular emphasis on Jamaica, the largest slave society in the English-speaking Caribbean. His subsequent academic interests moved in several directions, including a monumental comparative study of slavery in all times and places in the world, a study of the origins, elaboration and purview of the concept of freedom, especially in western societies, and an analysis of race and ethnic relations in the USA in the period since 1966.

Patterson's PhD dissertation was published as *The Sociology of Slavery* in 1967. In it he examines the structure and functioning of Jamaican slave society and the underlying facts that account for its development under British occupation. He examines the economic foundations of profit, the social relations of production, and the social institutions and mechanisms of resistance of the slaves. While the data are historical, the subject is sociological: it concerns itself with an analysis of social values and social change in this society, as well as the more fundamental theoretical concerns of social order and social control. *Slavery and Social Death*, published in 1982, is a work of prodigious scholarship and enormous breadth which draws on evidence from the tribal, ancient, pre-modern and modern worlds to discuss the internal dynamics of slavery in sixty-six societies over time. It begins with the compelling assertion that

> [Slavery] has existed from before the dawn of human history right down to the twentieth century, in the most primitive of human societies and in the most civilised. There is no region on earth that has not at some time harboured the institution.

These societies include Greece and Rome, medieval Europe, China, Korea, the Islamic kingdoms, Africa, the Caribbean islands and the American South. Patterson's goal is to 'define and explore empirically, in all its aspects, the nature and inner dynamics of slavery and the institutional patterns that supported it'. One of his principal conclusions is that the enslaved in all these societies, despite their differences, are desocialized and depersonalized; that is, they are socially dead and have no existence outside that of their master's existence. He confronts the enigma that slavery has been ubiquitous across all societies and that it has been a central defining factor in shaping some of western society's most cherished beliefs, for example civilization and freedom.

The first of a two-volume historical sociology of freedom was published in June 1991, entitled *Freedom: Freedom in the Making of Western Culture*. In this book he continues his analysis of the inextricable link between freedom and slavery, distinguishing several different types of freedom – personal, sovereign, civic – and analysing the potential evils that inhere in each one. He is at present completing the second volume of *Freedom*, dealing with the modern world.

His analysis of race, immigration and multiculturalism in the contemporary USA has been covered in two volumes, *The Ordeal of Integration* and *Rituals of Blood*. The first book examines the tremendous gains and progress made by African-Americans in achieving civil and economic equality, while the second considers the human cost of America's legacy of racism, focusing on the crisis of black gender relations as reflected in, for example, high rates of premarital childbirth and high rates of divorce, and on the range of images of African-Americans in society today. Patterson's main argument is that poverty, not race, is the main reason for the failure of integration. Large numbers of whites and blacks remain in poverty, even in families with two people working. His work criticizes national leaders and social scientists who benefit from the stereotype of a racially polarized society. Embracing a climate of optimism is the way forward, he argues, recognizing the real gains and the primacy of examining poverty and seeking changes in the national economy and in cultural practices – for example through challenging a romanticized and fashionable belief in teenage childbearing.

As a public intellectual Patterson has not hesitated to tackle politically charged issues, often intervening in debates on affirmative action and on gender relations in the black community. His position has most often been more nuanced than those of the traditional analysts, as he questions the received wisdom of most debates. For example, he questions whether evidence reveals that the benefits of affirmative action have outweighed the costs. He has highlighted the obstacles facing middle-class black women, who currently face a shortage of equally qualified and educated black men as long-term partners or husbands. And he has roundly criticized the lyrics of hip hop music, labelling them misogynist and hateful.

Patterson continues to have a significant influence in academic research on slavery and freedom and he is widely quoted by an entire generation of writers on these topics, in particular those trained in the wide range of departments of sociology and history across universities in Britain in the 1970s and 1980s.

See also in *Fifty Key Sociologists: The Formative Theorists*: Oliver Cox, Max Weber.

Major works

The Sociology of Slavery. An Analysis of the Origins, Development and Structure of Negro Slave Society in Jamaica. 1967. London: McGibbon and Kee.

Slavery and Social Death. A Comparative Study. 1982. Cambridge, MA: Harvard University Press.

Freedom: Freedom in the Making of Western Culture, vol. 1. 1991. New York: Basic Books.

The Ordeal of Integration: Progress and Resentment in America's 'Racial' Crisis. 1997. Washington, DC: Civitas Counterpoint.

Rituals of Blood: The Consequences of Slavery in Two American Centuries. 1998. Washington, DC: Civitas Counterpoint.

STEPHEN SMALL

EDWARD SAID

The Palestinian-American scholar, writer, activist and musicologist Edward Said was born in Jerusalem, Palestine, in 1935 and died in New York in 2003. A genuine Renaissance man in a world of increasing intellectual specialization, he is best known for work in literary and cultural criticism; on the Arab–Israeli conflict, especially his documenting and advocacy of the Palestinian cause; and in the field of Orientalism, which his groundbreaking work of the same name challenged to devastating effect. Among the more than twenty books he wrote during his life, including classic texts such as *Beginnings, Culture and Imperialism* and his autobiography *Out Of Place,* it is the work entitled *Orientalism* – aptly subtitled *Western Conceptions of the Orient* – that justifiably led to his international reputation as a critic and social theorist. Not least, this is because it consolidated the development of cultural studies while sparking the emergence of 'subaltern' and 'postcolonial' studies. Indeed, from the perspective of the social sciences, it is this controversial and challenging book that deserves greatest consideration.

Said contends that 'Orientalism' consists of a loose body of ideas and values stretching back to classical antiquity, evident in accounts of 'the East' by western travellers, colonial administrators and military leaders, as well as representations by novelists, artists and composers. Drawing on theorists such as Antonio Gramsci and **Michel Foucault**, Said understood European constructions of knowledge and stereotypical images of other cultures as 'discourses' in Foucault's sense of the term. This means that representations of the Orient by westerners are discursive practices that fix the meaning of the objects about which knowledge and truth are obtained. And fixing 'our' knowledge and meanings of an object such as 'the Orient' has, he argued, important social and political ramifications.

Said analysed four such implications. First, he argues, Orientalist discourses 'essentialize' the Orient by imposing an eternal, homogenous and thus ultimately erroneous form on to a heterogeneous and changing set of practices and institutions. In Orientalist discourse, therefore, 'the Orient' is constructed as fundamentally static, passive, non-autonomous, traditional and non-Occidental. This essentialism has the second implication of presenting the Orient as 'an Other' that is inherently opposed to the West. In this way, the relationship between the Occident and the Orient forms a binary opposition, in which the latter term and its alleged properties – such as a propensity for tyrannical forms of political rule (so-called 'Oriental despotism') – are used to construct a sense of western identity as external to the Orient. This identity is then reinforced by presenting the East as an antagonistic threat to the West and its values. In more technical terms, the Orient performs the role of a 'constitutive outside' that fixes the identity of the West while potentially destabilizing and subverting it.

Third, the vast archive of 'Orientalized' statements constitutes a powerful set of constraints on what can be said, thought and done about 'the Orient'. Said thus showed how a 'will to knowledge over the Orient' informs Orientalism as a body of representations by providing the intellectual and cultural means for appropriating the Orient by European colonization and imperialism. Even more, Said emphasized the *general* complicity of all knowledge and political institutions and practices. The final implication is directly and practically political, as Said argued that Orientalist representations actively impede a proper exchange and mutual interaction between East and West. This observation is vital for Said's understanding and criticism of Orientalism as a power structure, as his basic interest is to dissolve the misleading barriers that have been established by Orientalist writers and to furnish the possibility of a meaningful cultural exchange between different societies. For Said, this could be achieved in the name of a humanism that transcends cultural particularity, thus providing the universal vantage point for developing a satisfactory *modus vivendi* between different formations.

There are at least two critical issues raised by Said's account. The first concerns the way that Said thought about the connection between discourse/knowledge and social reality. This is a vital question because it raises questions about our knowledge of the world and the objects which knowledge seeks to apprehend. Here Said's work is ambiguous in deciding whether or not the discourse of Orientalism comprises a system of statements that *represent* the Orient, or whether Orientalist discourse actually *brings into existence* the object or reality it describes. Said's answer wavers between a weak and strong answer to the question. The weaker version suggests that the discourse 'is a *system of representations* framed by a whole set of forces that brought the Orient into Western learning'. In this view, '[t]he phenomenon of Orientalism ... deals principally, not with a correspondence between Orientalism and Orient, but with the *internal consistency of Orientalism and its ideas* about the Orient ... despite or beyond any correspondence, or lack thereof, with a "real" Orient'. On the other hand, however, especially after the failure of Napoleon's occupation of Egypt, 'the very language of Orientalism changed radically ... and became not merely a style of representation but a language, indeed a means of *creation*'. In this perspective, then, Orientalist texts '*create* not only knowledge but also the very reality they appear to describe'.

This ambiguity about the nature of the Orient has important consequences for his epistemological stance. If Said is to remain faithful to a conception of knowledge in which statements represent the way the world is, then he must assume that there is something to be represented and that a particular representation either represents or misrepresents social reality. By contrast, if he questions whether or not the Orient actually exists, as in his view that Orientalist discourse produces its own object of analysis, then he may be required to articulate a different conception of knowledge and truth – say a species of relativism, conventionalism or postmodernism. However, if he chooses the latter, then the category of representation itself is jeopardized, which Said half-recognizes towards the end of *Orientalism*, arguing that

Since Islam *has* been fundamentally misrepresented in the West – *the real issue is whether indeed there can be a true representation of anything,* or whether any and all representations, are embedded first in the language and then in the culture, institutions, and political ambience of the representer.

Here he accepts that representations are '*eo ipso* implicated, intertwined, embedded, interwoven with a great many other things besides the "truth", which is itself a representation'. This leads to the methodological observation that we are 'to view representations … as inhabiting a common field of play defined for them, not by some inherent common subject matter alone, but by some common history, tradition, universe of discourse'.

Nevertheless, despite these misgivings, Said never spells out the full implications of the last thought, and his reference to the '*mis-representation*' of Islam in the West itself undercuts the reservations to which he alludes. Instead, it is left to Timothy Mitchell to challenge the very concept of representation, arguing that it is important to understand how the West came to see the world as divided between a sphere of representations and a sphere of 'real' objects. In other words, the key issue is to grasp *how* the division of the social world into 'representations' and 'reality' was the product of modern Western discursive practices, which then served as templates for our knowledge and understanding of social reality.

The *second* issue concerns Said's critique of Orientalism, which is based on the affirmation of universal 'humanistic values' and the defence of 'human experiences' that are systematically denied by Orientalism. Said argues that 'Orientalist reality is both anti-human and persistent', thus constituting the major 'intellectual issue' raised by Orientalism, that of whether it is humanly reasonable to divide the world into clearly differentiated cultures or societies. In so doing, Said stresses the role of the intellectual as an 'independent critical consciousness' who employs 'humanist critique' to oppose the anti-humanist ideology of Orientalism.

One potential difficulty here is that the very universal values that Said invokes are themselves products of the western discourses that are allegedly complicit with Orientalism. Another is whether his affirmation of universal human values sits comfortably with his desire to affirm the particularity and heterogeneity of different cultures. And lastly there is the position and function of the humanist intellectual. While Said is unrepentant about affirming the role of the humanist critic in being able to recognize 'that the historical world is made by men and women, and not by God, and that it can be understood rationally', his view leaves open an account of the 'grip' which ideologies such as Orientalism exercise upon subjects, as well as the obstacles that stand in the way of dissolving such 'mind-forged manacles'.

In a world marked by the events of 11 September 2001, a global 'war on terror', where major western powers such as Britain and the United States have invaded Afghanistan and Iraq to secure 'regime change', in which the conflict in Israel between Jew and Palestinian shows no sign of being resolved, it is arguable that no book in contemporary social theory is more important than Edward Said's *Orientalism*. Though controversial in its argument and political implications, it has established its author as one of the key thinkers of the modern period.

See also: Michel Foucault, Gayatri Spivak.

See also in *Fifty Key Sociologists: The Formative Theorists*: Antonio Gramsci.

Major works

Joseph Conrad and the Fiction of Autobiography. 1966. Cambridge, MA: Harvard University Press.
Beginnings. 1975. Baltimore, MD: Johns Hopkins University Press.
Orientalism. 1978. New York: Random House.
The Question Of Palestine. 1979. New York: Vintage, 1980.
Literature and Society. 1980. Baltimore, MD: Johns Hopkins University Press.
The World, the Text and the Critic. 1983. Cambridge, MA: Harvard University Press.
Musical Elaborations. 1991. New York: Columbia University Press.
Culture and Imperialism. 1993. New York: Random House.
Out of Place: A Memoir. 1999. New York: Knopf.

Further reading

Timothy Mitchell. 1991. *Colonising Egypt.* Cambridge: Cambridge University Press.

DAVID HOWARTH

DOROTHY SMITH

A feminist sociologist, Dorothy Smith is best known for her influential text *The Everyday World as Problematic: A Feminist Sociology* and for the development of the methodological strategy of 'institutional ethnography'.

Dorothy E. Smith was born in Huddersfield, England, in 1926, the only daughter in a middle-class family of four children. Her teenage years were affected by war and her childhood education has been described as haphazard. She had a range of paid jobs, including clerical work for a publishing house in London, before deciding in her twenties to go to university. She completed her first degree in social anthropology at the London School of Economics in 1955. There she encountered a strong group of young lecturers and postgraduates in the social sciences, including Ralph Dahrendorf, **David Lockwood**, Norman Birnbaum, Asher Tropp and Leonore Davidoff, at a time when sociology was entering a period of rapid and exciting growth and when European sociologists were engaging critically with, and reinterpreting, the structural functionalism of **Talcott Parsons**. She also met her future husband, an American veteran, Bill Smith, and they decided to do postgraduate work in sociology at the University of California at Berkeley.

At Berkeley she took a wide range of courses, including one by Tamotsu Shibutani on the work of George Herbert Mead. **Erving Goffman**, then producing some of the texts that quickly became sociological classics – the essays published as *Asylums* and the books *Encounters*, *Stigma* and *Behaviour in Public Places* – was her PhD supervisor. Smith's thesis, which she completed in 1963, was entitled 'Power and the Front-Line: Social Controls in a State Mental Hospital'. Whilst in the United States, she also gave birth to her two sons and her marriage ended.

Following a period teaching at Berkeley, Smith returned to Britain as a single parent with her sons to take up a lectureship in sociology at the University of Essex in 1966. The University had been established as part of the early 1960s expansion of British universities and had admitted its first students only two years earlier. The new, lively sociology department, itself part of the rapid expansion of sociology in Britain, was headed by its first professor, Peter Townsend, who appointed academics from a wide range of disciplinary backgrounds to the department, including Paul Thompson, Geoffrey Hawthorn, Roland Robertson, Dennis Marsden, Peter Abell and Alasdair MacIntyre, the second professor. Encouraged by Smith, David Lockwood joined the department in 1968 and Art Stinchcombe was a visiting professor in 1969–70. Smith was the department's first woman lecturer and, in 1968, its first woman senior lecturer, and she was a key figure in the department's early history. However, she found it difficult to survive as a single parent in Britain alongside academic life and in 1969 she left Essex for a post in Canada at the University of British Columbia (UBC). She began to teach courses in women's studies and the sociology of knowledge, and she quickly established an excellent reputation as both scholar and teacher. In 1977 she moved to a professorship in sociology at the Ontario Institute of Studies in Education in Toronto; Toronto and Canada became her home.

By the early 1970s Smith had acquired a strong grounding in sociology and related disciplines, and she had the confidence and critical skills to start publishing. Some of the different strands of her thinking are visible in her early papers: the marked influence of symbolic interactionism and ethnomethodology, as well as of the Marxist ideas that were flourishing in sociology in the 1970s, along with the profound impact of feminist thinking. These were all combined with a strong intellectual commitment and a desire, whilst building on these foundations, to grapple with difficult issues and to think critically and creatively. Several of these early papers, appearing from 1973 to 1975, were highly influential, including 'Women, the Family and Corporate Capitalism', 'The Social Construction of Documentary Reality', 'Women's Perspective as a Radical Critique of Sociology, Feminism and Methodology', 'The Ideological Practice of Sociology' and 'K Is Mentally Ill: The Anatomy of a Factual Account'. The year 1975 also saw the publication of an edited volume with Sara J. David, *Women Look at Psychiatry*. This included a brief joint introduction and two papers by Smith, 'Women and Psychiatry' and 'The Statistics on Mental Illness: What They Will Not Tell Us about Women and Why', as well as a third with Rita MacDonald, 'A Feminist Therapy Session'.

A common feature of these early papers and of her subsequent work was her critical examination of concepts, categories and constructs. On the one hand, she was developing clear arguments about the discipline of sociology, contending that it presented itself as an abstract, rational, objective discipline, yet this claimed objectivity excluded the experiences of women and gave a distorted picture of social relations. In this we can see signs of her growing interest in the way knowledge of the social is developed and constructed. On the other hand, she was examining the practices that underpin the use of categories – later termed 'conceptual practices' – by professionals such as psychiatrists, showing a determination to unravel the way in which the specialized expertise of the powerful organizes and controls events and people. For example, in her paper on mental health statistics she offered an insightful analysis of the way the statistics are constructed, examining the relationship of psychiatric agencies, procedures and practices to the personal troubles individuals experience, and pointing out what cannot be learned about women and mental illness from them. We can see the influence of ethnomethodology in this unpacking of professional practices; yet Smith was also interested in the social relations and structures of power in which the practices are embedded. It is clear, too, that a concern with women, informed both by her own experiences as a mother and academic and by the teaching of women's studies courses at UBC, had become central to her academic work. For Smith, however, women's experiences – the standpoint of women – are only the starting point of the analysis.

Smith's distinctive feminist approach was developed, refined and generalized over the next decade and her ideas were brought together in her most influential text, *The Everyday World as Problematic: A Feminist Sociology*, published in 1987. This used her wide knowledge and understanding of sociology to offer a critique of the discipline that was written from the standpoint of men located in what she called the 'relations of ruling': 'a complex of organised practices, including government, law, business and financial management, professional organisation, and educational institutions, as well as the discourses in texts that interpenetrate the multiple sites of power'. This concept is close to **Foucault**'s notion of governmentality, which was being developed around the same time. Her task was to provide an alternative: a sociology constructed from the standpoint of women. This, she argued, looks at the everyday worlds (compare Goffman's *The Presentation of Self in Everyday Life*) in which women are located, but must also take explicit account of the gendered relations of ruling. In this context she introduced the concept for which she is now particularly known, that of 'institutional ethnography'. The term refers to the methodological strategy for doing sociological research, in particular research on women, that she had outlined in her earlier papers but which was now delineated more precisely. Institutional ethnography requires that sociologists begin by examining everyday social relations between individuals but go beyond this description and see these social relations as structured by relations of power. The focus is on exploring how institutional relations that are part of the ruling apparatus determine everyday worlds. She illustrates this strategy using a range of examples from her own experiences and through analysis of a number of social texts and surveys.

Smith further developed the ideas presented in *The Everyday World as Problematic* in two further books: a collection of papers written during the 1990s, *Writing the Social: Critique, Theory and Investigations,* and *Institutional Ethnography: A Sociology for People.* She also published two collections of her earlier papers (some reworked), as *The Conceptual Practices of Power: A Feminist Sociology of Knowledge* and *Texts, Facts and Femininity: Exploring the Relations of Ruling.* In *Writing the Social* she included an important paper, 'Telling the Truth after Postmodernism', in which she set out the grounds for her rejection of the postmodernist turn in sociology. She pointed out that whilst she shared a number of the postmodernists' assumptions about the importance of texts and discourses, she nonetheless accepted that it was appropriate to talk of truth and reality. The book also included a number of examples of the ways in which sociology could be carried out. In *Institutional Ethnography,* as the subtitle indicates, she made it absolutely clear that the method of institutional ethnography is a method of social inquiry that can be extended across all social groups.

Smith's methodological approach has become very influential not only in Canada but also more widely. As well as two awards from the Canadian Sociology and Anthropology Association, Smith has been honoured for her contributions to sociology in the United States, receiving the Jessie Bernard Award for Feminist Sociology in 1993 and the American Sociological Association's Career of Distinguished Scholarship Award in 1999; she has also been awarded numerous honorary degrees. There is now an Institutional Ethnography Division of the Society for the Study of Social Problems, with its own newsletter. Institutional ethnography had its birth in a strong feminist consciousness, but it has a wider relevance for sociology. By developing the approach and helping to ensure that it is embedded in the set of methodological approaches adopted by sociologists, Smith has made a distinctive and important contribution to the discipline.

See also: Erving Goffman, Michel Foucault.

See also in *Fifty Key Sociologists: The Formative Theorists*: George Herbert Mead.

Major works

Women Look at Psychiatry. 1975. Ed. with Sara J. David: Vancouver: Press Gang Publishers.
Feminism and Marxism: A Place to Begin, a Way to Go. 1977. London: Routledge, 1990.

The Everyday World as Problematic: A Feminist Sociology. 1987. Boston, MA: Northeastern University Press.
The Conceptual Practices of Power: A Feminist Sociology of Knowledge. (Essays of 1974–90.) Boston, MA: Northeastern University Press, 1990.
Texts, Facts and Femininity: Exploring the Relations of Ruling. (Essays of 1978–90.) London: Routledge, 1990.
Writing the Social: Critique, Theory and Investigations. (Essays of 1991–9.) Toronto: University of Toronto Press, 1999.
Institutional Ethnography: A Sociology for People. Walnut Creek, CA: Alta Mira Press, 2005.

Further reading

Marie Campbell. 2003. 'Dorothy Smith and Knowing the World We Live in'. *Journal of Sociology and Social Welfare* 30(1).
Patricia Ticineto Clough. 1993. 'On the Brink of Deconstructing Sociology: Critical Reading of Dorothy Smith's Standpoint Epistemology'. *Sociological Quarterly* 34(1).
Nicholas D. Spence. 2002. 'Publicly Engaged Knowledge: Dorothy Smith's Proposed Sociology'. *Western Journal of Graduate Research* 11(1).

JOAN BUSFIELD

GAYATRI SPIVAK

In 1976, Johns Hopkins University Press published Spivak's introduction to and English translation of Jacques Derrida's *Of Grammatology.* The book not only represented Spivak's formidable intellectual power but also brought Derrida's critique of the logocentric tradition of western philosophical enquiry and its heavy emphasis on Aristotelian arguments of identity and non-contradiction to the attention of Anglo-American academics. Against this debate Derrida revealed the pivotal centrality of *otherness*, or, in his own words, *difference.* Spivak has developed these themes in her own work since then.

Gayatri Chakravorty Spivak was born in 1942 in Calcutta before the partition of the subcontinent. Of Bengali descent, she attended Presidency College in Calcutta and achieved a degree in English before arriving in the United States in 1962 as a PhD student enrolled in comparative literature at Cornell University. Her PhD dissertation was on W. B. Yeats and was supervised by Paul de Man. Later, in 1974, her dissertation was published as *Myself I Must Remake: The Life and Poetry of W.B. Yeats.* She is currently the Avalon

Foundation Professor in the Humanities and director of the Center for Comparative Literature and Society at Columbia University, where she teaches English and the politics of culture.

In her engagement with Derrida's deconstructive philosophy, Spivak argues that, in the words of Sarah Harasym, 'deconstruction is the deconstitution of the founding concepts of the Western historical narrative'. Her encounter with Derrida's work had been accidental, but her interest in his work was deep because of her own biography and its relationship to the British colonial education system:

> Where I was brought up – when I first read Derrida I didn't know who he was, I was very interested to see that he was actually dismantling the philosophical tradition from inside rather than outside, because of course we were brought up in an education system in India where the name of the hero of that philosophical system was the universal human being, and we were taught that if we could begin to approach an inter-nalisation of that human being, then we would be human. When I saw in France someone who was actually trying to dismantle the tradition which had told us what would make us human, that seemed interesting too.

This self-reflexive account reveals that Spivak's attraction to Derrida's philosophical work was largely stirred by an intellectual desire to 'dismantle the hegemonic practice' of western thought that offered the rationalization for European domination and colonialism. In doing so, Spivak moves beyond the orthodox readings of Derrida's work by expanding his critique of western philosophical knowledge to address debates about colonialism, imperialism, literary criticism and western feminist representations of 'subaltern' women's lives, struggles and histories. Hence Spivak has been instrumental in deploying Derrida's deconstruction of the western humanist subject in the framework of postcolonial thought.

In June 1984, at a conference on 'Post Modernity' in Sydney, Australia, Spivak was a keynote speaker, discussing Derrida's thought, the problems of textuality and the domain of politics, and there she set out her most influential ideas. These were elaborated in her essay 'Can the Subaltern Speak?', which was originally published in the journal *Wedge* in 1985 and subsequently reprinted in 1988 in an edited collection of essays, *Marxism and the Interpretation of Culture*. The essay was an exceptional critique of the claims made by twentieth-century European intellectuals such as **Michel Foucault** and **Gilles**

Deleuze to represent and speak on behalf of the marginalized and of the sanctimonious claims of British colonialists to save native women from the tradition of Hindu widow sacrifice in nineteenth-century India. Without a doubt this essay not only confronted the universal claims of western feminism; it also contested its paradigms and focus. More importantly, it created a space for self-reflexivity and brought forward critical scholarship on issues relating to race, class, sexuality, religion and culture. In her essay Spivak chides the political representations of 'Third World' women by western feminism, and her work has yielded a deeper ethical understanding of the power dimensions of 'speaking positions' and has also brought a richness and complexity to feminist theory. Despite this contribution there have also been contemptuous critiques of her famous essay.

Spivak's literary criticism is encapsulated in her essays 'Imperialism and Sexual Difference', 'Three Women's Texts and a Critique of Imperialism' and 'The Rani of Sirmur'. According to Spivak, literature and, indeed, its teaching have been pivotal in the construction and propagation of the colonial mission and she considers it of special importance that texts such as Charlotte Bronte's *Jane Eyre*, Mary Shelley's *Frankenstein* and Daniel Defoe's *Robinson Crusoe* were permeated by colonial discourse. In a similar way to **Edward Said** and Homi Bhabha, Spivak lays emphasis on the argument that nineteenth-century English literature was entwined with the historical narrative of imperialism that offered a social perspective of England as both civilized and indeed progressive. Concomitant to this, Spivak has also, unlike Edward Said, established the rhetorical structurings of the aesthetic and political agency of postcolonial literary texts to elucidate and contest the poignancy of colonial master narratives. While Edward Said, Homi Bhabha and Gayatri Spivak are gratifyingly distinguished as the 'holy trinity' of postcolonial theory, Spivak is more renowned for her serious and thought-provoking engagement with postcolonial literature as a form of defiance against the colonial master narratives deployed in traditional English texts.

According to Spivak, culture was drawn on as a form of rhetoric in the civilizing mission of European colonialism. Basing herself on the deconstructive theories of Paul de Man, Spivak effectively claims that 'the basis of a truth claim is no more than a trope'. While a trope is merely a figure of speech, according to de Man all texts are conscious that they are metaphorical and symbolic and are therefore prone to the possibility of misconstruction. What is more, from Spivak's perspective any literary text can pose serious cultural, ideological, political and social injury.

While Spivak's influence in feminist theory, literary criticism, Marxism and cultural studies is widely recognized, it is important to analyse whether her theories – which were largely developed in the 1980s – are applicable to current debates about belonging, loyalty to the nation–state, Islamphobia and phenomenological studies of whiteness.

See also: Gilles Deleuze, Michel Foucault, Edward Said.

Major works

'Can the Subaltern Speak?'. 1985. In Cary Nelson and Larry Grossberg, eds. *Marxism and the Interpretation of Culture*. Chicago: University of Illinois Press, 1988.
In Other Worlds: Essays in Cultural Politics. 1987. London: Methuen.
The Post-Colonial Critic. 1990. London: Routledge.
Chotti Munda and His Arrow, ed. and trans. 2002. Oxford: Blackwell.
Death of a Discipline. 2003. New York: Columbia University Press.

Extracts can be found in Donna Landry and Gerald MacLean, eds. 1996. *The Spivak Reader: Selected Works of Gyatri Chakravorty Spivak*. London: Routledge.

Further reading

Sarah Harasym. 1990. *The Post-Colonial Critic: Interviews, Strategies and Dialogues*. London: Routledge.

SEVGI KILIC

CHARLES TILLY

Charles Tilly is a historian whose work has developed since the mid-1960s in relation to a set of clearly defined sociological and political issues, which he has investigated using a systematic variable-driven approach. He has examined processual dynamics and developed analytic frameworks, informed by the identification of social mechanisms that he analyses and compares across long historical periods. Few authors have been as productive. So extensively has he written on diverse topics and periods, often using very complex explanatory schemes, that any overview of his work can only be very partial. Tilly's work focuses on large-scale social change and its relationship to contentious politics, especially in Europe since 1500.

Tilly was born in Illinois in 1929 and studied at Harvard, Balliol College, Oxford, and the Facultés Catholiques de l'Ouest, Angers. He received a PhD in sociology from Harvard in 1958. He has taught in several institutions, including the University of Delaware, the Department of Sociology at Harvard University, and the MIT–Harvard Joint Center for Urban Studies. He was professor of sociology at the University of Toronto and taught in several departments at the University of Michigan. He was distinguished professor of sociology and history at the New School for Social Research and is currently professor of social science at Columbia University. He has also taught for shorter periods at several other North American and European universities. His work is widely cited and has received several prizes.

Tilly's work is characterized by its attention to structural, contextual and relational factors. This has entailed the identification of sequential processes often lost in macro approaches based on quantitative evidence and focused on a search for universal models. Conversely, Tilly's consideration of relational variables has required him to pay specific attention to the formation and transformation of networks in various historical contexts, and to the mediating impact of demographic and technological variables in the activation of political conflict. Much of Tilly's work concerns state/movements interaction, and specifically the role of nation-building and state-building in determining the features of movements, their emergence, changing action repertoires, the formation of political identities and network institutionalization processes.

However, he also examines broader issues, such as processes of state formation and democratization, and he has worked on the philosophical underpinnings of his relational realist approach. This he distinguishes from social constructionism, in which he sees the processual dynamics that guide the construction of issues as underspecified; or poststructural approaches, which he sees as neglecting the role of relational variables and unnecessarily abandoning attempts at causal explanations – a concern that has always been distinctive of his comparative method.

Comparisons across French regions organize Tilly's study of the anti-revolutionary movement of *The Vendée*. In this book he tackled the problem of why the counterrevolution developed in Vendée by identifying the distinctive sociological traits of a rural society in transition and comparing them to a different region – Anjou. He identifies the complex and changing relations between power-holders and peasants, differentially stressing the role of urbanization, class structure and associations in orienting reactions to the 1789 Revolution. He then examines issues of development and modernization typical of the social history of the period. But instead of searching for universal explanations he focuses on the factors that made up a radically different context and consequently led to different outcomes. Instead of seeing the Vendée as a prototypical backward region, he points out that peasants, the aristocracy and the clergy were not invariant categories with standardized interests and perspectives, and he examines their interaction on the basis of local variables and processual dynamics which vary between the two contexts analysed.

Another influential early book was *From Mobilization to Revolution*. Here Tilly studied the formation and transformation of collective action. He stressed the need to identify the specific contexts experienced by participants. These include the social structures in which shared interests can be mobilized, the political opportunities that emerge from strategic interaction with the authorities, and changing action repertoires. He argued that movements have shifted from a focus on reactive claims (that is, attempts to react to challenges) to a focus on to proactive claims in which movements increasingly assert claims that have never been expressed. He formulates the concept of 'movement action repertoire', which he sees as driven by strategic considerations of cost-effectiveness in interaction with governments.

The Contentious French is a book that in clear and evocative style examines the joint impact of state-building and nation-building on the everyday lives of ordinary French people. Tilly shows the implications of the development of capitalism and the industrialization, urbanization and proletarianization of work for the forms of social and political conflict – the invention of new forms and the abandonment of obsolete ones. He describes the impact of state-making activities such as the routinization of policing, the extension of military service and more accurate statistical reporting on individual lifestyles, and analyses the impact of the emergence of political parties and interest groups on the structure of political contention.

Durable Inequality is a bold book that formulates a theory at a high level of abstraction. It has attracted criticism from stratification specialists as well as attention and prizes. In *Durable Inequality*, Tilly examines the factors that reproduce structured inequalities among different social groups, that is, inequalities that persist over repeated social interactions. He investigates the dynamics that crystallize inequalities between such diverse groups as men and women, blacks and whites, and citizens and non-citizens, and argues that all inequalities are engendered by similar processes. These involve similar responses to organizational problems, albeit in different types of organizations. Irrespective of the size and type of an organization – which may range from a household to a government – Tilly sees inequality as rooted in the fact that on both sides of a categorical divide there are processes that make actors dependent on dominant unequal practices.

Tilly's book *Stories, Identities and Political Change* brings together some of his earlier work and strives to present it systematically. It constitutes a useful introduction to and general overview of Tilly's production. He classifies his work by focusing on three main areas: political processes, the role of identities in these processes and the role of stories in constructing identities.

In *Social Movements 1768–2004*, Tilly looks at social movements from a wider perspective, inquiring into their mechanisms of diffusion and their contribution to democratization. He investigates the changing nature of the social movement as a social category, examines the impact of new technologies and discusses globalization. He broadly discusses their impact in the contemporary world and their viability in different political regimes. This is extended in *Contention and Democracy in Europe, 1650–2000*, where Tilly conducts comparison between British and French history to identify the various mechanisms that lead to democratization and sometimes de-democratization. He stresses the unanticipated outcomes of complex interactions among actors with conflicting agendas, pointing out that democratic outcomes have resulted from struggles in which it was not the deliberate intention of the participants to create democratic institutions. He emphasizes the non-linear character of democratization processes, which are influenced by local-level dynamics, circumscribed changes in political environments, and social and political relations. Democratization resulted from complex historical dynamics which included several reversals and phases of de-democratization. On the basis of this analysis, Tilly takes a broad-brush approach to the issue of contemporary democratization trends in Europe and elsewhere. He again emphasizes processual variables such as internal disintegration and external conquest and economic crisis, which he connects to relational dynamics such as the collapse of relations between trust networks and governmental agents and the resulting new political opportunities for contentious politics.

Trust and Rule takes a more general approach and examines the formation and outcomes of the relation between trust networks and political regimes in history. Here Tilly emphasizes the role of structural political conflict over dispositional variables, showing that political identities result from relational dynamics, not from durable psychological dispositions as many approaches to political identity instead contend.

Major works

The Vendée. 1964. Cambridge, MA: Harvard University Press.
An Urban World. 1974. Boston, MA: Little, Brown.
The Rebellious Century, 1830–1930. 1975. With Louise Tilly and Richard Tilly. Cambridge, MA: Harvard University Press.
From Mobilization to Revolution. 1978. Reading, MA: Addison-Wesley.
As Sociology Meets History. 1981. New York: Academic Press.
Big Structures, Large Processes, Huge Comparisons. 1985. New York: Russell Sage Foundation.
The Contentious French. 1986. Cambridge, MA: Belknap Press of Harvard University Press.
Coercion, Capital, and European States, A.D. 990–1990. 1990. Oxford: Blackwell.
European Revolutions, 1492–1992. 1993. Oxford: Basil Blackwell.
Popular Contention in Great Britain, 1758–1834. 1995. Cambridge, MA: Harvard University Press.
Roads from Past to Future. 1997. Lanham, MD: Rowman & Littlefield.
Durable Inequality. 1998. Berkeley, CA: University of California Press.
From Contention to Democracy. 1998. Ed. with Marco Giugni and Doug McAdam, Lanham, MD: Rowman & Littlefield.
Extending Citizenship, Reconfiguring States. 1999. Ed. with Michael Hanagan. Lanham, MD: Rowman & Littlefield.
How Social Movements Matter. 1999. Ed. with Marco Giugni and Doug McAdam. Minneapolis, MN: University of Minnesota Press.
The Politics of Collective Violence. 2003. Cambridge: Cambridge University Press.
Contention and Democracy in Europe, 1650–2000. 2004. Cambridge: Cambridge University Press.
Social Movements, 1768–2004. 2004. Boulder, CO: Paradigm Press.
Economic and Political Contention in Comparative Perspective. 2005. With Maria Kousis. Boulder, CO: Paradigm Press.
Trust and Rule. 2005. Cambridge: Cambridge University Press.
Identities, Boundaries, and Social Ties. 2006. London: Pluto Press.
Why? 2006. Princeton, NJ: Princeton University Press.

Further reading

Donatella Della Porta and Mario Diani. 1999. *Social Movements: An Introduction.* Oxford: Blackwell.
Mustafa Emirbayer. 1997. 'Manifesto for a Relational Sociology'. *American Journal of Soociology* 103(2).
Theda Skocpol. 1984. *Vision and Method in Historical Sociology.* Cambridge: Cambridge University Press.

Dennis Smith. 1991. *The Rise of Historical Sociology.* Cambridge: Cambridge University Press.

Sidney Tarrow. 1994. *Power in Movement: Social Movements, Collective Action and Politics.* Cambridge: Cambridge University Press.

CARLO RUZZA

ALAIN TOURAINE

Alain Touraine, born in 1925, is and has for many years been one of France's key sociological theorists. He has researched and written on a wide range of central sociological topics, including work, post-industrialism, democracy and inequality. He is best known, however, for his work on social movements and both the theory of action and the methodological innovations which came out of it.

Through the 1970s Touraine wrote a series of studies on different social movements, including the movements and protests of May 1968 in Paris, the workers' movements and the peace movement. Aside from these specific studies, however, he was one of the first writers, if not the first, to claim that the underlying pattern of conflict in western societies had shifted from the capital–labour configuration described by Marx to a new one centred upon 'new social movements', or, rather, as his work tends to frame the matter, 'the' new social movement. He argues that post-industrial economic transformation and the rise of the welfare state have displaced labour conflicts, giving rise to a new type of society, a society that he calls 'the programmed society'. The new social movement, he continues, has emerged in response to the organizational features or 'mode of historicity' of this new type of society and the various strains, opportunities and incentives it has generated.

The meaning of Touraine's central concepts is notoriously difficult to tease out. What he means by 'mode of historicity', however, is the ensemble of cultural, cognitive, economic and ethical models and means by way of which society acts upon both itself and its environment in order to produce and reproduce itself. It is society's basic organizational form. A 'programmed society' is characterized by a much more intensive degree of self-production and management than the societies that preceded it. It is a post-industrial society that increasingly manages, in a reflective way and through the agency of specific organizational units and experts, the behaviour of its members, the organization and co-ordination of its own internal functions, and its relations with its external environment. There is an echo here of Theodor Adorno and Max Horkheimer's idea of the 'administered society', but also an anticipation of **Giddens**' 'reflexive modernization'. The programmed society is a society that is more aware of itself, *qua* society, and more actively involved in identifying and securing the conditions necessary to its own flourishing. How and why this type of society and its mode of historicity generate new forms of conflict is never spelled out clearly by Touraine, but the implication of much that he writes is, on one side, that the increasing control and complexity involved generate tension, which leads to conflict and movement formation, and, on the other, that the opening up of society to increased reflexive management calls the organization of society into question and generates competing claims as to how it should be managed. Active political administration of the family by way of social work and social policy, for example, both generates resentment about the interference of the state into its citizens' private lives and also puts the family into question in a way which can be taken up in extra-parliamentary channels by individuals, groups and such radical movements as feminism and anti-psychiatry. Intervention prizes open Pandora's box and interventionist agencies often get more than they bargained for.

In some respects Touraine was one of the earliest 'post-Marxist' sociological theorists, in that he argued that society had entered a new mode of historicity which could not be understood by reference to the old Marxist model. Aspects of the Marxist model find a trace in his approach, however, particularly in his apparent assumption that every mode of historicity involves a central social conflict and a single social movement relating to that conflict:

> the practical aim of our research: to discover the social movement which in programmed society will occupy the central position held by the workers movement in industrial society and the civil rights movement in the market society by which it was preceded.

He is not oblivious to the plurality of conflicts in the societies he studies (and lives in) but like the Marxists he is convinced, or at least was convinced in most of his major work on social movements, that beyond this appearance of plurality there is a single, key social movement that characterizes the mode of historicity to which it belongs and that has a historical mission to fulfil. In his more recent work Touraine has perhaps relaxed this belief a little. Still, however, there is a sense that he operates with a very specific, though not particularly clear, concept of social movements that he is unwilling to apply to the wide range of collective protest groupings that most sociologists quite happily call 'social movements'. There is a strong normative aspect to his conception of social movements that makes him inclined to limit its application quite stringently.

Much of Touraine's work was completed at a time when structuralism dominated the French intellectual climate. Interestingly, however, his work went very much against the grain of structuralism, emphasizing issues of agency, process and change. The decision to study social movements is, of course, integral to this and to some extent demands it. To study social movements, at least in the manner most people do, is to study the way in which individual social agents, working together, can achieve change. This is a far cry from the tendency of structuralist writers either to 'dissolve' agents – reduce them to mere 'bearers' of structure – or to explain them away as effects of ideological or political apparatuses. Agency is prominent in Touraine's account even relative to other theorists of social movements, however. Much of his work seeks to explore agency and bring it into the analytic foreground. An adequate conception of society and social change, not to mention social movements, he argues, presupposes a strong conception of agency.

Notwithstanding this focus on agency, however, movements are not always fully transparent to themselves in Touraine's view. For this reason he advocates what he calls 'sociological interventionism'. This is a form of engaged social research that involves working with social movements in an effort to allow them to clarify more fully their own nature and purpose. The sociologist becomes akin to a psychotherapist, albeit working with collective clients, allowing those clients to achieve the self-clarification that will enable them to pursue their projects and aims in a more fruitful manner. The training of sociologists, their research skills and also their outsider status (relative to a given movement) allow them to identify within movements aspects that may not be apparent to insiders. And they can feed this analysis back to insiders in an attempt to make their findings thematic within the internal conversations of the movement itself. Sociological interventionism is questionable in a number of respects but it is interesting because it is one of only relatively few attempts in contemporary sociology, certainly by a leading contemporary theorist, to spell out just what kind of a practical-political role sociology might play in ongoing political struggles and what use our skills and knowledge might have. Touraine is suggesting something much less grand and less presumptuous but also more specific than the role of the 'public intellectual' that his contemporaries are sometimes inclined to take up. It is arguable that, in the 'programmed society', sociology, along with the other social sciences, has a rather longer history of interventionism than Touraine's call to arms might suggest, often, as his critique of contemporary society suggests, with undesirable results. At the very least, however, he is opening up an important debate on the political and social role of the sociologist.

See also: Anthony Giddens.

See also in *Fifty Key Sociologists: The Formative Theorists*: Theodor Adorno, Karl Marx.

Major works

The May Movement: Revolt and Reform. 1968. New York: Random House, 1971.
The Post-Industrial Society. 1969. London: Wildwood House, 1974.
The Self-Production of Society. 1973. Chicago: Chicago University Press, 1977.
The Voice and the Eye. 1978. Cambridge: Cambridge University Press, 1981.
Solidarity. 1983. Cambridge: Cambridge University Press.
The Return of the Actor. 1984. Minneapolis, MN: University of Minnesota Press, 1988.
Critique of Modernity. 1992. Oxford: Blackwell, 1995.
What is Democracy? 1994. Boulder, CO: Westview Press, 1997.
Can We Live Together? 1997. Stanford, CA: Stanford University Press, 2000.
Beyond Neoliberalism. 2001. Cambridge: Polity Press.

Further reading

Alan Scott. 1991. 'Action, Movement and Intervention: Reflections on the Sociology of Alain Touraine'. *Canadian Review of Sociology and Anthropology* 28.

NICK CROSSLEY

IMMANUEL WALLERSTEIN

Immanuel Wallerstein was born in 1930 in New York into a politically conscious and aware family. His studies at Columbia University were interrupted by army service, and after returning to study he decided to complete an MA thesis on the right-wing McCarthyism sweeping through American intellectual life. A major influence on his work was the early work of **C. Wright Mills**. He received his PhD in 1959 for a thesis on politics in Ghana and the Ivory Coast. During an academic career in which he has taught at McGill University and the State University of New York at Binghampton and has held numerous visiting appointments – most notably at the Ecole des Hautes Etudes en Science in Paris – he has grappled with the political issues that arise from international economic struggles. Influenced by the work on comparative civilizations and the history of the long run undertaken by Fernand Braudel, he established the Fernand Braudel Center for the Study of Economies, Historical Systems and Civilization at Binghampton. From this base he produced the studies of *The Modern World System* that established his reputation and transformed the study of economic development. He retired from university teaching in 1999, but continues to write on aspects of the contemporary world system.

Wallerstein's early work built on his PhD concerned political change in Africa. He published a number of influential books in this area during the 1960s and early 1970s, and in 1973 he became president of the African Studies Association. This work led him into a critical consideration of the development literature and the then popular theories of modernization and 'underdevelopment'. Working in the same critical vein as André Gunder Frank, he began to develop the critical ideas that formed the basis of his 1974 study of the sixteenth-century origins of the modern capitalist world economy. This book became the first volume of a trilogy on *The Modern World System*, published between 1974 and 1989, successive volumes bringing the historical narrative up to date. The key ideas underpinning this work were applications of the arguments of Fernand Braudel, who had pioneered the historical study of long-term changes in the structures of economic, political and cultural systems. Wallerstein continued to explore the implications of his position in a series of essays, published as *The Capitalist World Economy*, and through collaboration with Samir Amin, André Frank, Giovanni Arrighi and Terence Hopkins. With these colleagues he produced a number of important works and established the study of world systems as a distinct specialism within sociology. Through all of this work Wallerstein has also engaged in methodological reflections on the nature of historical scholarship in the social sciences, the epistemological issues that arise in sociological investigation and the relationship between theory and practice.

Wallerstein holds that all but the very simplest societies are embedded in much larger economic, political and cultural structures and that it is essential to study the structures of these larger 'world systems'. A world system is a culturally differentiated system with a single division of labour. That is, the constituent social units are culturally distinct but economically interdependent. A world system may typically contain numerous ethnically distinct groupings. Wallerstein distinguishes between 'world-empires' and 'world-economies' as the two main forms of world system. A world-empire is a group of societies united through a common political framework: its units may remain ethnically distinct, but its economic interdependencies are tied into a larger political structure through which one society prevails over others. Examples would be the Chinese and Roman Empires. A world-economy, on the other hand, is politically differentiated – comprising a number of distinct political units – but economically integrated. The world system characteristic of modernity arose in the medieval period as a world-economy. It emerged as a system of states, or proto-states, that were involved in a complex network of economic transactions.

Across Europe there arose a world-economy centred on an extensive market for agricultural produce, handled through a network of trading cities, most notably those of Flanders and the Hanseatic region. Within these cities, a bourgeoisie of merchants dominated trade and built the structures of the modern world system. The European world-economy was surrounded by world-empires of varying strength, though the expansion of the modern world system led to their decay and incorporation into the world-economy. The development of a world-economy centred on England, the Netherlands and Northwest France was the basis of the capitalist industrialist take-off and the process that modernization theorists described as 'industrialization'.

Wallerstein recognizes three distinct sectors within the modern world-economy. These he calls the core, the periphery and the semi-periphery. The core comprises the most technologically advanced and most prosperous economies – the economies that benefit disproportionately from the way that the system operates. The core economies are the dominant agencies within the world system, shaping patterns of investment and trade flows. The core of the capitalist world-economy at its present stage of development comprises Western Europe, the United States and, most recently, Japan. The peripheral economies are those subject to exploitative trade relations and other imbalances in exchange through which characteristic forms of 'underdevelopment' are produced. Like André Frank, Wallerstein depicts development and underdevelopment as interdependent processes within a complex economic system. International economic relations are characterized by unequal exchange. Peripheral economies include much of Africa, Asia and Latin America. The economies of the semi-periphery share some of the characteristics of both core and periphery. They may be former core economies that are in decline and stagnation, or former peripheral economies that have achieved a degree of growth. Semi-peripheral economies include Eastern Europe, China and Brazil. A world-economy is a dynamic system, with particular economies within it subject to rise and fall or a shift from one sector to another. Patterns of alliance and geopolitical alignment, as also the struggles of social movements, reflect the changing fortunes of particular economies within the world system.

Wallerstein's recent work has centred more particularly on the current state of the capitalist world-economy and its major lines of social divisions. These divisions are those of race, nation, class, ethnicity and gender, and Wallerstein has explored the formation of 'antisystemic' social movements around these lines of divide. His study of *The Decline of American Power* explored the consequences of these divisions within the American economy itself as its position of global hegemony has declined since the late 1970s.

See also: Charles Tilly.

See also in *Fifty Key Sociologists: The Formative Theorists*: Karl Marx, Max Weber.

Major works

Africa: The Politics of Independence. 1961. New York: Vintage.
The Road to Independence: Ghana and the Ivory Coast. 1964. Paris: Mouton.
Africa: The Politics of Unity. 1967. New York: Random House.
The Modern World System, Volume 1: Capitalist Agriculture and the Origins of the European World-Economy in the Sixteenth Century. 1974. New York: Academic Press.
The Capitalist World Economy. (Essays of 1974–79.) Cambridge: Cambridge University Press, 1979.
The Modern World System, Volume 2: Mercantilism and the Consolidation of the European World-Economy, 1600–1750. 1980. New York: Academic Press.
World-Systems Analysis: Theory and Methodology. 1982. Ed. with Terence K. Hopkins. Beverly Hills, CA: Sage.
Dynamics of Global Crisis. 1982. With Samir Amin, Giovanni Arrighi and André Frank. London: Macmillan.

Historical Capitalism. 1983. London: Verso.
The Politics of the World-Economy. The States, the Movements and the Civiliza-tions. 1984. Cambridge: Cambridge University Press.
The Modern World System, Volume 3: The Second Great Expansion of the Capi-talist World-Economy, 1730–1840s. 1989. New York: Academic Press.
Antisystemic Movements. 1989. With Giovanni Arrighi and Terence K. Hop-kins. London: Verso.
Transforming the Revolution: Social Movements and the World System. 1990. With Samir Amin, Giovanni Arrighi and André Frank. New York: Monthly Review Press.
Race, Nation, Class: Ambiguous Identities. 1991. With Etienne Balibar. London: Verso.
Unthinking Social Science: The Limits of Nineteenth Century Paradigms. 1991. Cambridge: Polity Press.
Historical Capitalism, with Capitalist Civilization. 1995. London: Verso.
The End of the World as We Know It: Social Science for the Twenty-first Century. 1999. Minneapolis, MN: University of Minnesota Press.
Decline of American Power: The US in a Chaotic World. 2003. New York: New Press.
The Uncertainties of Knowledge. 2004. Philadelphia: Temple University Press.

Further reading

Dennis Smith. 1991. *The Rise of Historical Sociology,* ch. 4.
Thomas R. Shannon. 1996. *An Introduction to the World System Perspective.* Second edn. Boulder, CO: Westview Press.

JOHN SCOTT

WILLIAM JULIUS WILSON

Over the course of his four-decade career in American sociology, William Julius Wilson, the Lewis P. and Linda L. Geyser University Professor at Harvard University, has become one of America's best-known social scientists. He was born on 20 December 1935, in modest circumstances, in Derry Township, Pennsylvania. He earned degrees from Wilberforce University (BA, 1958), Bowling Green State University (MA, 1961) and Washington State University (PhD, 1966). After he received his PhD, he began his career in academia at the University of Massachusetts at Amherst, and then joined the faculty of the University of Chicago in 1972 (becoming the Lucy Flower University Professor in 1992). He joined the faculty of Har-vard University in 1996.

While trained in sociology, Wilson has helped bridge the fields of sociology and public policy by providing a litany of scholarly works that address issues of race and urban poverty in the United States. His most significant contribution in this area has been to elucidate the role that structural conditions play in the proliferation of urban poverty. These factors include urban labour market dynamics, the social organization and geographic locations of low-income residential communities, and the kinds of access that socio-economically deprived people have (or do not have) to social institutions and individuals embedded in, or related to, the formal world of work. Since the mid-1980s, Wilson has argued not only that structural conditions matter more than cultural factors in understanding why urban poverty endures in American cities and municipal regions, but that these conditions often shape the emergence of these cultural factors (which include the attitudes, beliefs and values maintained by disadvantaged people). In doing so, Wilson has striven to counter the pervasive culture of poverty logic that positioned cultural traits and psychological dispositions (such as elementary understandings of the world of work and the means of accessing good jobs; and internalization of feelings of despair and fatalism) as primary causal factors for American urban poverty.

Wilson's signature contribution to this area of sociology is *The Truly Disadvantaged: The Inner City, The Underclass and Public Policy.* Here he explored how the structural factors discussed earlier led to both the social isolation of the African-American urban poor from other sectors of the urban community that are more securely connected to the world of work, and to their being situated in concentrated poverty (or living in communities that are densely populated with other low-income residents). Social isolation refers to the lack of contact or sustained interaction with individuals or institutions that represent mainstream society. Wilson explains that such isolation makes it difficult for people who experience it to become tied to social networks that connect to jobs. It also generates behaviour that is not conducive to good work histories. For instance, as consistent employment mandates the maintenance of some degree of order and organization in everyday life, the absence of work leaves those in such a condition with little means of, or rationale for, maintaining such organization in everyday living. This latter state of being further reduces their potential for employability.

Another pivotal term in Wilson's lexicon was the 'underclass'. That term became a catch-all phrase for describing the hyper-socio-economically marginalized residents of American cities in the last third of the twentieth century. Although it was central to his early work on race and urban poverty, Wilson ultimately dispensed with the term due to its highly and unnecessarily pejorative implications.

Prior to *The Truly Disadvantaged*, Wilson published *Power, Racism, and Privilege; Race Relations in Theoretical and Sociohistorical Perspectives* and *The Declining Significance of Race: Blacks and Changing American Institutions*. The first book provided a historically grounded social theory of racism, by comparing the United States and South Africa. Here Wilson embedded conflict theory in a historical framework such that he could examine the different ways by which whites maintained superior positions in the socio-economic hierarchy in both countries.

In order to turn more fully to issues concerning mobility, stratification and the implications for class standing for both processes, Wilson then produced *The Declining Significance of Race*. This work often was mistakenly regarded as a refutation of the social significance of race in the post-civil rights movement era. Some of this had to do with the fact that this work appeared at a time when critical questions were being raised in the United States about the appropriateness of race-based policy initiatives and other social programmes that were perceived to have been designed for the specific interests of African-Americans.

Despite the criticism, Wilson argued in this book that African-Americans of the middle and upper classes had access to resources and information for socio-economic mobility that lower-income African-Americans did not. Hence, without refuting the social significance of racism, Wilson argued that by the end of the American civil rights movement era (*circa* 1970) class-specific issues affected the life-chance outcomes of African-Americans more than did race. *The Truly Disadvantaged*, then, became Wilson's response to what he saw as an increasing public assault on urban-based, low-income African-Americans, which was partly produced out of recognition of a seemingly stable, and at least partially integrated, African-American middle class following the 1960s.

More recently, Wilson has published *When Work Disappears: The World of the New Urban Poor*, which emphasized more thoroughly than did his earlier work what qualitative data illustrate about the lives of the urban poor. Finally, his most recent work, *The Bridge Over the Racial Divide: Rising Inequality and Coalition Politics*, reflects his return to thinking about race and racism and their role in contemporary social inequality.

The impact of William Julius Wilson's work has extended far beyond the confines of the academic community, making him a widely read scholar who has garnered extensive public recognition. *The Declining Significance of Race* won the American Sociological Association's Sydney Spivack Award. *The Truly Disadvantaged* was selected by the editors of the *New York Times* Book Review as one of the sixteen best books of 1987 and received the Washington Monthly Annual Book Award and the Society for the Study of Social Problems' C. Wright Mills Award. *When Work Disappears* was chosen as one of the notable books of 1996 by the editors of the *New York Times* Book Review and received the Sidney Hillman Foundation Award. Wilson also is past president of the American Sociological Association and an elected member of the National Academy of Sciences, the American Academy of Arts and Sciences, the National Academy of Education and the American Philosophical Society. In 1998 he was awarded the National Medal of Science, the highest scientific honour in the United States.

See also in *Fifty Key Sociologists: The Formative Theorists*: W. E. B. DuBois.

Major works

Power, Racism, and Privilege; Race Relations in Theoretical and Sociohistorical Perspectives. 1973. New York: Macmillan.
The Declining Significance of Race: Blacks and Changing American Institutions. 1978. Chicago: University of Chicago Press.
The Truly Disadvantaged: The Inner-City, The Underclass, and Public Policy. 1987. Chicago: University of Chicago Press.
When Work Disappears. 1996. New York: Alfred Knopf.
The Bridge Over the Racial Divide: Rising Inequality and Coalition Politics. 1999. Berkeley, CA: University of California Press.

ALFORD A. YOUNG, JR

INDEX

Entries in **bold** refer to principal entries in the book.

SOCIOLOGY: THE BASICS

Martin Albrow

This is a book for anyone who wants to know what sociology is and what sociologists do. In a subject that has changed dramatically over the last twenty years, *Sociology: The Basics* offers the most up to date guide to the major topics and areas of debate. It covers among other things:

- Sociology and society
- Laws, morality and science
- Social relations
- Power and communication
- Society in the future
- Becoming a socialist

Clearly written, concise and comprehensive, *Sociology: The Basics* will be an essential text for anyone thinking of studying the subject.

0-415-17264-0
978-0-415-17264-6

Available at all good bookshops
For ordering and further information please visit
www.routledge.com

SOCIOLOGY: THE KEY CONCEPTS

John Scott

Sociology: The Key Concepts brings together a strong group of well-known experts to review ideas from all areas of this diverse and pluralistic discipline. Exploring the key debates and founding ideas of this exciting field of study, the book is fully cross-referenced and covers such topics as:

- Community
- Childhood
- Emotion
- Discourse
- Race and racialisation
- Modernity
- McDonaldisation
- Gender
- Consumption
- Social capital
- Identity

0-415-34406-9
978-0-415-34406-7

Available at all good bookshops
For ordering and further information please visit
www.routledge.com